PATHWAY
THROUGH THE
PROVERBS

Pathway Through The Proverbs
Copyright © 2022
All rights reserved.

ISBN: 979-8-9853674-2-3

PATHWAY
THROUGH THE
PROVERBS

EDITORS

Kyle Bauer

Michelle Glush

CONTRIBUTORS

Fred Alvarado	Rachel Corcoran	Jose Nolasco
Jill Alvarado	Michelle Glush	Victor Miguel Rivera
Joshua Bauer	Karen Heimbuch	Jennifer Shank
Kyle Bauer	Rachael Hopkins	Debbie Speese
Teresa Bauer	Stephen Larkin	Lloyd Speese
Maureen Broderson	Bea Laufer	Chris Stanton
Juline Bruck	Martin Laufer	Kathleen Stevenson
Ricardo Chaidez	Gabriel Martinez	Alicia Suarez
	Cynthia Medrano	
	Amelia Montantes	
	Pat Nannarello	

Dedicated to the Family of
Pathway SFV

ACKNOWLEDGMENTS

I would like to acknowledge all of the Pathway SFV contributors. Thank you for your time, your insight, your dedication and your diligence. I know it was not an easy task, but you did a great job! Thank you for sharing your wisdom and life experiences to bless our Pathway family. Your contributions to this project are deeply appreciated.

I would also like to thank Martha Brantley, Karen Harrison, and Pat Nannarello for their long, meticulous hours of reviewing, editing, and "clean up" work.

Finally, a very special thank you to Michelle Glush who put more hours in than everyone. Your commitment to excellence and thoroughness is unparalleled. Your tenacity and focus to finish this project on time was inspiring. None of this would have ever happened without your attentiveness. Thank you for your love for the Lord, your wonderful disposition, which made it so easy to work with you, and your thoughtful insight.

Pastor Kyle Bauer

*Proverbs are persistently and perpetually
permeating my personality!*
—Pat Nannarello

INTRODUCTION

I am excited to introduce this special book, *Pathway Through the Proverbs*. The title of the book has a dual meaning. First, being a year-long devotional studying different proverbs, it is deciphering the pathway for the biblical worldview that makes for a happy, successful, significant, wise, and God-fearing life that will ultimately be fruitful in every way. Secondly, this book was written for our church, Pathway SFV, by more than 20 contributors from Pathway SFV's congregation. It is Pathway's "Pathway" through the Proverbs!

During nearly six months of Wednesday night services in 2022, I taught through Psalm 119, which makes explicit reference to God's Word in 173 of the 176 verses. In that study, we saw that God's Word is the foundational aspect of every part of our lives, and its wisdom and power is able to touch, comfort, sustain, and guide us in every season of life. Now, in 2023, by way of this devotional, we are going through Proverbs. As this book was edited, I realized just how much the wisdom offered in this book depends on consistent reflection and meditation on God's Word. I cannot help but sense the Holy Spirit has been calling to us in 2022, and now in 2023 and beyond, He is calling us to new heights and new depths of His Word. He is calling us to understanding of, dependence on, and fresh commitment to the authority of the Bible in our daily lives in the midst of the turbulent world that seeks to pull us into its way of thinking and living.

Solomon is said to have been the wisest man who ever lived. This attribution is not without merit. In 2 Chronicles 1:7-12, God appeared to Solomon and told him to ask for anything he wished. Solomon requested a wise and understanding heart to be able to rule over Israel. God was pleased with this request and granted divine wisdom and understanding. As we read through the Proverbs, remember two things: 1) The wisdom is from Solomon, but is really divinely given by God—this is God's wisdom for life, and 2) this is the Bible, the very Word of God!

Though I am quoting the first six verses of Proverbs verbatim, I have divided these verses into an outline format highlighting the purpose statements Solomon gives for his book:

"These are the proverbs of Solomon, David's son, King of Israel.

- Their purpose is to teach people wisdom and discipline, to help them understand the insights of the wise.

- Their purpose is to teach people to live disciplined and successful lives, to help them do what is right, just, and fair.

- These proverbs will give insight to the simple, knowledge and discernment to the young. Let the wise listen to these proverbs and become even wiser. Let those with understanding receive guidance by exploring the meaning in these proverbs and parables, the words of the wise and their riddles." (NLT)

Solomon, from the onset, gives us the explicit purpose for this book of the Bible. In writing this book, we are not attempting to add anything to what Solomon has said. The purpose is for each of these devotionals to "explore the meaning" of these proverbs. I find it interesting that Solomon also refers to these as "parables" and "riddles." In other words, each of these sayings contains a meaning that goes deeper than the mere surface-level understanding. I view each of these proverbs as individual treasure chests. As you explore the meaning, the deeper wisdom, and understanding of each of these proverbs, ask the Holy Spirit to impart to you the Spirit of Wisdom (Isa. 11:1; Eph. 1:17) to understand and apply a commonsense nugget of wisdom to what you read.

In His famous parable in Matthew 7:24-27, Jesus said, *"Everyone then who hears these words of mine and does them will be like a wise man who built his house on the rock."* (ESV) Later, Jesus says the converse that those who hear His words but do not put them into practice are like a foolish man who built his house on the sand. In the parable, it is interesting to note that both houses were subjected to howling winds, driving rain, and rushing rivers, but only the house on the rock stood firm. The fact is that, though we have joys, triumphs, and happiness in life, no one in this world is exempt from the storms of this life; we all go through tragedies, difficulties, disappointments, demonic assaults, tests, and temptations. It is also fitting to point out that both of these builders heard Jesus' words, but only one put them into practice. It is the solid rock of God's Word that gives us the security and stability through all of life's challenges. For this reason, we have written Pathway Through the Proverbs.

Though we have talked much about God's Word, some of what you will encounter may sound repetitious, in that there are constant reminders to go back to God's Word.

The Apostle Paul said in Philippians 3:1 (NLT), "…I never get tired of telling you these things, and I do it to safeguard your faith." I feel the same way. When something is of such importance that it is said many times and many ways throughout the Bible, it is worth the extra attention paid to the counsel.

Though it may seem repetitious, it is still valid. In the first eight chapters of Proverbs, King Solomon speaks directly to "my child," "my son," or "my children" 18 times. In speaking to his children, Solomon stresses the essential importance of their "hearing" and "putting into practice" his words in several different terms. He says to "listen, not neglect, treasure, tune your ears, concentrate, seek, store up, never forget, not lose sight of, pay attention, learn, never stray from, obey, keep, bind, follow, guard, love, write, and let penetrate" into their hearts the words of their father.

In the same way God, our heavenly Father, is stressing the importance of His Word in our lives. There is great wisdom and safety in going back to them again and again for His guidance, insight, and understanding. Many times in our lives we feel we don't have the answers, yet the wisdom literature of the Bible calls us back to the wisdom of God's Word, again and again and again and again and again, to the point where we may almost feel tired of listening to it. But in this lies God's answer to much of life's situations—His Word! It is important to point out that Solomon also exhorts his children to "cry out" for insight. To be hearers, we must also be seekers who desire to find the wisdom of our Father. Those who seek will find.

Pastor Kyle Bauer

JANUARY

My child,

listen when your father corrects you.

Don't neglect your mother's instruction.

What you learn from them

will crown you with grace

and be a chain of honor

around your neck.

—Proverbs 1:8-9

NO OTHER NAME

Proverbs 30:3-4

*"I have not learned wisdom,
nor have I attained to the knowledge of the Holy One." (NIV)
"Who but God goes up to heaven and comes back down?
Who holds the wind in his fists? Who wraps up the oceans in his cloak?
Who has created the whole wide world?
What is his name—and his son's name? Tell me if you know!" (NLT)*

*"No one has ever gone into heaven except the one
who came from heaven—the Son of Man." (John 3:13)*

What is His name?

Jesus.

Maker, Creator, Light of the morning, The Great I Am, Captain of the Lord's Armies, Messiah, Great Shepherd, King of Glory, Our Rock and our Fortress, Lion of Judah, Deliverer, Rose of Sharon, Crown of Glory, Rock of Ages, Wonderful, Counselor, Ancient of Days, Prince of Peace, Redeemer, Emmanuel…The Alpha…

> *"In the beginning was the Word, and the Word was with God, and the Word was God. He was in the beginning with God. All things were made through Him, and without Him nothing was made that was made. In Him was life, and the life was the light of men. And the light shines in the darkness, and the darkness did not comprehend it." (John 1:1-5 NKJV)*

Son of Man, Lamb of God, Bridegroom, Second Adam, King Forever, Holy One, Yahweh's Glory, Our Brother, Son of the Most High God, King of the Jews, Peacemaker, God my Savior, Rabbi, Light of the World, Healer, The Resurrection, The Way, The Truth, and The Life, The Risen Lamb…and the Omega…

> He who testifies to these things says, *"Surely I am coming quickly."* Amen. Even so, come, Lord Jesus! *"The grace of our Lord Jesus Christ be with you all. Amen."* (Rev. 22:20-21)

Jesus.

I think that says it all.

Michelle Glush

RIGHTEOUS RICHES

Proverbs 11:4

"When judgment day comes,
all the wealth of the world won't help you one bit.
So be rich in righteousness,
for that's the only thing that can save you in death." (TPT)

Psalm 118:8 is the exact center of the Bible.[1] The God-breathed, inerrant Scripture does not miss one detail. Indeed, at the very heart of the Bible is the very heart of the Gospel message:

"It is better to trust in the Lord than to put confidence in man."

The Gospel message is that we cannot save ourselves. We are not good enough, smart enough, rich enough, educated enough, connected enough, or anything enough to make ourselves right with God. It is simple faith and trust in the Lord, and the goodness He provides for us through Jesus Christ, that makes us right with Him.[2]

Jesus wrote a letter to the church in Laodicea rebuking and counseling it.[3] This church believed it was "enough" to impress God. The Laodicean church alleged, "I am rich and have need of nothing." They were big enough, rich enough, cool enough, and smart enough. Jesus, however, saw things quite differently.

"[you] do not know that you are wretched, miserable, poor, blind, and naked—I counsel you to buy from Me gold refined in the fire, that you may
be rich; and white garments, that you may be clothed, that the shame of
your nakedness may not be revealed; and anoint your eyes with eye salve,
that you may see."

Many people have a misguided theology similar to the church in Laodecia: only the wicked suffer, but the godly are blessed with riches.[4] This church's outward grandeur and riches inspired its great confidence in its own godliness. Meanwhile, this church was unaware of its impending judgment that Jesus was about to shut it all down. Jesus does not care about what we have gained for ourselves—He is thoroughly unimpressed. He is moved by righteous living. In the end, money—or anything else we depend on in this life—means nothing. Live in faithfulness and obedience to Jesus; it is the only thing worthwhile.

Kyle Bauer

---

1   Some will dispute this claim, but that is not important here. In our modern Bibles, it is the center.
2   See Ephesians 2:8-9
3   Revelation 3:14-22, (NKJV)
4   See the book of Job

BE LIKE JESUS

Proverbs 18:21

"Death and life are in the power of the tongue,
and those who love it will eat its fruit." (NKJV)

With our words, we can encourage or destroy. Build up or tear down. Bring laughter or tears. Elevate or eviscerate.

I was really good at the latter. The Lord taught me through an experience with my husband that my calling him a jerk was only reinforcing what he already thought of himself. When I finally gave up and said to God, "YOU fix my words," HE moved me right out of the way and literally put His foot on my mouth to shut me up. Then, He made me start complimenting my husband for the most mundane and inane things (which I hated to do), but through those compliments, my husband was beginning to have a better view of himself which helped him not to be a jerk. Praise God!

I also used to work myself into a rage when some inconsiderate bozo would cut me off or drive too slowly or do something incredibly stupid. When I became a believer and realized that all those lovely words that were coming out of my mouth were making ME ugly and unlovely, I stopped yelling at other drivers and started blessing them. It did wonders for my blood pressure, and actually made me feel better, because I was not pumping all that bad vitriolic juice into my body while the bozo drove merrily on. More importantly, I realized those words were hampering the weight and effectiveness of my prayers. *"The effectual fervent prayers of a **righteous** man avails much."* (James 5:16)

When people are yelling and berating one another, the response it elicits is negative. But, when people are kind, loving, and complimentary, the response is positive. Today, our prayers are more important than ever. So, to have your prayers carry weight and have Holy Spirit authority, curb your tongue. Be kind, be prayerful, and be fruitful. Be like Jesus.

Pat Nannarello

STAY ON THE PATH

Proverbs 10:9

*"He who walks with integrity walks securely,
but he who perverts his ways will become known." (NKJV)*

I recently read a news article about a local non-verbal teen who went missing while hiking with family members in a heavily wooded area. Search and rescue teams were desperate to find where the teen had gone off the marked path. After six hours of searching, a Sheriff's deputy heard the distinct sound of clinking rocks down a steep ravine. The teen was successfully rescued after falling more than 400 feet over the side of the fire road off the hiking trail.

The news article doesn't touch on it, but I wonder how the teen felt about being the subject of a news story? Turning off the marked path may not only be dangerous, but also may result in unintended or undesired recognition. Those "Stay On Marked Path" signs along hiking trails are there for your protection, designed to enable you to safely reach your destination.

Did you know that God has cut a path through the wilderness of life for you and marked the path with His signposts? God repeatedly warns us throughout the Bible to stay on the path He has marked out for us by His Word. He has made a smooth path that averts the wide-mouthed jaws of the enemy's snares of iniquity. All you have to do is stay on the path. When you follow God's wisdom, gain His understanding, and grow in the knowledge of God, then you will walk safely. In fact, the Lord directs the steps of those who are godly, and He delights in every detail of their lives (Ps. 37:23). You can walk in confidence when you walk in the ways of the Lord, for He will keep your foot from being caught up (Prov. 3:26). But if you go off the path that God has marked out by His word, if you twist God's Word, or allow sin to pervert your way, then the Bible says you will suddenly fall (Prov. 28:18), and you will be found out. You will become known, but not in a good way. Stay on the path, walk in the security of God's protection, and enjoy the journey!

Rachel Corcoran

SOONER OR LATER

Proverbs 16:27

An ungodly man digs up evil,
and it is on his lips like a burning fire. (NKJV)

In my professional career, I used to travel throughout North America regularly. I recall a trip from Northern California to Boise, Idaho. Uniquely, of a plane with 137 seats, only two were taken. One other gentleman and I were the only people on the plane. Of course, we began a conversation. I distinctly remember something he said while we were discussing how best to deal with the variety of personalities within our businesses. He said, "If you talk long enough, sooner or later you say the wrong thing." How true.

We continued our discussion and began exploring why some people say the wrong thing regularly and do not seem to care who it damages. He also poignantly noted that this kind of person continually says the wrong thing because the wrong thing is in them, and they look for whatever is negative.

Solomon appears to be making a similar point in this text. A certain kind of person, an ungodly person, is always looking for evil and the wrong thing. An ungodly man searches for and digs up the wrong thing, evil things. Clearly, he routinely finds them, because they (the wrong things) are right on his lips, and he has a burning, uncontrollable desire to speak the negative and to say the wrong thing. This is because evil is his true nature.

Matthew 12:34 reads, "…out of the abundance of the heart, the mouth speaks." Does your mouth burn with the wrong words? It is a reflection of what is inside of you. Guard your words. Guard your heart. Let your lips and your heart burn with goodness. Sooner rather than later, this becomes who you are, and you do not have to worry about talking so much or saying the wrong thing.

Lloyd Speese

FEAST ON GOD'S GREATNESS

Proverbs 17:1

*"Better a dry crust with peace and quiet
than a house full of feasting, with strife." (NIV)*

No matter how beautiful the table is or how good the food tastes, the meal is no longer enjoyable when tension is also being served at the table.

It is difficult to find pure joy and peace in the temporal things of this world. The things we can buy with money, the things we can feast on from riches, will fade away. Many seek worldly riches thinking it will solve their problems or make life easier. It might for a while, but at what cost?

When we pursue riches or things that are not eternal, we will never feel satisfied, because God has placed eternity in us. (Eccles. 12:13) When we try in our humanness to fill that space with the world or other relationships, we never find the peace God can offer us. Even filling our lives with fancy dinners, business dealings, sports, friends or family, new cars, nicer clothes, the latest technology, or bigger houses, we can still find an emptiness that drives us to find more, get more, and fill up the space that is meant for God. In our search, we can become dissatisfied, bitter, irritable, and full of tension and strife, and we never really feel deep contentment.

In Romans 8:6, Paul reminds us that peace comes from God and not in our flesh.

Success is not more. It is contentment with what you have (1 Tim. 6:6). A simple dinner or a meal for a king, we should learn to be content regardless of what is being served (1 Phil. 4:11-12). Do you feast on God's greatness and His blessings, or do you put more value on worldly things?

Take a moment and reflect on where you may have sought out worldly pleasures. Make an effort to find contentment with what God has given you, and you will find real and lasting peace in your life, feasting on the goodness of God.

Jill Alvarado

QUICK TO LISTEN

Proverbs 18:17

"The first to speak in court sounds right —
until the cross-examination begins." (NLT)

Over nearly 20 years of ministry, Teresa and I have sat and counseled many couples. Usually, it begins with one person in the relationship calling my wife or me asking for counseling, and he or she proceeds to tell us the situation and their perspective on it. It always sounds reasonable, and I am always tempted to take the person at their word. However, experience has taught me that there are always two sides to the story, and marriage is always a two-way street. Marital problems usually go something like this: She is right—and so is he. She is also wrong—and so is he. Both people have valid points, and in some way or another, both are at fault and have contributed to the communication breakdown. Though taking sides when the first version of the story comes out is tempting, it is unwise to rush to judgment until the whole story comes to light. Only then can wisdom be implemented in a way that satisfies the needs of both people, and marital restoration can begin its process.

The same is true in the social and political spheres. Inevitably, something tragic happens, and politicians will rush the public into some opinion that best suits their particular political and social engineering agenda before all the facts are clear. The rush to judgment and knee-jerk, emotional reactions are not only unwise, but also they are dangerous. They rush to unfounded public verdicts that destroy a person's reputation and often unfairly judge a person or a situation when only a fraction of the evidence has been revealed. A situation can appear one way and be spun to favor one point of view, but this rarely favors justice, fairness, understanding, or wisdom.

It is wise to be quick to listen, slow to speak, slow to judgment, and weigh all the evidence of any situation, whether it be with children, our marriages, co-workers, or anything we see on the news. Being quick to listen will keep us from foolish and unjust judgments.

Kyle Bauer

OUR WORDS CAN PRODUCE LIFE

Proverbs 15:4

*"When you speak healing words, you offer others fruit from the tree of life.
But unhealthy, negative words do nothing but crush their hopes." (TPT)*

We can so quickly speak the first words that come to mind in response to situations or people we encounter. We need to ask the Lord to guard our lips in those situations so we only speak life-giving words that will bless the hearer and return to bless our hearts as well.

Words, like good seeds, can bring forth life and healthy growth, and deadly seeds, sown like thorns, can tear at the heart and bring destruction. Empty words, like seeds casually sown, bring forth no fruit and far more often do more damage than good.

Oh, that we would live and abide in our Abba Father's love, that only those words that He would want to speak would come forth. He created all things with His Word, and all things that He created were good!

In the Garden of Eden, God spoke to Adam about two trees planted in the center of the garden. He told him not to eat from the Tree of the Knowledge of Good and Evil because it would produce death. Unfortunately, Adam and Eve chose to eat from that tree—and death was unleashed as a result. Proverbs 18:2 says, *"Death and life are in the power of the tongue, and those who love it will eat its fruit."* (NKJV) Our words produce life or death, and we get to choose which one we feed to people and nourish ourselves.

Let's follow the wisdom and direction found in this proverb and take heed to the admonition given in James 3:10, that from our mouths can come forth both blessing and cursing. We, therefore, pray for the Lord to set a guard on our tongues so that we will bless and speak life!

Kathleen Stevenson

BLESS AT ALL TIMES

Proverbs 11:26

"People curse those who hoard their grain,
but they bless the one who sells in time of need." (NLT)

So, what is one guy going to do with all that grain? What I imagine is a man gripped by fear, and having thoughts of "what if I lose it all?" "What if someone tries to steal it?" "What if there is a flood?" "What if the end of the world happens?" "What if….".

This man has cursed himself. His unwillingness to sell shows contempt for the needy. That is kind of heavy and displays a disdain for the needy. His pride in his "grain" is all he has, and he is unwilling to sell it despite a need in his community. I imagine the people cursing are not just praying curses on him, but they are actually yelling choice nouns and adjectives at this hoard of grain. And the more they curse, the less likely he will be willing to sell.

Then you have the other guy. The one willing to sell. The blessed guy. There is a small jewelry store in Lahaina, Maui, called Lahaina Gems. It is run by a woman who initially seems like the first person in our story. She is unwilling to haggle with me—hard, coarse, a little on the mean side. But once you get talking to her, she begins to open up, and she will begin to "talk story" as they say in Hawaii. Jill and I were surprised at how open and friendly she became. We still did our haggling, but I left with a new friend, got a better deal, and she sold more than what we came in for. She was blessed. We were blessed. I look forward to seeing her next time we go back.

It is interesting the proverb notes that "people curse" and "they bless." It is not just about the guys with the grain. It's also about the ones who curse or bless. We, the people, can either bless or curse. But just as there are many ways to curse, there are many ways to bless. Be sure to bless those who are willing to sell, but as Jesus said, bless even those who curse you. In other words, just bless at all times.

Fred Alvarado

A FRIEND LOVES AT ALL TIMES

Proverbs 17:17

*"A friend loves at all times
and a brother is born for adversity." (NKJV)*

Long ago, English Pastor Charles Spurgeon observed, "Friendship is one of the sweetest joys of life. Many might have failed beneath the bitterness of their trials had they not found a friend."

My husband and I recently moved. We left the home we had lived in for over 40 years; the home where we raised our two daughters; one filled with thousands of loving memories. Though we were excited at the prospect of being closer to some of our family, one of the most difficult things we experienced was leaving so many good, long-time friends behind. Friends who had happily celebrated the wonderful, happy times of life and faithfully stood by us in the dark, challenging times. We have learned during this season that no matter if our friends are near or far, God will show us new ways to intentionally stay connected with them.

God's Word has much to say about friendship. The Lord teaches us to celebrate one another's joyous occasions and extend our hands to lift our friends' heads and hearts as they navigate life's challenges. Most significantly, God asks us always to choose love and patience and to treat others how we hope to be treated.

Friendships are not always easy. For many, the pandemic has sadly given way to a loneliness epidemic, and isolation has become the norm. Differences in opinions, busy schedules, and distance can make nurturing our friendships a sacrifice. But we are assured it is a sacrifice well worth it. Our God is a God of community, and He never intended us to live our lives alone.

Are you holding something against a friend? If so, reach out and do all you can to make amends. Extend your heart and hand in forgiveness. Today, ask the Lord to show you how you can love, support, and encourage a friend.

Prayer: "Lord, help me be the friend who loves as You loved. Help me be a source of strength, comfort, and joy. Teach me to listen, understand, support my friends in their struggles and celebrate their successes as if they were my own."

Maureen Broderson

HONOR YOUR PARENTS

Proverbs 10:13

"Wisdom is found on the lips of the discerning,
but a rod is for the back of one who has no sense." (NIV)

There are three keywords in this proverb: WISDOM, LACKS, and JUDGMENT.

Out of the mouth of a wise person will come smart words or judgment, but he who lacks wisdom inevitably places himself on a path of unpleasant consequences.

This brings to mind something I did when I was around 12 years old, the age when you think you know everything (lol). Now that I am older and have my own children, I understand.

We were living in Puerto Vallarta, and my mom was washing dishes when I approached her to ask if I could go out with my friends—to which she answered NO. Here is where the other two words come into play. When she said NO, I made a disdainful noise by clicking my tongue. Without any warning, my mom turned around and backhanded me across my mouth. I was astonished! I did not know she was that fast, and then she gave me a word of warning: "Never do that again! I am your mother."

That day I learned two things: 1) I was not as smart as I thought I was, and 2) my mom was faster than I thought. I could have avoided all of that by honoring my mom, but my lack of wisdom…you know the story.

Gabriel Martinez

MOTIVES VS. APPEARANCES

Proverbs 16:2

"Humans are satisfied with whatever looks good;
God probes for what is good." (MSG)

It is the constant struggle of our flesh—Motives vs. Appearances. The entire message of Jesus in the Sermon on the Mount (Matt. 5-7) deals with the heart of a person rather than the outside appearances of the person. Jesus speaks of anger in the heart as the real motive that leads to the sin of murder; of the sin of lust in the heart as the real motive that leads to the sin of adultery. It is the motive that spurs the actions. Jesus also speaks of prayer, fasting, and giving—outward actions that may hide true motives. We can pray, fast, and give to either 1) be lauded by people or 2) do the same in secret and be rewarded by the God who sees the inside of our hearts. If we merely cover ourselves with a facade of goodness, the true motives will eventually bleed through.

Our lives are like trees: the hidden roots feed the growing, outside leaves. If we do not like the leaves, I suppose we could either pull them off or cut off the branches and get rid of them. However, the leaves will only sprout again the following season because the healthy roots that feed the growth of the outward appearances remain intact. To change the tree, so it no longer produces the undesired leaves, the root must be cut off. Instead of the dead works of our sin, Jesus plants the seed of His Word and Kingdom in our hearts that begins to grow deep roots of righteousness that produce not a facade but equally righteous leaves on the outside.

C.S. Lewis said, "We can only [live God's new life] for moments at first. But from those moments the new sort of life will be spreading through our system: because now we are letting Him work at the right part of us. It is the difference between paint, which is merely laid on the surface, and a dye or stain which soaks right through."

Kyle Bauer

EMBRACE DISCIPLINE

Proverbs 19:27

"If you stop listening to instruction,
my child, you will turn your back on knowledge." (NLT)

In one of the seasons of my life, when looking to the Lord for a new career, I embarked on the soul-crushing task of interviewing for a new job. During that season, the catchphrase that headhunters would ask a potential candidate was "are you an educated person? Or are you a lifetime learner?" As I understood it, I believed that they were looking to find those who not only had the knowledge and formal training in a specific line of work, but also had the desire to continue to grow. I believe the eagerness to learn strikes at the heart of this proverb.

If we are ever to walk wisely and consistently in the knowledge of God, we must embrace discipline. For that, we need to be like professional athletes who have knowledge and experience in the game and consistently continue to develop. Their primary focus in life is mastering their sport, and as such, they never stop learning about it. For them, continually gaining knowledge and understanding in their field is indispensable. If they are to remain at the highest level of the game, they can never stop learning and never cease doing the very disciplines that brought them to this level.

In like manner, the knowledge of God and His ways are not, as my pastor likes to say, a one-and-done experience. Instead, God desires our walk with Him to be continually vibrant and life-giving, one that grows strong and flourishes.

Jesus, being our greatest example, never stopped moving forward. He never failed in the disciplines He knew would bring him to that eternal life-altering moment of the cross. Instead, he made sure that the disciplines of being alone with the Father, prayer, and gaining knowledge of the Word never ceased to be a priority.

Let us also not stop listening, growing, and moving forward so that we might walk worthy of the Master and not stray from His Word and knowledge.

Jose Nolasco

TRUE FRIEND OR FALSE FRIEND?

Proverbs 12:26

"The godly give good advice to their friends;
the wicked lead them astray." (NLT)

Have you ever received bad advice from a well-meaning friend? Advice on relationships, car problems, plumbing issues, childcare, finances, or other things? We can become temporarily upset by bad advice but quickly forgive it because they mean no harm. I used to be on the receiving end of people who gave bad advice just to hurt me.

"The godly give good advice to their friends," because the godly care about their friends, families, and neighbors. The godly will instruct us in the things of the Lord (even when we do not want their advice). The godly, though not perfect, will always try their best to be there for their friends and give us godly counsel. However, even when the wicked have friends, they will purposely lead them astray. They encourage us to "try some recreational drugs, recklessly drink alcohol, give in to substance abuse, steal a car with them, talk back to our parents, lie to the authorities, cheat on exams," and the list goes on. These were some things my "friends" said to me over the years. Following some of this bad advice got me arrested and hauled into court.

The sobering reality is that there are people, as victimized as they may have been in their own lives, who do not seek the best interests of others. As far back as I can remember, I was always extremely hesitant to call anybody a "friend." My classmates encouraged me to engage in high-risk activities, and I usually suffered several forms of punishment for following their directions. I often asked myself, "how can these people be my friends? They constantly seek my harm and never encourage me to do a single positive thing. Do they truly want the best for me, or are they only using me for their own personal gain and entertainment?"

I never want to make anyone feel the way I often felt growing up regarding false friends. It is always a great reminder to become the friend we always wanted. We should seek to become a true brother and true sister in Christ to all around us. Then, we can cultivate that culture of sincere love, fellowship, and friendship. Jesus said to do unto others as you would have them do unto you.

Victor Miguel Rivera

HIDING HATRED

Proverbs 10:18

"He who hides hatred has lying lips,
and he who spreads slander is a fool." (AMP)

My dad told me that when I was young, we were at a gas station where I stole a small piece of chocolate. I immediately hid it, but when we got home, my dad saw the stolen candy, and we went back to the gas station, where I returned and paid for it. I learned a great lesson that day.

Like guilty children or even Adam and Eve in the garden, we hide because we know we have done something wrong and do not want anyone to find out.

Jesus teaches us not to hate because unresolved hatred festering in our hearts is the attitude that could lead to actions such as murder (Matt. 5:21-22). Though we may not commit murder, if we conceal hatred in our hearts, we allow sin to persist within us. Concealing sin and pretending everything is fine is living a lie.

Foolish people spread slander, and it is hard for them to keep track of their lies. Remembering the details can be difficult, because it is not the way it really happened. It is unwise to lie and slander because the truth always comes out, and when it does, the liar will be left naked and exposed like Adam and Eve, desperately looking for cover.

But the Bible says that the truth will set us free. The Ten Commandments tell us we are not to lie and give false witness, and we are not to murder. You may not have murdered someone physically, but if you hide the sin of hatred, murder is alive in your heart. So, let's put aside the sin of lying or hiding hatred in our hearts and put on the spirit of love, which does not harm our neighbor.

Heavenly Father, forgive me for hating others, even if I feel my hatred is justified, though I know my hatred is **never** justified in light of what you have done on the cross for me. You have called me to love and to be truthful as You are.

Stephen Larkin

BE STILL

Proverbs 20:3

*"It is to one's honor to avoid strife,
but every fool is quick to quarrel." (NIV)*

Have you noticed that everyone wants to win? I have seen that even in children. There is a tendency always to want to be the winner, whether right or wrong. One time a parent told me that her daughter had to win all the time, and if she did not, she would throw a fit. A word to the wise—do not let your child act like that. There are times when you, as the parent, have to win the battle of wills with your child.

Proverbs 20:3 tells us that avoiding strife and fighting is the mark of an honorable person. Disagreements are inevitable, but it will be up to us to represent Jesus well in the way we behave and speak. Next time you are faced with a situation or tempted to start an argument, be still in the Lord.

Before I was called into the ministry, there was a situation where accusations were leveled against me. These charges had no basis or foundation. I decided to stay still and trust in the Lord. By not following the argument, God honored us (my wife and me) by giving us the privilege of being the founders of a new church in Mission Hills, California. Had I defended myself and fought my cause, the outcome for the ministry would have been different.

Do not despair if you are in a situation where you think that fighting will solve this matter! Remember, the fight belongs to the Lord!

Ricardo Chaidez

RUN TO THE FORTRESS

Proverbs 18:10

"The name of the Lord is a strong fortress;
the godly run to him and are safe." (NLT)

There have been countless times in which I have witnessed my daughter run to her father when he gets home. She screams with joy and shouts, "Daddy!" Whether he is gone ten minutes or ten days, she is filled with exponential excitement upon his return. There is no one on this planet that could ever replace her father, and that is the same feeling our Heavenly Father wants us to have about Him.

I know, however, not every father is the same. Some people may only have bad memories of a father coming home drunk, or perhaps receiving a cold slap from the back of their dad's hand, or hearing callous words spewed from a critical mouth. Perhaps the only memory they have is of their father walking out, never to return. This is NOT who God is. He is a good and perfect Father. He is a protector and a shield of safety for his children.

Proverbs 18:10 speaks to the strength of God the Father and the protection He longs to provide to His children. God is a fortress that cannot be shaken. He provides His children with a shelter for us to run to, not just in times of trouble but simply to be in His presence. His arms are a place for us to receive His loving embrace and take refuge as He valiantly defends us from the chaos of the world.

Whether we were brought into a home with an exemplary father or otherwise, let us be reminded that our Heavenly Father cannot compare. His unconditional love will always find a way to protect us in the ways that we need. Run to His fortress and embrace the safe haven that He longs to provide.

Jennifer Shank

WISDOM COMES TO REST

Proverbs 14:33

"Wisdom rests in the heart of him who has understanding,
but what is in the heart of fools is made known." (NKJV)

Sadly, in today's world it is disheartening to see how quickly so many will mock anything having to do with God. It seems like all the best-selling books will often take swipes at the Church, the people of God, and anything having to do with the Creator. Yet, no matter how hard one tries to reason with people who have this cultural mindset, it is far too much of a stretch for them to accept the goodness and reality of who God is, even amidst verifiable phenomena, living testimonies, and scientific support for God's truth and His reality. Those who are disposed to resist and reject God's grace go to great lengths to discount His existence. Sadly, for these the chasm is far too deep and the divide too wide for them; God and His Wisdom find no place in them.

Yet for those who love God and search for His truth, wisdom finds a place of rest in their heart. This is a great promise that one can count on. You may not have a theological background or think you are capable of great wisdom, but God makes His Wisdom readily available to those who ask Him. The Word assures us that wisdom will find a resting place in those who are teachable. Seek, and you will find understanding about the ways of God.

This verse assures us that if we humbly seek God with soft and teachable hearts, with love for Him, wisdom will come to rest in our very hearts.

Jose Nolasco

PATHWAY THROUGH THE PROVERBS

DISTINCTION OF A LIFETIME

Proverbs 25:3

"As the heavens are high and the earth is deep,
so the hearts of kings are unsearchable." (NIV)

It was the lockdown for everyone else, but for me, it was a writer's dream, a retreat of quality time! The manuscript lay before me like the wardrobe closet leading into Narnia. There was just one problem. It was locked. I needed a voice for the hero of the story. I went deeply into research, conducted interviews, and met the person who would become my version of the character. This one had come from the military, was groomed for command, and had impeccable discipline. After listening carefully to the premise, he agreed to help. I was suddenly impacted by the bluntness of his wisdom. He was the one I was considering for the protagonist of the story when this verse in Proverbs came to my awareness. Once I completed the consultations, I found that I missed our conversations and the larger-than-life imprint this military expert had provided. His insights went far beyond the development of my manuscript. I felt as if I had become his trainee.

In the glare of his inspection, I suddenly had a sense of how it is when God reviews my life. In a very similar way, when coming into the Presence of the Lord, consider yourself most carefully! His ways are beyond all searching out. The Lord's intelligence is massive beyond any human standards. How do you regard God when you pray? Just like the military expert being consulted for specific details for a book, communing with God is a very high honor…being near Him…hearing His voice… the distinction of a lifetime! Yet, how many regard it as such?

I hope you understand how our GOD is AWESOME, exceedingly far beyond what we may experience in daily, temporal ways!

Juline Bruck

GET UNDERSTANDING

Proverbs 17:10

"One word of correction breaks open a teachable heart, but a fool can be corrected a hundred times and still not know what hit him." (TPT)

Nobody likes discipline in the moment, and on that, I think you would agree with me. Correction hurts and causes you to humble yourself, but only if you are willing to accept the correction. Even though I cannot say that I like discipline, I can say that I love being disciplined, because I know that it will make me wiser as a result.

Those with a teachable heart are wise, understand correction, and love knowledge. They accept discipline because they want to become better and learn from their mistakes. A moment of constructive criticism is like a key that unlocks their heart to deeper wisdom. But the foolish do not understand discipline, because they refuse to accept it. There is no key of constructive criticism that can open their heart. The foolish hate correction and refuse to learn from their mistakes, so they stay as fools who hate knowledge. *"Whoever loves discipline loves knowledge, but whoever hates correction is stupid."* (Prov. 12:1, NIV)

The foolish refuse to accept discipline, so if anyone tries to correct a fool, they will only be pushed aside and hated by him. This is because the foolish do not want to change. *"Anyone who rebukes a mocker will get an insult in return. Anyone who corrects the wicked will get hurt. So don't bother correcting mockers; they will only hate you. But correct the wise, and they will love you. Instruct the wise, and they will be even wiser. Teach the righteous, and they will learn even more."* (Prov. 9:7-9, NLT)

Love correction and discipline, and you will do your soul a favor. He *"who disdains instruction despises his own soul, but he who heeds rebuke gets understanding."* (Prov. 15:32, NKJV).

Joshua Bauer

ASLEEP OR AWAKE?

Proverbs 20:13

"Do not love [excessive] sleep, or you will become poor;
open your eyes [so that you can do your work]
and you will be satisfied with bread." (AMP)

Children rarely look forward to bedtime. They will invariably insist, "But I am not sleepy!" Of course, if it were a Friday night, special occasion, or holiday, our parents might relax and give in to our pleas. But for the most part, we did not argue with them.

In the summertime, when we were still young and on school break, Mom would make us take a nap every day. I was always surprised when I awoke to discover just how long I had been asleep. I was completely unaware of the passage of time while I was sleeping.

When we continually press the "snooze button" on our daily tasks and life work, we will later be shocked to realize how much precious time has forever slipped by us. According to this verse, to be asleep is to be lazy; to be awake is to be productive. This scripture is not criticizing the physical necessity of sleep; it is a warning against excessive sleep.

"Do not love sleep, or you will become poor"—literally, "deprived of inheritance." One should not be sleeping when there is work to be done. "Laziness casts one into a deep sleep [unmindful of lost opportunity], and the idle person will suffer hunger." (Prov. 19:15, AMP)

Let us guard our souls from becoming oblivious with excessive sleep. Let us shun the apathetic temperament that renders us half asleep and never fully awake. Let us learn to keep our eyes open so that we can accomplish our work, put bread on the table, and enjoy the rewards of true satisfaction.

Karen Heimbuch

POINT A TO POINT B

Proverbs 20:24

"The Lord directs our steps,
so why try to understand everything along the way?" (NLT)

The shortest route between the starting point and the ending point is a straight line. That is what we want—a nice and easy road toward our ultimate destiny, but you and I know very well that life does not work that way. I have heard it said that if you want to make God laugh, tell Him your plans!

Over the past 20 years of Teresa's and my ministry, we have served in five different pastoral positions, and in four of those, I made predictions. I was only 22 years old the first time, and I felt like I could have done that job forever. Five years later, we went to Texas. I told Teresa we would be in Texas for *at least* ten years. Three-and-a-half years later, we moved to Mexico as missionaries; I was only 31 years old. In Mexico, I told Teresa that we would be in Mexico *at least* until I was 40. Seven months later, we found ourselves back in the United States, not knowing what to do with our lives or what God was doing with us. In 2014, we began the Spanish-speaking side of a church in Santa Clarita, and I told Teresa that we would be there *at least* until I was 40. Five years later, we moved on from that ministry assignment. In June 2019, we came to Pathway SFV, and I told Teresa, ***"I ain't sayin' nothin'!"***

For all my planning to get from point A to point B in a straight line, for all the understanding I had (which was not much), and for all my trying to figure out everything God was up to, I have given up trying to anticipate everything He does or trying to make my plans happen.

But most importantly, however, I have learned along the way that at each step, God has immensely valuable life lessons for us to walk through. It is okay not to know the entirety of God's purposes for our lives all at once. Our job is to be obedient followers and be content to know that He will get us to where He wants us to be!

Kyle Bauer

THE BATTLE IS THE LORD'S

Proverbs 21:31

"The horse is prepared for the day of battle,
but deliverance is of the Lord." (NKJV)

Battles rage all around us. They can come in the form of a belligerent boss, a broken marriage, sickness, facing fear, opening a business, gang violence, substance abuse, financial instability, etc. Unfortunately, as much as I want to tell you otherwise, we will not win every battle on this earth.

If God is for us, how could it be that we could lose any battles? It is impossible to see what God sees. We only see imperfectly through our own limitations. So why prepare for battle if God will do what He pleases? We were not created to carry God's load of omniscience and sovereignty. Our human eyes only see through the lenses of what we are capable of seeing. God can foresee every facet of a situation and consider every precious person involved. When Jesus died on the cross, the disciples thought they had been abandoned, but Jesus showed up and reminded them that He was all He said He was, and He was fulfilling all He told them He would fulfill (and more). Yet, after all Jesus said, all of His apostles died as martyrs—in fact, James was martyred within 10 years of Jesus' resurrection. To our worldly, limited vision, this seems like a lost battle.

But it wasn't.

Where many see loss, God sees victory. God's currency is sacrifice; this does not mean we are fated to torture, but many see loss where God sees victory. No matter how prepared, resourceful, smart, or equipped you may be, God is still working all things for good. He is your redeemer, and not a single battle is yours to win. God is doing so much more in the battle than you can possibly know. What may seem like a loss to us is God working behind the scenes in other situations and lives, and the battle is HIS to win.

Rachael Hopkins

HONEST WORDS FROM A FRIEND

Proverbs 27:6

*"Faithful are the wounds of a friend
[who corrects out of love and concern], But the kisses of an enemy are deceitful
[because they serve his hidden agenda]." (AMP)*

Receiving sincere and honest correction from a loved one, close friend, or authority figure can sometimes feel daunting. The sting that we feel in our spirit, as they tug on deep-rooted insecurities, fears, or past experiences, is not always pleasant. However, that loving correction can often address the spiritual wounds that are residue from past hurts. Just as physical wounds are visible, the fears, sins, and events of our past, buried deep within us, are now also on display. But do not fret, for the Lord uses these wounds to reveal His truth about our life and heart. Through faithful friends, God wants to show us areas in our life that need correction, and He is able and willing to heal that wound and our spirit, mind, and heart in the process.

On the other hand, an enemy will actively work against us, disguising whispers and lies under a facade of something as pleasing or tempting as a kiss. This enemy will try to lure us in with this false display, but there is an alternate agenda behind the mask.

When my sister expressed concern about an area of my life that had been taken over by fear, I felt a tear in my soul, and it opened up a wound I had been concealing. I knew she was right, and I knew the Lord wanted me to surrender this area of my life to Him, but I was stubborn and would not listen. Instead, I was lured in by temporary happiness, the enemy's kiss, and sought healing from this wound through unhealthy habits. The enemy's facade sought only to steal my freedom away from me, the freedom for which Jesus died on the cross. Finally, I realized that the discomfort I felt from this wound was God's way of telling me that any form of temporary happiness would not make the ache go away.

The more we seek the Lord and ask Him to help us work on what needs to be changed or corrected in our lives, the more we will be healed instead of the further destruction that comes from our enemy's deceitful kisses.

Amelia Montantes

HEARING AND LISTENING

Proverbs 29:19

"Words alone will not discipline a servant;
the words may be understood, but they are not heeded." (NLT)

Have you ever tried to reason with a two-year-old? You get nowhere fast. A child understands a discipline event much more than disciplining words. Events are concrete, painful, and eye-opening. Words are abstract and difficult to envision. But when events are combined with potent words, transformation happens.

Proverbs 29:19 is clear that words alone are not enough to adequately transform us. We receive God's Word through many sources—the Bible, teaching, classes, pastors, and church services. How many of us have heard the Word but still struggle in our personal lives with belief, temptation, sin, anger, lust, selfishness, and many other things? How often have we heard God's Word but not listened? Just as a two-year-old can hear, they need extra help to learn to listen through discipline. Take account of moments where you truly learned a life lesson. Did it happen through mere words, or was there also an event surrounding it?

I learned to trust God with my finances, not because someone told me to, but because God brought me through a season where my paycheck was gone the moment I got it. I was constantly irritated, angry, and frustrated. I was a real ray of sunshine in everyone's life. One day I was griping about my situation when the Holy Spirit said, "You don't trust Me, do you?" I thought I did, but now I was not so sure. He continued, "If you trusted Me, you wouldn't be in such a foul mood all the time!" My eyes were opened. I saw my lack of trust. I repented, changed my attitude, and within a week, my entire financial life radically changed. The financial event was what gave the words their transforming power.

God orchestrates events in our lives. When things come to a critical point, He lets us see the truth in His Word that relates to our situation, and transformation happens. Do not ever despise the situations you cannot understand. The process is not done. His Word will breakthrough, give meaning to it, and change your life. His wisdom is found in the process.

Kyle Bauer

DISCIPLINED CHILDREN ARE HAPPY CHILDREN

Proverbs 23:13-14

*"Don't fail to discipline your children. The rod of punishment won't kill them.
Physical discipline may well save them from death." (NLT)*

Discipline in our children's lives is very important because it teaches them that in life, there are limits that must be respected and our actions have consequences. For example, they must wait for the traffic light to signal to cross safely when they want to cross the street. If they cross the street ahead of the light without obeying, they put their lives at risk. Corporal discipline is like the signal that prevents them from being run over, and parents are the ones who teach them to respect the signal. When the child disobeys, parents talk to the child first. If the child does not follow the instructions, we confront the disobedience by requesting that our words be obeyed. Sometimes talking works, but most of the time, talking with a spank on the bottom has more effect in the child's mind for quicker obedience. Spanking should only be given on the rear end, where God gave a cushion. The spanking will hurt, but it will not harm them. Pain is an effective reminder to obey.

Some parents do not want to spank their children because they were mistreated by parents who either hurt or abused them—I am not at all advocating for anything abusive. My husband and I gave corporal discipline to our children when they were little. The method of discipline implemented with them has been healthy and created wonderful relationships within our family. Our kids remember the spankings, but they were not harmed by them. If you only try to reason with your children, you will learn that the kids will not be as fast to obey as if they were corrected with the method of love and discipline suggested by this proverb. I want to encourage you to search what the Bible says about correcting with a biblical understanding. A byproduct will be that you get to enjoy obedient children who know how to respect authority and the limits established by God. Ultimately, discipline is for their well-being.

Teresa Bauer

GETTING TO BE A HABIT

Proverbs 23:26

"O my son, give Me your heart.
May your eyes take delight in following My ways." (NLT)

God wants your heart, which means all of you. He loves you and wants only the best for you. Because of this, He wants you to follow His instructions with joy. Just like tithing. The Lord asks us to trust Him with 10%, but He wants us to give it not because we have to but because we want to, and in giving, we choose to do it with joy! "The Lord loves a cheerful giver." (2 Cor. 9:7)

How many times have I tried to do daily life my own way? Too many. It ended up in disaster, or at the very least, not as good as it could have been if I had done it God's way. Usually, that was because I forgot to ask Him in the first place! I did not want to bother Him with my insignificant daily issues. I forgot that the Bible says He cares about everything! (1 Pet. 5:7)

I finally figured out that asking God needed to become a habit, so I began a practice of asking Him for everything. What should I wear? What socks? What shirt? What pajamas? What to eat? And He would answer! The more I asked about those things, the more of a habit it became to go to Him for everything—not just the little things but also the big things. I have learned we can bring our daily issues before God with confidence. How am I going to pay this bill? How am I going to discipline my child? How am I going to save my marriage? But the questions turned into: Will You please provide so I can pay this bill? Will you please give me Your wisdom so I can discipline my child? Will you please give me faith to save my marriage?

Once you give God your heart (all of you), you are truly allowing Him to rule over your life. In the same way you take delight in looking at a glorious sunset, noticing all His shades of green, or feeling the presence of the Holy Spirit, that is how God will delight you when you follow His instructions. You will always be blessed by Him when you do.

Pat Nannarello

ARE YOU TRUSTWORTHY?

Proverbs 11:13

"A gossip betrays confidence,
but a trustworthy person keeps a secret." (NIV)

Having a trustworthy reputation can only be achieved with time and experience. However, it can be destroyed in a moment when confidence is betrayed. The pain of a betrayed trust is deep, and the relationship can suffer greatly. When it is broken, it can be difficult to repair. A reputation is like ice on a hot day. Once it is gone, it is not coming back. In a church community, it is even more important to be trustworthy because members of a church family are more vulnerable and open to each other, making the pain even deeper when we gossip.

Many years ago, I confided in a Christian friend. Normally, I had a lot of energy and enjoyed volunteering, but one day everything changed, and I hit "burn out." It was an unfamiliar experience, and I felt very guilty and ashamed of my feelings. I needed to talk to my friend who was involved in the same activities that I was. I asked her to please not tell anyone we knew about my feelings. After I shared them with her, I felt much better. About three days later, three of our mutual friends came to console me. I was shocked and felt very betrayed by her repeating what I had told her in confidence. I was also angry at my friend and shared my feelings with her. She apologized sincerely, and I forgave her, but I did not trust her anymore with personal details I did not want to be made public. I learned that it was possible to love my friend and do things together, just not expect her to keep confidence. God has given me people I can trust in confidence, and I appreciate that gift more now than ever. This experience has also made me more aware of being faithful to keep a confidence with someone else because of how damaging breaking trust can be. I have learned that it is important to keep your friend's secrets, even in casual conversations.

Martin and Bea Laufer

RUN TO THE BATTLE

Proverbs 24: 11

"Rescue those who are unjustly sentenced to die;
save them as they stagger to their death." (NLT)

I have to admit, after I chose this proverb to write about, I hesitated—shrank back, thinking, "who am I to write something to encourage the Body of Christ to action?" I am just one small voice. But I heard a minister say, "Run to the battle," and God lit a fire inside me.

My mom used to say "the world is going to hell in a handbasket"! I don't know what the handbasket had to do with it, but the statement is true—the world is willingly on its way to hell. Those who are pushing it in that direction are not only aiming for us, but they are aiming for our children.

When David heard about Goliath, the giant speaking blasphemies against God and Israel, he was incensed and indignant that some godless Philistine would utter such things. His anger turned to action, and with the consent of King Saul, he picked up five stones and ran to the battle. When others around him, even his own brothers, mocked him, he knew His God would give him the strength to defeat this enemy. David swung his slingshot and, with one small stone, felled a giant twice his size. In the face of all his naysayers, God gave him the victory.

There are spiritual forces working in this world trying to steal the hearts of our children and young people. They are the same demons who manifested their evil as pagan gods in the time of antiquity. They are calling evil good and good evil. They are trying to confuse our young children into believing lies about who God created them to be. They are seducing our young people into sexual immorality and perversion.

The Lord has been using the events since 2020 to expose the evil of the enemy. As we, the Church, become wise to the strategies of the devil, it is our turn to rise up, run to the battle, and kill the spiritual goliaths that are trying to take the lives of the ones we love.

Part two continues tomorrow…

Michelle Glush

RUN TO THE BATTLE, CONTINUED

Proverbs 24: 11-12

"Don't excuse yourself by saying, 'Look, we didn't know.'
For God understands all hearts, and he sees you.
He who guards your soul knows you knew.
He will repay all people as their actions deserve." (NLT)

Because of the Supreme Court decision overturning Roe v. Wade, there is now a crack in the altar of idolatry, convenience, and self. However, there is still a battle as it pertains to the states. It is a step in the right direction, but there is a long way to go.

Sixty-three million voices, who never had a chance to be, are calling to us saying, "It is time to stand for those with no voice. Enough! Do not allow another child to be killed, mutilated, abused, or deceived. Speak up for those who cannot speak for themselves. Speak the truth, tell them about the love of Jesus who died for them, and give them a chance to choose life."

Let's stand up and no longer allow hell to seep into our lives and culture. Let's ask God for boldness and open doors, willing hearts, and a spirit of repentance to fall on our nation. I believe God is calling us to light the fire in our hearts and fan the flame of passion for the lost and to save souls.

Ask God how you fit into His battle plan. Not everyone is called to preach, but we all have a part to play, and God will show you what that is. Are you an intercessor, willing to fight the battle for purity and life in the spirit? Are you the next public servant who will pass laws based on biblical principles and righteousness? Are you willing to use your voice or your gifts to draw the next generation to the love of Christ? Even something as simple as voting for biblical values can change the culture.

Whoever God has called you to be, Rise Up, take up your sword—the Word of God—and pray for His will to be manifest here on earth. Pray for the enemy to be defeated, silenced, and for the people who are willing participants to repent and turn to God. Rise up, take up your shield and defend the innocent, the unborn, and those who have been deceived.

Let's stand on God's side—the little ones are counting on us.

Rise up and run to the battle!

Michelle Glush

GOOD MEASURE

Proverbs 11:25

"A generous person will prosper;
whoever refreshes others will be refreshed." (NIV)

This is a proverb with a promise. The promise is received by faith and does not designate any timeline for when the promise will come to pass, but we can believe if God said it, it will surely happen. Luke 6:38 records a similar passage to this proverb: "Give, and you will receive. Your gift will return to you in full—pressed down, shaken together to make room for more, running over, and poured into your lap. The amount you give will determine the amount you get back." (NLT) When we give to others, we demonstrate an aspect of God's character and nature, His unfailing love, and generosity.

I have heard it said that you cannot outgive God, and I have found that to be true in my life. A while ago, my husband and I were attending a church that was having a building fundraiser. It required an immediate down payment of a certain amount of money to secure the land. The Pastor asked the congregation to give a certain amount, and to us, the amount was very challenging. We had given our tithes and offerings and had a certain amount left to take care of other obligations. By faith, we agreed to give the amount requested, and a few days later, we received an unexpected check in the mail that was above what we had given. God is faithful. We just need to stand and believe with expectation and watch Him move.

Acts of generosity do not just have to involve money, but can also include your time, your prayers, and even just the simple ministry of your being present with someone to share your heart with them. When we give to others, whether at church or to someone in need, God takes notice of our hearts and our faithfulness. Not only do the ones you help get refreshed, but God is blessed and takes joy in returning the blessing to you.

Debbie Speese

FEBRUARY

My child,

listen to what I say,

and treasure my commands.

Tune your ears to wisdom,

and concentrate on understanding.

Cry out for insight,

and ask for understanding.

Search for them as you would for silver;

seek them like hidden treasures.

Then you will understand what it means

to fear the Lord,

and you will gain knowledge of God.

—Proverbs 2:1-5

FLATTERY WILL GET YOU NOWHERE

Proverbs 29:5

"A man who flatters his neighbor
spreads a net for his feet." (NKJV)

Flattery will get you nowhere…except in politics, sales, and dating apps.

Many of us are of an age where we remember the adage above was something that was meant to help us or protect us from harm. I mean, flattery itself feels pretty good for the person receiving it, and, in our contemporary society, if it feels good, what could be wrong with it, right? (Wink! Wink!)

Now add to that question the reality that this proverb describes flattery as laying out a net. Flattery means smooth or slippery; it also means to divide and plunder. The primary thought behind this word is that of being faithless, flattering someone, or being smooth in speaking. Flattery is a smooth and slippery speech that aims to lull someone into a false sense of security, and once they are disarmed and cannot see the trap, they can be plundered. You see, the person giving the flattery is spreading a net for the person receiving it so that, if it's successful, the recipient will haplessly and unwittingly fall into this trap!

Interestingly, every use of the word flattery in the Old Testament carries a negative connotation. It is a complement with an agenda; the flatterer uses his words to find favor and gain access to important people. The Bible warns us against the wayward and flattering woman who would use glowing comments to seduce a victim to fall into her trap. Here is a simple way to remember the difference between flattery and a compliment: Flattery gives you a big head, while a compliment builds your character and confidence. "Knowledge puffs up but loves builds up." (1 Cor. 8:1)

Jose Nolasco

A SOURCE OF LIFE

Proverbs 25:23

"The north wind brings forth rain,
and a backbiting tongue an angry countenance." (NKJV)

Have you ever been caught in a rainstorm while driving or hiking? For me, it was the latter. My friends and I were walking back from a hiking trip when we felt droplets of rain on our heads that soon turned into a brutal rainstorm. It was as if the rain were angry at us as we ran back to our car, getting soaked from head to toe. This hiking trip and the rain that followed remind me of the countenance of a person when we allow our tongues to gossip about them.

A backbiting tongue hurts not only the "gossipee" but also the "gossiper." The pain is not in the physical but in the heart. When we gossip, even if it is not with malicious intent, we are not spreading the life that God calls us to sow with our tongues. Instead, we are allowing our hearts to conform to the culture of this world when we should guard our hearts with the truth of God's Word.

God knows the incredible power of our tongue, which is why He gave us one. The tongue has the power to bring life and praise to our Lord. But when we gossip, we also bring pain to the Lord, and our spiritual life becomes like stormy weather. God's pain is justified because our hearts are "the wellspring of life," which is why He does not want to see anything destructive come from that bountiful source of life.

Proverbs 25:23 is a reminder to tame our tongues, thus guarding our hearts. Before speaking about someone who is not present, pray to the Lord: "May these words of my mouth and this meditation of my heart be pleasing in your sight." (Ps. 19:14, NIV) When we use our tongues as a source of life instead of one that produces backbiting remarks, it brings a smile to God's face.

Amelia Montantes

EAR TO THE TRACKS

Proverbs 22:17

"Pay attention and turn your ear to these sayings
otherwise apply your heart to what I teach." (NIV)

Can you listen to two people talking loudly at the very same time? Can you be in a room that is full of light and darkness? Can you stand on your head while you are walking down the street?

There are some things that just cannot be done at the same time. This choice proverb describes God's wisdom as "shouting" to us right now, "You cannot listen to me and learn my ways while listening to the world's wisdom, philosophy, and lifestyle; it is one or the other!"

Proverbs 22:17 in The King James version says, "Bow down your ear and hear these words." The Hebrew carries the meaning "to bend the ear." In other words (in the Chris Stanton version!), "Grab the broad part of your ear and pull it down to the ground and pay attention to what I will speak!"

In the early days of our country, people would put their ears to the railroad tracks and listen for the train, and they would be able to hear it coming long before they could see it. I believe that if we bend our ear to the Lord, He will teach us things that are to come (see Jer. 33:3). He will give us understanding. He will solve the mysteries that are in our hearts. He will teach us the way to go when we do not know. He will show us where we need to go. He will give us direction, comfort, and counsel... but we must put our "ear to the track." With the ear to the track, we will hear the plans God has for us.

What is more, I have a simple map of the three railroad tracks where we can hear what God's good plans for us are:

1. Find a place to be alone, be quiet, and prepare your heart to listen for God's voice.
2. Pray and speak with God about all the questions on your heart.
3. Read the Bible, look up the subject of the question you are concerned about, and read until He speaks with an answer from His Word.

Pay attention and put your ear to that track.

Chris Stanton

WHAT GOD REALLY LIKES

Proverbs 21:3

*"The Lord is more pleased when we do what is right and just
than when we offer him sacrifices." (NLT)*

Eugene Peterson, in his dynamic equivalent translation of the Bible, "The Message," translates this verse:

> *"Clean living before God and justice with our neighbors mean far more to God than religious performance."*

In my marriage, I can be a dutiful husband for my wife, making sure her needs are provided for, and mechanically do "things" without passion and desire, or I can live a life of dedicated, passionate, open, and honest love with her, simply because I want *her* for her own sake. It is a life lived out of love, not performance or mere duty. Similarly, it is out of thankfulness, not obligation, that we serve the Lord. Did you ever consider that just as my wife wants my passion, desire, openness, and honesty in a deeply intimate and personal relationship, perhaps God wants the same with us? Psalm 119:7 says, *"As I learn your righteous regulations, I will thank you by living as I should!"* (NLT)

A while back, in a time of prayer, I was lamenting the damaged and foul state of our world, and I felt so small. My desire is to see the world change, and I have dedicated my life to the ministry to impact people with the Gospel of Jesus Christ. Yet even with that desire to change the world, it seems like nothing significant is happening. As I was pondering this, the Holy Spirit spoke to my heart, saying,

> When you live thankful, and when you do what is right, you bless Me. A world that is so damaged and corrupt hurts My heart, but when I see people doing what is right, it is like a breath of fresh air to Me. Even if that was all the impact you ever had in this life was to bless Me, it would be worth it.

This began to change my view on my life's significance in the eyes of the Lord. Neither you nor I are the saviors of this world. Our primary job is to love the Lord our God with all our heart, soul, and strength. Obedience, belief, humility, and thankfulness bless God's heart more than anything else.

Kyle Bauer

PARTYING WITH THE DEVIL?

Proverbs 16:12

"Good leaders abhor wrongdoing of all kinds;
sound leadership has a moral foundation." (MSG)

During my college years, I was the captain of the dance team. I danced at many stadiums, in front of thousands during football games, and occasionally would be seen on TV when we had national coverage. I performed with confidence and enthusiasm, but I had a little secret: behind my smile was a young woman who struggled with self-image issues. I wrestled with negative thoughts about my weight and was always comparing my body to other women. I never had a full-blown eating disorder; however, I had a horrible relationship with food. I wish I could say that those damaging ideas never entered my mind anymore, but sometimes the devil sneaks up on me, and I begin to entertain those same critical notions once again.

Have you ever struggled with unfavorable thoughts about yourself? In giving in to those thoughts, we are engaging in unnecessary conversation with the devil and giving him entrance to hold us in deception. Instead, we need to focus on the Word of God, concentrating on things that are true, pure, praiseworthy, noble, and lovely (Philippians 4:8). If we believe the devil's lies rather than God's truth, then we are missing the mark. Listening to the lies of the devil can lead to wrongdoing which is exactly what he wants. We simply cannot give him the entrance to do that!

According to Proverbs 16:12, good leaders should hate all wrongdoings. Good leadership is not just about confronting the wrongdoing of others; it is also about recognizing the same in ourselves. Standing on the moral foundation of God's Word will help us process through our struggles, and when those thoughts begin to arise, we have two options. Option A: We can take the thoughts captive and lay them at the feet of Jesus (2 Cor. 10:5), or Option B: We can blow up some balloons and have a party with the devil.

If you are unshakeable in your faith, then the answer should be obvious.

Jennifer Shank

LET GOD TELL YOU WHAT TO DO

Proverbs 13:13

Ignore the Word and suffer;
honor God's commands and grow rich. (TMB)

A part of me hates being told what to do. As a child, I used to say to myself that I could not wait until I was an adult and could do what I wanted and would not have to listen to anyone else force me to do what they wanted me to do. Well, there's a saying, "youth is wasted on the young." How true. In my youth, because of my youth, from a youthful premise (no experience), I believed I knew what was best for me and what I did and did not want to do. I felt others were just too pushy in telling me what to do.

As an adult, not enjoying being told what to do usually means I do not appreciate folks ordering me to do something, especially if I have a better understanding or, frankly, do not respect their position or premise over or above my own. However, in my adulthood, I have learned it is best to modify that disposition. In a spiritual context, I am to obey those who have rule over me (Hebrews 13:17). In secular contexts, I am to agree with my adversary to keep the peace (Matt. 5:25). I also must maintain a godly testimony by being obedient, often when I do not want to. Adulthood has a way of teaching you that.

Solomon speaks in a spiritual and natural context about accepting instruction, doing what you are told to do, doing it by choice, and liking it. Follow God's instructions in His word, or you suffer. Harsh but true. Honor, reverence, enact, take joy in following God's commands, yes, commands, and grow rich. Notice becoming rich is not positional, meaning immediate and infinite. Rather, it is progressive, earned, literally, and abstractly.

Well, the young lad who hated being told what to do, became a teen, young adult, and adult whose mother often said to him that even as a young lad, he was obedient and mature. So perhaps following God's commands causes the intended outcome to sort of rub off on you, even if you do not see it. By the way, one could infer being rich is not to suffer. Selah.

Lloyd Speese

DISCIPLINE DELIVERS

Proverbs 20:30

"Physical punishment cleanses evil;
such discipline purifies the heart." (NLT)

Why do parents oftentimes let their children "run the show" by throwing tantrums or making snarky remarks? It is literally a show, and a test of wills, that the kids put on at the store, at church, or wherever they can get away with it. In the Bauer house, we never allowed our kids to throw tantrums, either when they were young or now that they are teenagers. We have taught them that things are not obtained that way. If this behavior is not confronted and corrected, they will not "grow out of it," it will only follow them into adulthood.

Corporal punishment confronts the sinful nature. When we talk about corporal punishment, we are talking about spanking on the bottom and "time out" on a chair or their bed. When our children were young (only up to 12 years old), my husband and I corrected them with a spanking. This is in no way a "beating" or abuse. It is done mildly (and only on the rear end) with love and understanding. Our parental philosophy was that most corporal discipline should be done by the age of five. We have experienced that after five years old, having been diligent, there are very few instances of corporal discipline needed through the ages of six to 12. We spanked them not because we were angry but to teach them that disobedience to our instructions was not acceptable.

It is our responsibility to teach our children obedience and discipline so that their hearts, as the proverbs say, are purified through correction and not allow foolishness to take root. This kind of discipline teaches children that there are consequences for their actions. We have told our now older children that the older they get, the more severe the consequences are. Corporal discipline as a child is nothing compared to the life-changing consequences as an adult.

The "terrible twos" or "teenage rebellion" are not a given. Properly implemented discipline requires a different way of living and thinking in a family. Now that our children are teenagers, my husband and I enjoy being with them and seeing them doing good, loving Jesus, obeying their parents, and respecting authority.

Teresa Bauer

FEAR IS IDOLATRY

Proverbs 10:24

"What the wicked dread will overtake them;
what the righteous desire will be granted." (NIV)

Only days after God freed the Israelites from slavery in Egypt with many miracles, they camped by the Red Sea. When the Egyptians attempted to recapture them, the people broke out in a panic, and despite the miracles they had seen God work, their response was anything but faith. "Weren't there enough graves for us in Egypt?" they cried.

Their contention was the exact opposite of God's intention. He intended a life of promise and goodness for His people, but they accused Him of bringing them death. In fact, five times they accused God of trying to kill them.[1] Finally, the Lord had had enough. His response to their lack of faith and enduring fear was final: "… I will do to you the very things I heard you say. You will all drop dead in this wilderness!"[2] The very thing they feared became their reality.

People who live in fear—both Christian and not—find themselves overtaken by the fears they confess, whether it be sickness, loss, trouble, or lack. It is as if confessing and holding on to fear becomes a self-fulfilling prophecy. In his book *Why Zebras Don't Get Ulcers*, Sapolsky writes, "…disease emerges…out of the fact that we [allow stress/fear] for months on end, worrying about mortgages, relationships, and promotions."[3] In other words, our fears literally sicken us—and overtake us.

All people desire the same things: satisfaction, love, health, and safety. But such things are a double-edged sword. We can pursue them in this ephemeral life and live equally in fear of losing them—idolatry at its core—or we can live for something eternal that can never be lost. In talking about this life, Jesus said that if we will "lose it for [His] sake," we will find the real thing.[4] Idolaters live holding on to the fleeting things of this world, while the godly have an eternal inheritance that will never be lost awaiting them. So, "do not throw away your confidence, for it will be richly rewarded."[5]

Kyle Bauer

1   Exodus 14:10-12;15:22-24; 16:1-3;17:1-4; Numbers 14:1-3
2   Numbers 14:28-29 (NLT)
3   Sapolsky, R. M. (1998). Why Zebras Don't Get Ulcers: An updated guide to stress, stress-related disease, and coping New York: Freeman, 7
4   Matthew 10:39
5   Hebrews 10:35-36

SWEETER THAN PERFUME

Proverbs 27:9

"Oil and perfume make the heart glad;
so does the sweetness of a friend's counsel that comes from the heart." (AMP)

Finding true friends is like finding treasure. They are better than the riches of oil and the sweetness of perfume!

I have some wonderful friends in my life who are jewels. We laugh together, cry together, pray together, and love to go out for Mexican food. These wonderful people have also walked with me through the most difficult times of my life. Their sweet counsel has brought me comfort, a listening ear, wise words, and sometimes a swift kick in the pants.

One of my treasures is a friend who has been in my life for 40 years. He is a continual prayer warrior on my behalf, always pointing me to Jesus, bringing me to the Word of God, and giving me godly counsel in times of need or distress. (And, he's even chased me around the house with a garden hose until I picked up his 12-string guitar to defend myself!) He has been a picture of God's faithful love and character throughout my life.

Another jewel in my treasure chest is a friend whose hospitality brought me back to life. In a time of great need and confusion about the future, she opened her home and her heart to give me a place to stay while Doctor Jesus worked in my life to bring me back to wholeness. Her friendship showed me the kindness and unfailing love of God.

Who is our greatest friend (treasure)? Jesus.

Not only is He our Savior and Lord, not only is He our brother, but at the Last Supper He gave us the opportunity to call Him our friend. He wants to laugh with us, comfort us in times of distress, be our rock and our fortress, and share the deepest secrets that only true and best friends share. (Ps. 25:14 NLT)

Just like the sweet scent of oil and perfume will make you glad, the sweet counsel of a true friend will bring you joy. They love you for who you are, and instead of trying to make you into their image, they help you to become more like Jesus.

Michelle Glush

HONEST HEARTS

Proverbs 16:11

"The LORD demands accurate scales and balances;
He sets the standards for fairness." (NLT)

Accurate scales and balances have to do with honest business practices (and honest taxes!). Honest dealings and personal integrity in everything we do are God's standard for living daily in righteousness.

Do you make things just slightly unfair in your favor? Do you report *all* of your taxable income? Do you tell a little white lie here and there, so you come out looking better than others?

I am reminded of the time years ago when I held a meeting at a church, and only five people came. I reported to the pastor that "five or six" people came. Later the Lord told me I was a liar because exaggeration was a lie! It was FIVE, not SIX people. I added one more person so I could look just a bit better. My internal "scales" of integrity were off balance.

At the end of the day, honest dealings come down to the motives of the heart. We can be outwardly flawless but impure on the inside. In Matthew 5:21-28, Jesus redefines murder and adultery as not merely outward actions but sinful intentions; murder begins with anger harbored in the heart, and adultery begins with lust harbored in the heart. It is easy to say, "Well, I never actually committed murder or adultery." However, Jesus is pointing out the state of the heart. Though these *actions* were not technically committed on the outside, the fact is that the *sin* is still lurking underneath the surface.

Let's take this a step further. *Why* do we do the things we do? We could do something that is outwardly good and biblical, but what is the motive that drives the good work? Position? Accolades? Was the good work truly for the Lord, or was it for some other motive?

The "honest dealings" and "accurate scales" are balanced by the Lord, whose standard of fairness is weighed by His Word, which discerns and judges every intent, motive, and thought of the heart. Are our hearts truly lined up with our actions, because good actions with sinful motives are not aligned? Are we being honest with ourselves and before God in the motive of everything we do?

Kyle Bauer

WISE IN WHAT WE SPEAK

Proverbs 10:31

*"From the mouth of the righteous comes the fruit of wisdom,
but a perverse tongue will be silenced." (NIV)*

Have you ever said something and thought, why did I say that? Usually, that means it was either something dumb or cruel that came from your lips. Words spoken cannot be taken back. The same can be said of email or social media posts, which can never be deleted entirely (everything electronically can be discovered, and nothing is ever truly gone). Whether you say it or think it, Jesus is still listening. Jesus said "[*it is]* not what goes into the mouth defiles a man; but what comes out of the mouth, this defiles a man." (Matt. 15:11 NKJV) As believers, it matters to Jesus how we talk, what we say, and how we say it.

I had a situation arise at a job long ago where the manager hired a person into a position where I was supposed to be promoted. They gave the position to a new hire, and the manager never gave me an explanation. I wanted to tell everyone how upset I was and how much I did not appreciate it, but the Lord gave me the grace to shut my mouth when I started to say something. So, I decided to trust and obey the Lord by keeping my mouth closed lest I say something unfitting.

As we trust God and believe that he directs our path, as we walk by faith in Him and lean on His understanding and not our own, we will have the strength to walk in His knowledge and be wise in what we speak.

Debbie Speese

PLAN TO DO GOOD

Proverbs 14:22

"If you plan to do evil, you will be lost;
if you plan to do good, you will receive unfailing love and faithfulness." (NLT)

Have you ever planned to do evil? Have you ever concocted a plan to hurt, steal, damage, destroy, deface, vandalize, or inflict any other type of harm? Or have you ever planned to do good? Have you planned to help, heal, rehabilitate, repair, clean, restore, or do any other act of kindness? What happened?

Plans of evil, according to Proverbs 14:22, will cause you to become lost. As a child in elementary school, I remember planning all sorts of crimes. As a teenager, I acted out several of them. As this proverb says, I truly became lost in my plans to commit evil. We become lost because our minds can so quickly become depraved and desensitized, skewing our view and blurring our judgment. Planning evil, no matter the scale, will always lead us astray, and, in addition to hurting ourselves, it will hurt others as well.

However, Proverbs 14:22 gives us hope. If we plan to do good, we put ourselves in a position to receive God's unfailing love and faithfulness! With all the blessings He has for us, we also open ourselves to receive favor and blessing from those around us. When we plan to do good, it is not only for the promise from the Lord to obtain blessing, but also it is out of a thankful heart for what the Lord has done for us.

Have you ever been so captivated by the Lord and so in love with Jesus that good deeds flow out of you in love to God and love for your neighbor? As we continue to plan for good, the Lord promises His unfailing love and faithfulness upon our lives. The Lord will bless our paths as we meditate on Him. So, out of our love for Jesus and love for our neighbors, let's be a people who always plan to do good!

Victor Miguel Rivera

LOVE FULFILLS THE LAW

Proverbs 21:10

"The soul of the wicked desires evil;
his neighbor finds no favor in his eyes." (NKJV)

In Luke 10:29, a teacher of the law asked Jesus, "…who is my neighbor?" In reply, Jesus answered with the parable of the Good Samaritan (Luke 10:30-37), a story of a traveler robbed, badly beaten, and left for dead on the side of the road. Jesus went on to say that none of his fellow Jews stopped to help, but only a foreigner, a Samaritan man, was kind enough to care for and help him. He took pity on him and bandaged his wounds and carried him on his donkey to the nearest inn, and took care of his financial needs while he recovered. By his actions, he showed love to this man and thereby fulfilled the second commandment that Jesus gave us, to "love your neighbor as yourself."

This leads us to an interesting question. What is a neighbor? In American culture, we think of neighbors as the people who live around us in our "Neighborhoods." But the Vine's Expository Dictionary defines a neighbor as, "according to Christ, any other man irrespective of nation or religion with whom we live or whom we chance to meet." Our neighborhoods just got a whole lot bigger!

So, while a wicked person would seek to harm anyone other than himself because he has no regard for and finds no favor in a neighbor, we are called to love our neighbors just as we would love ourselves. How do you love your neighbor? Read the parable of the good Samaritan again for a refresher. Love truly fulfills the Law (Rom. 13:8).

Heavenly Father, thank You for loving and favoring me. Help me to love those around me as You love them. Let me favor them as You favor me and not harbor evil in my heart by ignoring their suffering.

Stephen Larkin

KEEPING IN STEP WITH GOD'S WILL

Proverbs 24:30-34

"One day I passed the field of a lazy man, and I noticed the vineyards
of a slacker. I observed nothing but thorns, weeds, and broken-down walls.
So, I considered their lack of wisdom, and I pondered the lessons I could learn
from this: Professional work habits prevent poverty from becoming your
permanent business partner. And: If you put off until tomorrow the work
you could do today, tomorrow never seems to come." (TPT)

As a stay-at-home mother, it is difficult to structure my unstructured time, because I do not have my mother next to me tapping her foot, insisting that an extra half-hour spent scrolling on the internet is a poor choice. (To be honest, there are some adjustments that I will be making as a result of rereading this posting.)

Time management is not my major struggle, as I organize much of my time well. This day's offering could easily be secular and not differ from reading something from *Seven Habits of Highly Effective People* by Steven Covey.

My life has a higher dimension in that God helps me distinguish between loitering in unproductive matters versus fine-tuning my focus to His intentions for my time. I sense that God is revealing some next steps for my future. I am learning to be productive with my time by spending more time with God so I can hear His "still, small voice." This will move me toward more fruitful actions, work, and decisions that will make the future much more productive. In other words, what we do today matters for tomorrow. Spending time in God's presence to keep in step with His will for our lives is always productive. He will faithfully lead us into fruitfulness!

Juline Bruck

A CRUSHED SPIRIT…

Proverbs 18:14

"The human spirit can endure a sick body,
but who can bear a crushed spirit?" (NLT)

God is our Healer, Restorer, and Redeemer. In our God, we have HOPE, even in sickness. In Romans 15:13, Paul says,*" Now may the God of hope fill you with all joy and peace in believing, that you may abound in hope by the power of the Holy Spirit."* (NKJV) In February of 2022, first my wife and then I came down with the Omicron variant of Covid-19. Since we are both in a high-risk group, we took it seriously, stayed at home, treated each other, and prayed over each other. Our bodies were sick, but our souls were healthy. During that time, our faith and hope were in God, and he carried us through. Today there are no residual effects on either of us. We have lived through many sicknesses and some surgeries, all with faith and trust in our God. Our soul was secure in Him.

Years ago, I went through a dark season of time with depression. It was a very different struggle than any physical illness I had experienced. Doctors did not help me. I realized at the time that I felt no hope. Hope was simply missing. I didn't know why it was missing or even why I needed hope, but I knew I needed it. I felt crushed by the weight of the depression. I prayed to God through faith to restore my hope and my life. It did not happen overnight, but God was there for me and continued to restore, assure, and embrace my soul until I was again hope-filled. I have heard it said that the mind is much harder to heal than the body. I can honestly say that having an established faith relationship with my Heavenly Father, with many past experiences to strengthen my faith, made it possible for my hope to be restored and the crushing burden lifted from me. My answer to King Solomon's question is this: The one who can bear a crushed spirit is one who has an established solid faith foundation in God. One who knows and loves the Lord God, and has an established prayer relationship with Him, can be restored. May God grant you that faith walk in your life that can uphold you through all things.

Martin and Bea Laufer

REFLECTING JESUS

Proverbs 17: 3

*"The refining pot is for silver and the furnace for gold,
but the Lord tests the hearts." (NKJV)*

In 2020, when our church was fasting and praying for issues affecting our nation, the Lord gave me a picture. I saw my reflection in a large and very ornate shiny oval mirror made entirely of gold. As I stood looking into the mirror, a finger touched the surface, and the molten gold became ripply and chaotic, and I could not see myself anymore. But when the chaos subsided, and the mirror became calm again, instead of my reflection, I saw Jesus.

We all go through seasons when we search for God but cannot seem to hear His voice or see where He is taking us. We deal with what appear to be unanswered prayers. However, God is not lost. He has not forgotten His way, His Word, His promises…or ours.

Ephesians 6:10-13 says, *"Finally, my brethren, be strong in the Lord and in the power of His might. Put on the whole armor of God, that you may be able to stand against the wiles of the devil. …Therefore, take up the whole armor of God, that you may be able to withstand in the evil day, and having done all, to stand."*

It is during times of adversity that we learn to stand. We stand on His Word, on His promises, on His goodness, on His unchanging love, and unchanging character.

1 Corinthians 15:56 says, *"Therefore, my dear brothers and sisters, stand firm. Let nothing move you. Always give yourselves fully to the work of the Lord, because you know that your labor in the Lord is not in vain."*

When you walk through times of testing, God has not left you. He is giving you the opportunity to grow deeper in Him, to reach further for Him, and to seek Him with all your heart. When life seems so chaotic that you cannot keep a grasp on who you are, hold onto Him, because when the chaos fades to calm, you will see Jesus looking back at you through the mirror.

Michelle Glush

GROWING STRONG KIDS

Proverbs 23: 13-14

"Do not withhold discipline from a child;
if you punish them with the rod, they will not die.
Punish them with the rod and save them from death." (NIV)

I have worked in children's ministries for the past 17 years. I have been blessed to meet different kinds of personalities and beautiful individuals. Our focus in children's ministries is to guide these wonderful little souls to Jesus.

Children like to test boundaries. They can push the teacher's buttons to try and see what they can get away with. Kids want their way and will use whatever is in their power to get it. As parents, discipline reminds children that for every action, there is a reaction, and every choice has a consequence—either good or bad. Our fallen nature always tends toward sin, and we all need a Savior.

When I think about punishment with the rod, I find it helpful to see it as a support. Think of young, flexible trees that are tied to a support pole. This keeps the small, fragile trees upright and prevents them from falling over and breaking or growing crooked and outside the boundaries set for them. Sometimes the simple act of taking a toy away from a child is not enough of a punishment. Punishment with the rod is more direct and instructive.

The support we provide to children is fundamentally for their healthy growth in the Lord. Teaching kids is always challenging, because, at the end of the day, it is a life-and-death situation. As parents, teachers, and caregivers, it is our responsibility to guide, correct, and support our kids, so they grow into adults who love and follow God. They are our future generation, and they need us, and we need them. Let us instruct them in the ways of the Lord by not withholding the necessary discipline that will help them grow healthy and strong.

Alicia Suarez

THE RECIPROCAL GOD

Proverbs 15:29

"The Lord is far from the wicked,
but he hears the prayers of the righteous." (NLT)

The Lord hears the prayers of those He is pleased with, and He is far from the wicked. *"The eyes of the Lord watch over those who do right, and His ears are open to their prayers. But the Lord turns His face against those who do evil."* (1 Pet. 3:12, NLT) God is a reciprocal God. To reciprocate means to give or do in return. Psalm 18:26 says, *"With all who are sincere, you are sincere, but you treat the unfaithful as their deeds deserve."* (CEV)

The Lord is pleased with those who seek Him, and because they seek Him, He will be near to them. They are the righteous. The Bible says that *"without faith, it is impossible to please Him, for he who comes to God must believe that He is, and that He is a rewarder of those who diligently seek Him."* (Heb. 11:6, NKJV).The righteous accept His decrees and obey Him. But the wicked do the opposite.

The psalmist writes, *"Salvation is far from the wicked, for they do not seek out your decrees."* (Ps. 119:155, NIV) Proverbs 1:24-26 further says, *"But since you refuse to listen when I call, and no one pays attention when I stretch out my hand, since you disregard all my advice and do not accept my rebuke, I, in turn, will laugh when disaster strikes you; I will mock when calamity overtakes you."* (NIV)

God is near to those who are listening, obeying, and seeking Him. He is also a God of grace, mercy, and forgiveness. He desires to be near to everyone and that all come to Him so He can show them His favor.

Joshua Bauer

WISDOM CONQUERS

Proverbs 21:22

"The wise conquer the city of the strong
and level the fortress in which they trust." (NLT)

Wisdom sees beyond the natural. Oftentimes societies and individuals put their trust and devotion into one major thing. We were created as worshipping creatures. When anything other than God is at the center of our being, false worship starts to happen, a pseudo-worship of a false god (objects, ideas, self) that becomes the foundation of what our lives revolve around. When your foundation is the truth, God Himself, you will win everything ultimately. But it may not seem that way in all cases from human eyes but solely through wisdom's eyes.

Let's say you're in battle, and an all-out ripped man in armor twice your size stands before you. You may think, "I'm toast." This might be true in the physical. But a wise man will see beyond the obvious obstacle, like physique or shallow words, and find the weak points of the current threat before him. Is he weak-hearted? Tempted by greed? Easy to distract?

Spiritual strongholds often hide behind grandiose physical gestures. God may assign something to you as simple as making someone's day brighter with a smile or as complicated as going up against a city and not only overtaking the physical space, but also doing spiritual warfare to destroy the spiritual stronghold of the enemy over it.

Whether the spiritual stronghold is led by the flesh or the demonic realm, the bottom line is that by allowing God to use you as a vessel submitted to Him, He will give you the resources you need to complete the task He gave to you.

Rachael Hopkins

69

TWO HEADS ARE BETTER THAN ONE

Proverbs 12:15

"The way of fools seems right to them,
but the wise listen to advice." (NIV)

The person who lacks understanding and wisdom—the fool—listens to his own counsel above everyone else. He takes his own advice as if he alone were the most sagacious of the learned and the only one worth listening to.

By no means does this indicate that we cannot use our brains or come to decisions on our own. But the adage applies here that "two heads are better than one." It is supremely arrogant to believe that your counsel, and yours alone, is sufficient to navigate the circumstances that come up in the family, or a project at work, not to mention the treacherous waters of this life.

God created us for community, and He has gifted people differently in each community. Each person has a different temperament, a different way of seeing things, different specialties and education, a different way of perceiving a situation, processing it, and interests in it. As we cooperate with one another, honoring and listening to what each person brings to the table, we will be able to make wiser decisions that take into consideration the full scope of an issue that one person alone cannot see completely.

Several years ago, I was on a church team charged with building a small group ministry. I was very focused on the recruitment and training of leaders and curriculum. After all, that is what is going to make or break this ministry. In one meeting, a woman said, "But where are we going to put people's coats when they get to the houses?" In my mind, I was immediately dismissive of what I considered to be a foolish question that had little or no bearing on the success or failure of the small groups. I was right regarding the ministry's success, but for many people, these details, which my mind does not naturally gravitate towards, are things that, if thought through, make for a more hospitable and considerate home group. This is something that I most certainly would overlook. But in a team, listening to the advice and honoring the gifts in each other bring greater wisdom and success.

Kyle Bauer

BEHIND THE FACADE

Proverbs 17:20

"One whose heart is corrupt does not prosper;
one whose tongue is perverse falls into trouble." (NIV)

Have you witnessed a person who seems to always be in the right place, say the right things, and maybe even have all the pleasures the world can offer? But then you see who they are behind the scenes. Underneath the facades, corruption has seeped into their heart, and the words coming out of their mouth display the real motives and character of who that person truly is; a corrupt and deceitful person. Proverbs 10:9 reminds us, "Whoever walks in integrity walks securely, but he who makes his way crooked will be found out." (ESV).

We can see corruption, perversion, and deception all around us. Sometimes it feels good to point it out in others because at least we are not that bad, right?

It is easy to slip into a lie to make yourself look better or cover up gossip with "we need to pray for…" and justify our lies to get what we want or save ourselves the uncomfortableness of the truth. Yet those "white lies" can lead us onto a slippery slope toward a corrupt heart.

The Bible is full of examples where people have lied or acted from a place of corruption, some bigger than others, but still, they are all the same—sin. Romans 6:23 says, "For the wages of sin is death." Praise God that those who are in Christ are saved from eternal death, but one day we will all account for our lives (1 Cor. 5:10). Matthew 12:37 also reminds us that by our words, we will be justified, or by our words, we will be condemned.

This verse warns us that corruption will not prosper us, it may seem that way, but the tongue that is perverse and lies will bring trouble to whoever entertains their sinful nature. Therefore, we must guard our thoughts and words, seeking the renewing of our minds through Christ, and not fall down the slippery slope of corruption in our hearts.

Ask God to reveal where corruption has slipped in to areas of your life. Then ask the Lord for deliverance and forgiveness for things you may have thought or spoken that go against the goodness of God.

Jill Alvarado

CHOOSE YOUR WORDS WISELY

Proverbs 21:23

"Watch your words and hold your tongue;
you'll save yourself a lot of grief." (MSG)

The few fights that I remember breaking out on my elementary school playground during recess were not an automatic reflex to an unintentional shove. Most physical fights began over taunting, careless, unbridled words.

This verse strongly urges self-awareness and self-control regarding our words. We must be intentional—not only with the words that we choose to speak, but also the words from which we choose to refrain. To rephrase Shakespeare's Hamlet: "To speak, or not to speak: that is the question…"

Although a horse can be controlled by a small bit in its mouth and a ship can be turned by a small rudder, "no one can tame the *human* tongue; it is a restless evil [undisciplined, unstable], full of deadly poison" (James 3:8, AMP). Just as a spark can set a great forest on fire, so your tongue "can set your whole life on fire, for it is set on fire by hell itself" (James 3:6, NLT). The potential damage of reckless speech cannot be overstated.

> *"Watch your words…"*— Be restraining.
> *"…and hold your tongue…"*— Be abstaining.

If you restrain offensive and provoking words, and abstain from unkind and hostile language, then *"you'll save yourself a lot of grief."* Let us be vigilant in guarding the words of our mouth. As Matthew Henry advises: "Keep thy heart, and that will keep thy tongue from sin; keep thy tongue, and that will keep thy heart from trouble."

Karen Heimbuch

A KIND WORD

Proverbs 12:25

"Anxiety weighs down the heart,
but a kind word cheers it up." (NIV)

Have you ever carried a bag of rocks? They are heavy, awkward to handle, and unless you have a specific use for them, have little to no value. This is what anxiety is like, a burden. In other translations of the Bible, anxiety is described as weighed down, heaviness, and depression. So why do we choose to carry around a bag of rocks called anxiety?

The answer is in the second half of the verse" but a kind word cheers it up." Have you ever walked around with a bouquet of balloons? Or have you ever seen a child receiving a balloon? It's lighter than air, colorful, easy to carry around, and it sure makes kids happy.

In Matthew 6:34 Jesus reminds us saying, *"So don't worry about tomorrow, for tomorrow will bring its own worries. Today's trouble is enough for today."* Jesus, the Son of God, understood and knew about worry or anxiety. Philippians 4:6 (NIV) says, *"Do not be anxious about anything, but in every situation, by prayer and petition, with thanksgiving, present your requests to God."*

What I have found in my life is that I tend to go around picking up "rocks." Each day, I pick up a new and heavier rock; before I know it, I am weighed down. My heart is heavy, and I wish someone would give me a balloon, a kind word, a compliment, something encouraging—anything to replace the rocks I am carrying.

This proverb is doubly insightful. Be careful not to allow anxiety, worry, or depression into your daily life, and a kind word helps to lighten someone's load. God has given you the ability to replace someone's "rocks" by giving them a balloon. The Holy Spirit will give you plenty of opportunities to provide a kind word to someone who needs it. So don't miss out on blessing that person.

The more balloons you hand out, the fewer rocks you will carry. So today, go out and hand out that balloon and lighten someone's heart. You will find that as you do, your load will lighten.

Fred Alvarado

DON'T PLAY FAVORITES

Proverbs 28:21

"To show partiality is not good,
because for a piece of bread a man will transgress." (NKJV)

The definition of partiality is to show an unfair bias in favor of a thing or person compared with another thing or person.

Deuteronomy 10:17 says, *"For the Lord your God is God of gods and Lord of lords, the great God, mighty and awesome, who shows no partiality and accepts no bribes."* In addition, Romans 2:11 states, *"For God does not show favoritism."*

I have worked in the entertainment industry most of my life, and it is definitely a place where partiality rears its ugly head—a lot. I consider myself a hard worker and trustworthy, but in the "biz," that means bupkis (that's Yiddish for nothing)! No one cares about who you are just what you can do for them. I have been thrown under the bus by a co-worker because they messed up and needed to save face and their job. My boss, who trusted me with his life, chose a bigger name over me because this "less than lovely" person could ultimately put money in his pocket. Being on the receiving end of someone else's partiality is no fun.

Basically, this translates to "for a piece of bread (for a buck), a person will lose their integrity." Every person has their price. This is not the "do unto others as you would have them do unto you" instruction that Jesus gives us. (Matt. 7:12)

Partiality is inconsistent with God's character and incompatible with Jesus. If I am trying to be like Jesus, why would I even think not to respect each and every person? He gave His respect to Caesar, to the prostitute, and to the tax collector.

In Proverbs 23:1-3 it says, "The enemy lays a trap for us every time we are exposed to the wealth of the world, and we need to stay diligent." Whenever we are nice to someone because they can do something for us, it will not end well. The Lord loves it when we love others the way He loves us. Remember, "That which you do to the least of these your brethren, you do unto Me."(Matt. 25:36-40)

Pat Nannarello

TODAY IS NOT THE END OF THE STORY

Proverbs 24:19-20

"Do not fret because of evildoers or be envious of the wicked,
for the evildoer has no future hope,
and the lamp of the wicked will be snuffed out." (NIV)

Have you ever heard the saying "The grass is always greener on the other side"? People are never satisfied with their situation; they always think others have it better. Unfortunately, this happens in professing Christians when they see the evildoer prosper.

Proverbs 24:19-20 tells us not to be envious of the evildoer. Our human nature is always competing with others who seem more prosperous than us. But the Word of God reminds us that He cares for all our needs according to His riches in glory. This scripture reminds us not to envy the riches of the wicked, for their riches are only temporary.

Many times in my Christian life, like the Psalmist in Psalm 73, I would question the Lord regarding my financial situation, career, and even the ministry He called us to serve in his kingdom. But just like the Psalmist says in verses 16-17, *"When I tried to understand all this, it was oppressive to me till I entered the sanctuary of God; then I understood their final destiny."* Today as I write, I am reminded of the blessing of knowing the Lord, despite the difficulties every one of us face. So, before we fret about the blessings of others or envy their lives or riches, remember we have the promise of God's blessings and strength and grace in our lives today and in the life to come.

Ricardo Chaidez

PROMISE AND PERFORMANCE

Proverbs 20:6

"Lots of people claim to be loyal and loving,
but where on earth can you find one?" (MSG)

What term did Jesus use most often when addressing the Pharisees? Hypocrites: Those who put on a false appearance of virtue but act in contradiction to their stated beliefs. In other words, they do not practice what they preach (Matt. 23:1-12). Not only do they do whatever it takes to look good in public, but also they expect to be served at the expense of everyone else.

It seems that the Pharisees of the Bible can easily be found in the politicians of today. They love to boast their noble intentions yet typically fail to follow through on any of them, often doing the opposite.

This is precisely what Proverbs 20:6 addresses: Just because you *say* you are loyal or good or merciful or kind, do you back up your words with your actions? Do you have a proven track record? Are you truly steadfast, reliable, trustworthy, faithful?

The word for "*loyal*" in this verse is the Hebrew word *hesed,* which literally means "*unfailing love.*" Boasters are unreliable.

Peter boasted that he would never lose his faith in Jesus, even if everyone else did. He boasted that he would never disown Jesus, even if it meant dying with Him. So said all the other disciples (Matt. 26:31-35).

Although Peter failed three times that very night to keep his promises, Jesus always keeps His word! His name is Faithful and True (Rev. 19:11), and He places a premium on faithfulness:

- "I will search for faithful people to be My companions." (Ps. 101:6, NLT)
- "Well done, good and faithful servant! You have been faithful with a few things; I will put you in charge of many things. Come and share your master's happiness!'" (Matt. 25:21, NIV).
- "He is Lord of lords and King of kings—and with Him will be His called, chosen and faithful followers." (Rev. 17:14, NIV)

Karen Heimbuch

CONTROL YOURSELF

Proverbs 17:27

"He who has knowledge spares his words,
and a man of understanding is of a calm spirit." (NKJV)

Knowledge is defined as facts, information, and skills acquired by a person through experience or education.

Have you ever noticed that someone who runs off at the mouth usually has nothing to say? For all their many words, they do not have any understanding of what they are talking about, and they certainly do not have a calm spirit about them.

Proverbs 13:3 says, *"Those who guard their lips preserve their lives, but those who speak rashly will come to ruin."*

In 1 Kings 3:9, Solomon asked God for "an understanding mind" so he could govern the people of Israel and be "able to discern between good and evil." Throughout the Book of Proverbs, Solomon tells us that knowledge and wisdom give life.

Proverbs 3:21-22 tells us *"…do not let wisdom and understanding out of your sight, preserve sound judgment and discretion; they will be life for you…."*

Have you also noticed that Solomon's proverbs are short and sweet? His instructions are not in long, complex sentences; they are priceless jewels that get right to the heart of the matter. They are short, but they are deep. So, as you seek the wisdom that comes from God's Word and gain an understanding of the knowledge He has provided, you will not be tempted to run off at the mouth or get your shorts in a knot.

Therefore, get wisdom. Get understanding. Read Proverbs.

Pat Nannarello

DO YOURSELF A FAVOR

Proverbs 15:32

"Those who disregard discipline despise themselves,
but the one who heeds correction gains understanding." (NIV)

Let's face it, no one *likes* to be disciplined. It is painful and humbling. No one wants to go through it, yet wisdom suggests that we willingly submit ourselves to the process. It is interesting to note that this proverb says that the people who blow off discipline as unnecessary or beneath them, those who have the know-it-all attitude, actually hate themselves. They are literally doing harm to themselves by rejecting correction.

Discipline has a purpose. Discipline is not done out of anger, but God disciplines us out of love.[6] Psalm 119:75 says, *"You disciplined me because I needed it."* (NLT) Discipline's purpose is to form our character and correct behavior that could ultimately destroy our lives. We are born with a sin nature that desires to live contrary to the way God created life to be lived. Perhaps this is why God put our spirit and soul into a physical body. The suffering we often experience in our bodies is the impetus for our spiritual formation. The Bible says that even Jesus, in his humanity, learned obedience through the things he suffered.[7]

I have taken up a hobby that requires some woodworking skills. I have been learning to use machinery and tools and how they interact with different types of wood. My teacher shows me what needs to be done, then lets me do it. Since I am a novice, he frequently corrects things I am doing wrong, not because he is angry, but because he wants to see me succeed and grow in my abilities. If I reject his counsel and correction, I and the piece I am working on will eventually suffer for it. On the other hand, if I listen, I will grow and become much better. It is the same principle every time we come to God's Word. He gives us the correction, discipline, guidance, and counsel we need for success.

Do yourself a favor: Keep a humble and teachable spirit that loves correction and discipline, and you will grow into a marvelous man or woman of God.

Kyle Bauer

---

6   See Hebrews 12:4-11
7   Hebrews 5:8

MARCH

My child,

never forget the things I have taught you.

Store my commands in your heart.

If you do this, you will live many years,

and your life will be satisfying.

Never let loyalty and kindness leave you!

Tie them around your neck as a reminder.

Write them deep within your heart.

Then you will find favor with both God and people,

and you will earn a good reputation.

—Proverbs 3:1-4

ANSWERING THE FOOL, PT. 1

Proverbs 26:4

"Do not answer a fool according to his folly,
or you yourself will be just like him." (NIV)

Inevitably we all run into the foolish "know-it-all" types who love to run their mouth and spout their infallibly wise opinions in every circumstance. Wisdom dictates that there are times to keep the mouth shut, and other times when the right response needs to be voiced. If we say nothing when stupid things are said, we give agreement by our lack of response and are then consenting and counted among the fools.

"Do not answer a fool according to his folly," in this case, does not mean to keep one's mouth shut. On the contrary, the implication is not to answer silly, foolish opinions with more silly, foolish talk, or you, too, will be seen as a fool. Not answering a fool is not to engage such a person in his endless speculations and arguments. The wisdom of Proverbs instructs us not to entangle ourselves in silly, destructive, ridiculous talk, or we will only be hurting ourselves and gaining a reputation for foolishness. If we confront a fool on his terms, we will be caught in the tornado of stupid arguments that mean nothing, go nowhere, and only cause animosity. For example, "Can God make a rock so big He can't lift it?" Such "gotcha" foolishness threatens to suck you into an endless debate of idiotic and fallacious questions.

How do we answer when foolishness is present? I believe it depends on the context. If someone or a group is deciding on the correct course of action to follow, foolishness should be answered with kindness, truth, and godly wisdom. But, if someone is spouting their foolishness to make themselves look important or push their viewpoint on others in your presence, in public, or on social media, leave it alone and let them be the fool by themselves. Don't get drawn into the vicious vortex of their arguments. Walk away!

Stay tuned for tomorrow's proverb that will shed more light on this issue.

Kyle Bauer

ANSWERING THE FOOL, PT. 2

Proverbs 26:5

*"Answer a fool according to his folly,
or he will be wise in his own eyes." (NIV)*

This proverb, at first glance, seems to contradict the previous one. Proverbs 26:4 says not to answer the fool according to his folly, and 26:5 says to answer the fool according to his folly. So, which is it? We observed in 26:4 that we are not to answer foolishness with more foolishness, or we will become as the fool. However, Proverbs 26:5 tells us that answering a fool according to his folly is not returning foolishness with more foolishness but confronting foolishness with wisdom.

If you speak wisdom in response to foolishness, you will put foolishness in its place. If you let a fool, deceived by his own wicked heart, speak his folly, there will be people who are spiritually blind and who will believe his deception. Further, if a fool's absurdity goes unanswered, then that person could eventually rise to leadership. The opinion of the unanswered voice is the one that rings the most in people's ears. If people cannot discern between godly wisdom and worldly foolishness, which parades itself as wisdom, they may be fooled by the fool and follow him.

Matthew 15:14 says, *"…They are blind leaders of the blind. And if the blind leads the blind, both will fall into a ditch."* (NKJV)

There are times when a godly rebuttal is necessary, lest the fool be the one who has the last word, and you are forced to go along with his foolishness. One fool deserves another—so don't be the other fool. Be the voice of wisdom and reason; be the adult in the room.

Kyle Bauer

MEMORIES AND LEGACY

Proverbs 10:7

"The memory of the Righteous will be a blessing,
but the name of the wicked will rot." (NKJV)

Have you heard the saying "Viviendo la Vida Loca" (Living the crazy life)?

Our youth do not seem to care about the future or the generations that come after them, even if the tragedies of life point them to reflect on their lifestyle. Even tragedies in the lives of other generations do not seem to affect their behavior.

Proverbs 10:7 tells us that there are people that disregard godliness and righteousness. It seems that leaving a legacy for future generations is not a priority in our present world. But time and circumstances will bring the realization that a life lived without restraint will be remembered for generations as a wasted life. Selfishness only thinks about one's self and not future generations.

As I watched my children and my grandchildren grow, I learned I was not setting as good an example as I needed to. One of my loved ones made me aware that I needed to make some changes in how I was leading my family. I realized that I had fallen short of the legacy I wanted my family to have. I was encouraged to read the stories of so many men and women of the Bible who made mistakes but were called righteous and "Heroes of the faith" and remembered for many generations. God is always faithful to help us in our struggles and forgive our faults in our walk with Him. I repented of my actions and made changes.

The memory of the righteous is a blessing. Jesus tells us to be "Salt of the earth and Light of the world." (Matt. 5:13-16) Both of these are a blessing! Salt blesses food with flavor, whereas wickedness brings rottenness. Light gives the blessing of sight, whereas wickedness brings darkness. We can bring these blessings to our families and the world around us by living in His righteousness.

Ricardo Chaidez

THE RIGHT KIND OF DREAMING

Proverbs 13:19

*"It is pleasant to see dreams come true,
but fools refuse to turn from evil to attain them." (NLT)*

We all have dreams. At one point or another, we all have had objectives and goals we have wanted to achieve. We have career goals, relationship goals, and even ministry goals. We all dream, and our dreams are often limited only by our imaginations. Many of us dream big, such as wanting to be the greatest, run the fastest, achieve the most, etc. But would we do anything to obtain them; would we turn to evil to make them come true?

Proverbs 13:19 clearly states that fools turn to evil to obtain their dreams. Cheating on exams does not fulfill us the same way earning an honest grade does, and it will not benefit us in the future. Stealing can grant our immediate material dreams but will never help the spirit and will hinder our relationship with the Lord. Obtaining our dream job will satisfy us for a moment, but lying on a resume or betraying a friend for a promotion will only end up in bitterness and broken relationships. Trying to accomplish dreams in our flesh, using evil tactics, is foolish and will never benefit us in the end.

Unfortunately, we have even seen this within the ministry. Some leaders have been so obsessed with their dream of massive attendance and monetary gains that they are willing to water down the Gospel, preach a prosperity message, and ignore all biblical subject matter dealing with sin, all to see their dream come true.

The Lord sees it all. People who foolishly "refuse to turn from evil to attain [their dreams]" will not benefit, either in their earthly or spiritual lives.

What is the answer? Let's put our trust in God and His Word. Learn how to dream big with the Lord and ask Him to bring about His dream—His will—for us. Also, to see God's dreams for us fulfilled requires steps of obedience. As we walk step by step in obedience, God will lead us to the ultimate destination.

Victor Miguel Rivera

HAIR ON FIRE

Proverbs 16:32

"Better a patient person than a warrior,
one with self-control than one who takes a city." (NIV)

Some people have what is referred to as "a short fuse"—like me. An ignorant person or frustrating event can set my hair on fire in a nanosecond (Nanarello second!). God can even set my hair on fire. And He has.

Without patience (or a short fuse), an argument usually ensues, and sometimes it can look like a war. Arguments bring zero resolution. Early in my marriage, I realized that every time my husband and I argued, it was about the same thing—usually money. We re-hashed the same problem over and over without any resolution, just heartburn. I also realized the discussions were always at the wrong time. They usually happened when one or the other got home from work, where you typically take a moment to relax and not jump into talking about the heavy stuff right away. So, we began to make appointments to talk to each other about the heavy life stuff. FINALLY, we started to get somewhere. We both discovered that being patient in the beginning ended in resolution, which was the goal in the first place!

As Christians, we aspire to be like Jesus. As His disciples learning to be like Him, we are also learning to be patient as He is. Becoming like Jesus is NOT easy. And if you are like me, then you are also learning self-control, because Jesus takes his sweet time about EVERYTHING! I finally figured out that prayer (surprise) can greatly help in acquiring patience. If you are praying and asking God to intervene, you are not arguing, fighting, yelling, or just being stupid.

If someone wins an argument, no one is happy, but with patience comes wisdom, with wisdom comes knowledge, and with knowledge comes the ability to agree without going to war.

Pat Nannarello

EARS TO HEAR

Proverbs 15:31

*"If you listen to constructive criticism,
you will be at home among the wise." (NLT)*

First of all, I love that listening to constructive criticism means that we will be "at home" among the wise. Think of all the wise people you know in your life. They got that way *because they listened to constructive criticism*. In other words, this is a way of life. The wise listen to constructive criticism and grow even wiser. There is an implied converse to this: The wise do not listen to *destructive* criticism.

When I was 19 and 20 years old, I was at a crucial juncture between my teenage and adult years. Though I was still an adult (just barely), I thought like a teenage boy. My father knew this, and he needed to help his boy become a man. As long as I live, I will never forget the conversations we had over those two years. He challenged me and pointed out specific areas of lack, tunnel vision, childish thinking, and dangerous pitfalls I could have potentially fallen into. They were hard and difficult conversations that I did not particularly enjoy. Would you enjoy all of your faults being pointed out to you? I think not.

I specifically remember thinking to myself that I had an important decision to make: Either dad was crazy, and I could disregard his constructive criticism, or I could trust that he loved me, knew more than me, and I would listen and make the necessary changes and imitate the life he lived. I chose the latter.

My dad had always been a wise person, and as such, he was pointing out deficiencies in my life for the purpose of inviting me to live in the same wisdom that marked his life. These conversations happened more than 20 years ago. As a result, I have seen much of the same wisdom in my life and family that my dad's constructive criticism formed in me more than two decades ago. God offers the same wisdom to us, and it is ours if we have ears to hear. James 1:5 says that if we need wisdom, God will generously supply it!

Kyle Bauer

SINFUL GAIN WILL ALWAYS BECOME BITTER LOSS

Proverbs 20:17

"Bread gained by deceit is sweet to a man,
but afterward his mouth will be filled with gravel." (NKJV)

Unfortunately, the world's way of doing things is often easier than doing things God's way. Evil deeds or wrongfully achieved ends sometimes have fewer obstacles than doing things the right way. No matter how tempting this may be, it is important to know that our approach to anything we do matters to God. We are to do things as He would. He sees it, He knows it, and He counts it.

This accountability is important not because God is breathing down our necks to do what He wants us to do, but because there is a price to pay for neglecting to do things God's way. He does not want us to experience the consequences of reckless behavior.

For instance, running across the street is all fun and games until someone does not look both ways. Solomon is essentially giving us the same type of warning in this proverb. He is telling us that anything gained by perverse means may seem wonderful at first. If you do it deceitfully, you may quickly get what you want and feel good and comfortable. You may even gain more opportunities and be seen by others with envious eyes, wondering how you attained your success. But, give it some time, and that success quickly gained will soon be corrupted and will fall apart. It is worth heeding this warning, bread gained by deceit is sweet but later turns to gravel in the mouth.

Rachael Hopkins

KINGS LOVE CHILDREN

Proverbs 22:11

*"He who loves purity of heart and has grace on his lips,
the king will be his friend." (NKJV)*

It is amazing to watch the impact of a toddler on a group of people. We adults see their purity in every way. We are amazed at their innocence, their awe of every discovery, their excitement with what is often simple, and their simplicity in determining what is joyful. In essence, we love the purity of heart in a child. We are immediately drawn to them and instinctively become or attempt to emulate what they innately exude. Adults become childlike.

At first glance, one might see this proverb at face value and interpret purity of heart as essentially a destination, something to achieve. One should aspire to have purity of heart.

Let's challenge that interpretation by seeing the word love correctly, as a verb—as action. This augments the understanding of the text. Specifically, we now love (embrace, demonstrate, act) the purity of one's heart. We also now love (enjoy, appreciate) the end result—purity of our own hearts. We love the joy of the toddler. We show love toward the toddler as a reaction, a reciprocation of what we see or experience. Ultimately, we become the toddler.

Solomon advises us to develop this, which in turn elicits grace on one's lips. What you have now emanates from you toward others. Consequently, you have an impact on others. Solomon suggests you will have favor with great people—kings. Meaning someone who can impact your life with their influence, and they will do so as your friend. Toddlers have lots of friends.

Lloyd Speese

IMPATIENCE AND A BROKEN BRUSH

Proverbs 15:28

"The heart of the righteous thinks carefully about how to answer
[in a wise and appropriate and a timely way],
but the [babbling] mouth of the wicked pours out malevolent things." (AMP)

Raise your hand if you have ever responded to your child's tantrum with your own adult tantrum.

[Picture me raising my hand.]

About a month ago, my level of patience with myself was running rather thin. In addition to various responsibilities piling on my plate, my daughter, who was six at the time, had also been testing my patience on multiple occasions. One day she had been acting up and wasn't getting dressed to leave the house as fast as I needed her to. I could feel both of our temperatures rising. I asked her to come into the bathroom so I could comb her hair, and she reacted with a HUGE attitude. That's all it took. I snapped right back, I began yelling at her for her attitude, and in an attempt to "control" my own attitude, I broke the hairbrush I was holding into two pieces! This definitely was not my best parenting moment.

Proverbs 15:28 had completely left the building! There was no "thinking carefully" in my response, and neither was it wise, appropriate, or timely. My mouth was uncontrollable, and my actions were anything but righteous. I knew I had faltered; my own impatience was the cause of my reaction. Nevertheless, by God's grace, He convicted both my daughter and me to talk through our hurt, apologize to one another, and grow from our misbehavior.

Looking back, I am so thankful that we have a Heavenly Father who parents us way better than we parent our children! He thinks carefully, and He is wise about how to respond to our tantrums. He is the epitome of unconditional love and responds to His children with unfathomable grace, mercy, and patience. I am blessed to have the opportunity to glean from His example. I pray you choose the same.

Jennifer Shank

THE JOKE ISN'T FUNNY

Proverbs 26:18-19

"Just as damaging as a madman shooting a deadly weapon
is someone who lies to a friend and then says, 'I was only joking.'" (NLT)

This proverb is very sobering. To equate a madman shooting a deadly weapon and a person lying to a friend, saying they were only joking, means that lying carries some serious consequences with the Lord, not to mention the other person.

People can get away with saying things in humor that they could not normally say in polite conversation. I have blurted out things that people have laughed at, but at the root, they were completely true. Truth can sometimes be funnier than fiction.

But when a person uses humor to tear down their friend—a person made in the image of the Creator and bought by the blood of Jesus—essentially lying about them, and then saying it was only a joke is not a friend. They are not a person of integrity or to be trusted and have just revealed their selfish human nature. They have shown they do not love or even care about their friend, using them as the butt of a joke and ruining their reputation.

There are very few situation comedies I care to watch anymore because they almost always are based on lying, cheating, sexual immorality and innuendo, stealing, and deception. I do not know where the funny went, but they stopped being funny a long time ago. They use humor to tear each other down, to lie and deceive, and to create a culture of selfishness. If you want to see what not to do, watch one. They are a good study of how the enemy works.

But that is not who God calls us to be.

We are to love one another. Prefer one another. Speak the truth and edify one another. The Bible says in Proverbs 17:17, *"A friend loves at all times, and a brother is born for adversity."* In John 15:15, Jesus said to his disciples, *"No longer do I call you servants… but I have called you friends…"*

"Greater love has no one than this,
than to lay down one's life for his friends."—John 15:13

Michelle Glush

ETERNAL REWARDS

Proverbs 23:4-5

"Do not wear yourself out to get rich; do not trust your own cleverness.
Cast but a glance at riches, and they are gone,
for they will surely sprout wings and fly off to the sky like an eagle." (NIV)

HE WHO DIES WITH THE MOST TOYS WINS! Recognize the phrase that became popular from bumper stickers in the 1980s? The love for money became all-consuming for many Americans after experiencing years of financial limitations. In the 1970s, dramatic changes started happening as more and more women started working full-time jobs and earning better incomes. Many families found themselves with extra spending money and chose to spend it.

In the 1990s, things in the housing market were changing fast. Many people had computers, real estate was now online, "affordable mortgages" were being offered, and many people decided it was a great time to buy. Without much money in our pockets, people approached our young family to purchase a home. With "clever" ideas on paperwork, a world of opportunity opened up to own a home or make money by renting or flipping houses. But many people who purchased a house ended up losing everything in the 2000s when the economy changed, and a recession hit.

We desire security, owning a home, and money in the bank, and there is nothing wrong with that. Yet, we must show caution as we strive to improve our financial gains. As many learned in the early 2000s, what can be gained can be lost. Spending all your time seeking the gain of money or possessions can become a never-ending obsession that is never satisfied.

In Matthew 6:19-20, Jesus tells us, *"Do not store up for yourselves treasures on earth, where moths and vermin destroy, and where thieves break in and steal. But store up for yourselves treasures in heaven, where moths and vermin do not destroy, and where thieves do not break in and steal."* (NIV)

For many years I have had the simple words on the screen of my phone that say, "Eternal Rewards," reminding myself that material things, including money, should not be my goal in life. Instead, I should focus my attention on what God is doing and building up His Kingdom and not my own. What is your focus?

Jill Alvarado

91

ACT ON GOD'S TIMING

Proverbs 20:25

*"Don't trap yourself by making a rash promise to God
and only later counting the cost." (NLT)*

One of the tendencies that God has been helping me change is that I act quickly when I feel compelled to do something. For example, when I was a teenager, one day, I wanted to get a haircut. Instead of asking my mother to drive me to the salon, I asked one of my best friends to cut my hair right then and there. She was certainly not a certified beautician. In fact, she didn't even know how to cut hair! She tried to talk me out of it, but I was desperate, and I wanted my hair cut NOW. So, I said to her, "Just cut it!" Well, she cut it off, and it was horrifying! This happened to me because I was desperate and rushed to make a decision that I later regretted. I ended up needing to go to the hairdresser to have her try to fix the disaster.

Rushing into emotion-based decisions is not a good thing. Believe me, I speak from experience! It is not good either to make a promise to God and then not be able to keep it. Sometimes we try to manipulate God through a promise (if You do this, then I'll do that). Other times we sincerely want to please God, but we act in our humanity and strength. On the contrary, when we seek to honor God and work with Him, we bring the decisions before God and wait to hear from Him what He wants us to do, then He will give us the ability, the power, the strength, and the resources to be able to fulfill it.

Maybe God is going to ask you to give up other things that are occupying your time so you can fulfill what He has for you. Sometimes we must wait for God's timing and not our own. We should not be people who are carried away by our emotions, but let our yes be yes, and our no be no.

Teresa Bauer

IT MATTERS

Proverbs 19:25

"Strike a scoffer [for refusing to learn],
and the naive may [be warned and] become prudent;
reprimand one who has understanding and a teachable spirit,
and he will gain knowledge and insight." (AMP)

Hush! Don't offend! Stop doing that! Avert your eyes; nonsense abounds!

It is nice to be in charge, and it is good to be a school field trip chaperone.

As a stay-at-home mother, I went as a school field trip chaperone over 30 times. Oh, the stories I could tell! It is hard to pick just one…wait…wait…there are some beauties here.

While standing less than two feet away from me, a youth struck his classmate and then looked defiantly at me in a clear refusal to accept responsibility. I took his picture and said to him, "I don't know you, but I bet the principal does." Oh, here's another one. On a field trip to a posh and stately art museum, a student decided to run away from the main group. With my track shoes on, I ran right after him. That's right! A middle-aged woman was treading across the manicured lawns in high pursuit. Suddenly, he turned around to see me barreling towards him; the air went out of him, and the look on his face could have killed dandelions right on the spot.

These students might not remember me, but I do remember them. There were other moments, such as a youth who did not receive much attention at home and leaned in for some loving focus on the bus. It matters that you are involved, especially in matters of the heart. Whether you are chasing down a miscreant, correcting a recalcitrant, or comforting the needy, God will place you in situations where you can be the catalyst for change and growth in someone else's life.

Juline Bruck

MORE THAN YOU CAN ASK OR THINK

Proverbs 16:9

*"A man's heart plans his way,
but the Lord directs his step." (NKJV)*

We all have hopes and dreams that we keep close to our hearts and do not always share with others. This might be because others might laugh or discourage us from pursuing those dreams, or we are afraid they might not come true.

Proverbs 16:9 speaks about how a man's heart plans his way, and then we quickly see the word *but*. Usually, when we see that word, it feels as though bad news is following it. In this case the Word says *"the Lord directs his steps."* God cares about what is hidden in our hearts. He is committed to leading us one step at a time. When we share our plans and thoughts, we invite Him to do something with our lives even greater than we can ask or think.

I am naturally a strong-willed person, and that has, at times, made it difficult to be open to God's plan in my life, especially when it felt so contrary to my timeline, my plan, my desire, my heart, my thoughts, my, my, my! However, that type of thinking is limiting because I ended up boxing God into a very linear timeline, and it caused me to lose sight of the fact that I get to include the Creator of the Universe in my life, my hopes, and my dreams. When I shifted my focus from my plans to God's ways, I experienced surprises and adventures I could not have imagined.

God directing the path does not mean that He does not take our heart into consideration—quite the contrary. Instead, we get to lean on Him, renew our strength in Him, and find true freedom as we live out all He created us to be.

Cynthia Medrano

THE GLASS HALF FULL

Proverbs 15:15

"All the days of the afflicted are evil,
but he who is of a merry heart has a continual feast." (NKJV)

Our attitude greatly affects how we experience the events of our lifetime. This is true of the good and the not-so-good. Some live and behave as if nothing bad will befall them, while others cannot find the light even in a lamp store.

I had the opportunity to volunteer at a relief agency providing food for those less fortunate. It became apparent that in the very same room and the same distressing situations, there were attitudes that were worlds apart. In one case, a young man was homeless and facing food scarcity. While others with similar situations were in the same room waiting to be served, he was thankful and cheerful for everything being done for him. While others complained with a sort of "that again" attitude about the food and assistance they received, this young man could not help but explain to everyone around him how useful and beneficial every single one of his "blessings" was. Even the items that appeared insignificant seemed to have so much good and potential in his eyes. While to his peers "every day" was afflicted and bad, he rejoiced in the blessings he received.

There were two sets of people in that room—the "afflicted" and the "cheerful." The afflicted saw nothing good or worthy of praise. Not only did they see the glass was half empty, but also it was perpetually half empty. It was clear that no matter how much was put into that glass, their disposition would not allow them to see anything else.

On the other hand, this young man illustrated the second half of this scripture very well. A "cheerful heart has a continual feast!" He ministered to my heart though my situation may have been less distressing than his at the time. Truly his cheerful heart was at a banquet while mine was eating out of a brown paper bag.

Let us learn from this cheerful-hearted young man, and may our hearts be at a continual feast in the Lord!

Jose Nolasco

RISKY VS. SAFE

Proverbs 11:15

*"There's danger in putting up security for a stranger's debt;
it's safer not to guarantee another person's debt." (NLT)*

Solomon gets straight to the unvarnished point: Guaranteeing someone else's debt is essentially guaranteeing your own suffering. Just listen to these various translations: "It's a dangerous thing" (CEV); "It goeth ill with him" (DARBY); "will surely suffer harm" (ESV); "will get into trouble" (GW); "you will regret it" (GNT); "is sure to get burned" (MSG); "will suffer loss" (NCB); "trouble compounds" (VOICE); "shall be tormented with evil" (WYC).

But doesn't this warning contradict the promise found in Psalm 112:5?

*"Good comes to those who lend money generously
and conduct their business fairly." (NLT)*

Not at all. Psalm 112:5 is addressing those people who understand stewardship and the importance of investing in the lives of others. They *know* the people to whom they are lending their money, that their character has already been proven. Generous folks lend their money directly, not through a bank.

Again, note the distinction: *"a stranger's debt"*; an outsider, a foreigner. "Be sure you know a person well before you vouch for his credit! Better refuse than suffer later" (TLB). It is foolish to become legally liable for the debt, default, or failure in duty of a stranger. Avoiding such financial entanglements will guard against the unnecessary loss of your hard-earned assets, even possible bankruptcy.

Remember: Jesus was the guarantee for us when we were strangers—even enemies—and He suffered for it. *"Yet the Lord was willing to crush Him, causing Him to suffer…"* (Is. 53:10a, AMP)

Karen Heimbuch

THIS MAKES NO SENSE

Proverbs 10:27

"Living in the worship and awe of God will bring you many years of contented living. So how could the wicked ever expect to have a long, happy life?" (TPT)

This proverb uses the phrase "worship and awe" which is also understood as living, having discipline, existing, persisting, and residing with God. Other similar biblical contexts use the word "fear" rather than these descriptors. In some instances, using these other terms is needed and correct. However, the broader understanding is noted here and promises an unbelievable reward with many years of contented living. The question becomes, how do we actually accomplish this state of being, living, respectfulness, worship, and awe of the Lord? The verses preceding verse 27 refer to the life of a sluggard (a slothful, lazy person by choice) in the context of pain and agitation. Verses beyond verse 27 refer to a reverent lifestyle as glad, joyful, and strong. Perhaps this is the answer?

Notice how one state of being or living generates another state of living. In this case, living in the reverence of God creates contented living, for a long time. Also of note, contented living does not suggest perfect living in every way, hence the surety of many years. Meaning it infers a state of mind, and a state of existence wherein sometime things may seem perfect, and one is glad, joyful, and strong. However, when some things are not as perfect as we would prefer, we can still enjoy the same state of contentedness. The worship and awe of God also involve trusting Him in all situations, which then creates the contentedness in all situations. Gladness, joyfulness, strength. What an "awe"some place to exist!

Contrarily, Solomon asks the painful but obvious next question: "How do the wicked ever expect to have a long, happy life?" Dare I say he almost sounds dumbfounded by the lack of wisdom? Might the answer be found by simply reversing the thinking? Specifically, living without reverence, fear, worship, and the awe of God innately breeds a depth of ignorance that blindly expects long, happy lives. I suggest, YES. It is just that simple. Choosing not to worship and respect God causes a lack of wisdom so damaging, daft, inept, and destructive as to fool one into believing they have the possibility of a long, happy life or life at all. True happiness and life are found only in God's presence. Food for thought.

Lloyd Speese

IT IS BETTER TO BLESS THAN TO CURSE

Proverbs 11:9

*"With their mouths the godless destroy their neighbors,
but through knowledge the righteous escape." (NIV)*

Too often, we have seen how a very good friendship or family can be torn apart and destroyed because of something that was said—a curse word or simply the wrong word. But when there is knowledge of the Word of the Lord, you are more careful of the words you speak. Luke 6:45 says, "For the mouth speaks what the heart is full of." (NIV) So if your knowledge is from the Word of God, and that is what is in your heart, words of blessing will come out of your lips.

My sister, Teresa, gave me a book called *"Enjoy Your Journey with God."* When I started to read it and applied the knowledge to my heart, I did not realize that others would see a difference in me. Even my family noticed how I was speaking, and the words coming out of my mouth were different. One day my brother Jorge asked my mom, "have you seen how Gabriel speaks? He sounds so nice and peaceful, and the advice he gives always goes together with a verse from the Bible." I have seen a significant change in my life as God's Word has grown in me. My mouth brings blessing instead of destruction, and I am starting to see the fruit of it. This proverb says that the righteous escape through knowledge, and the blessings of God's Word in our lives keeps our neighbors and us from harm!

Gabriel Martinez

WORKS EQUALS ABUNDANCE...

Proverbs 12:11

"He who tills his land will be satisfied with bread,
but he who follows vain persons is void of understanding." (MEV)

Farming is a life of faith and trust: You hold back seed from your harvest one year to plant in the spring the next year and then must wait until late summer or the fall to harvest what you planted months ago. Year after year, it is a successful way to put food on the table and money in the bank, yet it is without any guarantees. Nevertheless, it is a system that has worked for centuries, and King Solomon saw it as wisdom to act in faith to plant and tend crops.

From Solomon's day until now, people have followed promises of, "Get rich quick with little or no work involved." Those promises come from people who only try to separate you from your money. Anyone who follows them is void of understanding, or more bluntly, has no sense. The Los Angeles Police Department says, "If it sounds too good to be true, it probably is." It is human nature to look for the easy way out. After all, it sounds so good! But this is not God's way or His plan. Simply put: Do not go there! God has a way and a plan for our lives, and He is Who we should go to for guidance.

Crypto Currency is the latest get-rich-quick scheme that has fallen flat. I, too, was drawn like a moth to a flame but, after prayerful consideration, decided not to invest in it. I Thank God for His guidance that I avoided the temptation. It just sounded too good!

To put Proverbs 12:11 concisely, it would be: It is wisdom to do what you know works and do not follow vain hope.

Martin and Bea Laufer

GROW IN WISDOM

Proverbs 14:28

"A growing population is a king's glory;
a prince without subjects has nothing." (NLT)

It is an age-old dilemma; we do not like to work harder. Sometimes my coworkers and I wish for business to slow down and give us a break. The rush can feel overwhelming, and it is more comfortable when business is slow. But when business stays slow, people get laid off, and businesses shut their doors.

A growing population brings new challenges for those in charge, so a king over many needs to have the wisdom to lead his people properly. Solomon asked the Lord for wisdom to lead God's people. He had a huge responsibility, and no man knows enough to govern perfectly. The wisdom of God can lead us through the uncertainties of life and help us shepherd His people. Those who function without wisdom will drive people away from them and end up with no subjects and no one to lead. What is the point of a prince without a people?

Proverbs 14:4 says, *"Where no oxen are, the trough is clean, but increase comes by the strength of an ox."* It will require hard work if we want to get a lot done. We have to take care of the oxen. In my line of work, we have to clean the espresso machine often to keep it working properly. It may be easier to give everyone a cup of regular "drip" coffee, but if we want more customers, we have to offer the types of coffee, tea, and food they want. Each of those requires its own setup and cleanup.

In the same way for us, it will take more wisdom, hard work, and determination to grow into everything God has for our lives. But, just like Solomon grew in wisdom, and his kingdom grew as a result, we too will have more to offer others as we seek God's guidance and grow past our comfort zones.

Stephen Larkin

CROWN OF GLORY

Proverbs 16:31

*"The silver head is a crown of glory,
if it is found in the way of righteousness." (NKJV)*

For as long as I can remember, gray hair has always been considered a negative thing, something to be ashamed of. A sign that you are "old!" Yes, you are getting older, aren't we all?

The author believes that it is something special, in fact, glorious! But the more important statement is how you attain the glory—"if it is found in the way of righteousness."

If you, like me, have gray hairs, have you ever stopped to think about how you got them? Think of Abraham. Having a newborn baby at the young age of 100 would definitely give me gray hair, but I am sure he already had some. Then there is Paul, who went from killing Christians to being imprisoned for sharing the Gospel. Or Moses, from Prince of Egypt to murderer to exiled sheepherder to the leader of the people of Israel in the Exodus. That would have sprouted a few grays in his lifetime. Finally, I think of Mary, Jesus' mother, who experienced the virgin birth, watched her Son being worshiped by the crowds, and agonized over His death on the cross. Imagine her anguish.

The proverb does not say that a gray head was found the easy way but "in the way of righteousness." Living a righteous life is no easy task. In fact, it is a more challenging way to live. If you are young, praise God! He is going to give you opportunities to grow some gray. If you are old, praise God! He has brought you through it and will still give you opportunities to grow grayer. Romans 5:3 says, "and not only that, but we also glory in tribulations, knowing that tribulation produces perseverance."

In those tribulations, and during good times as well, let us continue to live righteously, reaching up to God in every moment, and wearing that crown of glory well.

If you are bald, that is another story!

Fred Alvarado

THE RIGHTEOUS WILL FLOURISH

Proverbs 11:10

"When the righteous prosper, the city rejoices;
when the wicked perish, there are shouts of joy." (NIV)

I love to watch old western movies. A good old-time western film always has a band of villains wreaking havoc in the town, and the people hide until the cowboy hero comes in and kills all the wicked evil men and saves the day! Then, the entire city comes out with shouts of joy, because the wicked are gone, and now they can live free without their evil deeds.

When the righteous are in charge, the city rejoices! Just as our small old-time western town can get back to the business of life, so can a city whose leadership walks in righteousness. When the leadership acts with integrity, deals fairly and justly with its responsibilities, the people of the city can prosper. Righteous leadership sets a positive tone for a city to grow and thrive. When people can trust those in charge, they can focus on family and business and create a favorable environment for all. But if they need to be concerned about riots, thieves, murderers, high taxes, no police support, and the government trying to tell them how to run their business, rejoicing is not at the forefront of their thinking.

Just as we see in the western towns in the movies, when the bad guys are "driven out of Dodge," everyone is happy because good has won. God, our cowboy-hero, is the one who drives out the evil before us. Psalm 5:11-12 says:

"But let all those rejoice who put their trust in You;
let them ever shout for joy, because You defend them;
let those also who love Your name Be joyful in You.
For You, O Lord, will bless the righteous;
with favor You will surround him as with a shield." (NKJV)

When there is peace in a city, the righteous will not only rejoice, they will flourish.

Debbie Speese

SEEDS AND FRUIT

Proverbs 11:18

"Evil people may get a short-term gain,
but to sow seeds of righteousness will bring a true and lasting reward." (TPT)

In addition to this proverb, read Psalm 73, because it complements it and asks (and answers) the same questions many of us have when we observe the world today: Why do evil people prosper, get rich, and seem to get away with everything? Why does there seem to be a two-tiered justice system: one for the powerful elites and another for the rest of us? If they prosper and I don't seem to, why do I serve the Lord and do right? Is it all for nothing?

The way of this sinful world is to look out for yourself and do whatever is necessary to get on top and stay there. At the end of the day, selfishness and pride are the main roots of evil. People can manipulate circumstances, betray people, do many sinful, ugly things, and prosper for a time.

Despite all this, God has given us wonderful clues in the natural world of how He works—and one of His favorite natural metaphors is about seed and fruit. Genesis 1:11 says that seeds reproduce after their own kind. Apples produce apples. Oranges, oranges, etc. Jesus said in John 3:6, *"That which is born of the flesh is flesh, and that which is born of the Spirit is spirit."* In other words, reproduction is not only for the natural world but for the spiritual one as well. Good reproduces good, and evil, evil. Though wicked people may prosper for a moment, Galatians 6:7 gives finality to the issue: *"Do not be deceived, God is not mocked; for whatever a man sows, that he will also reap."*

If we plant seeds of selfishness, pride, immorality, betrayal, greed, and wickedness, or righteousness, goodness, kindness, faithfulness, peace, joy, and self-control, then in the long run, that will be produced in our lives. One will produce a long-term reward; the other will produce a short-term reward and long-term judgment. Jesus is looking for fruit in our lives, and He will judge us by that fruit.[1] What are you planting?

Kyle Bauer

---

1   See John 15:1-5, 16; Luke 13:6-9

LET GOD KEEP SCORE

Proverbs 20:22

"Don't ever say, "I'll get you for that!"
Wait for God; He'll settle the score." (MSG)

Even in humanity's sinful state, people are still deeply motivated to right wrongs. Although God is the original and ultimate Judge, our fallen nature would rather take things into our own hands instead of entrusting them to God's. Yet this verse, as well as Proverbs 24:29 (NIV), expressly forbid us to return evil for evil: "Do not say, 'I'll do to them as they have done to me; I'll pay them back for what they did.'" We are not to avenge ourselves. We are not to pay back. We are not to get even.

Vengeance belongs to God. He says: "I will take revenge; I will pay them back. In due time their feet will slip. Their day of disaster will arrive, and their destiny will overtake them." (Deut. 32:35, NLT)

Also, Romans 12:17-19 (NIV) plainly states:

> Do not repay anyone evil for evil. Be careful to do what is right in the eyes of everyone. If it is possible, as far as it depends on you, live at peace with everyone. Do not take revenge, my dear friends, but leave room for God's wrath, for it is written: "It is mine to avenge; I will repay," says the Lord.

When we have been injured, we must not allow a root of bitterness or resentment to take hold. Instead, we should wait in patient hope for our just God to intervene on our behalf *in His time and as He sees fit*. If we wait for the Lord, He will save us. He will make things right.

Karen Heimbuch

A WARM BLANKET OF DEBT

Proverbs 19:2

*"Desire without knowledge is not good -
how much more will hasty feet miss the way!" (NIV)*

With newfound freedom, free from credit card debt, a new house, and young children, a weight had been lifted off this young family. However, with this freedom came an uneasiness; being in debt for so long, the debt had become a warm blanket to them. Being in debt is awful, but it became a comfortable, known, and regulated way to live. Not fully understanding or accepting how to manage financial decisions practically, the parents began to miss the comfort of the debt blanket unconsciously. Instead of devoting themselves to learning how to manage their money correctly, the only thing that felt right was being in debt. This family did not want to be in debt again, but out of lack of knowledge and the desire to feel the comfort of what was known, they hastily slipped back into debt again. The desire to stay free of debt was there, but the parents did not truly accept the knowledge, and they found themselves back in debt again and again. This was the pattern until they acted on the knowledge and the wisdom of what God's Word teaches about finances.

It is easy to rely on yourself, especially if you think you have the answers and do not seek godly wisdom. We can get by for a while depending on our own knowledge or worldly wisdom, but if we do not submit our ways to Christ and seek His desires, we can find ourselves wanting the "warm blanket" feeling again without understanding why. Facing difficult circumstances, walking into sin, or being unsatisfied, we could miss out on something the Lord has for us by not seeking His knowledge first. Proverbs 3:7 says, *"Don't be impressed with your own wisdom. Instead, fear the LORD and turn away from evil."*

Take a moment and consider your life. Where have you depended on your own wisdom or wisdom from the world, and where have you made a decision without seeking God's wisdom? Do you have an issue in your life that needs to be submitted to God's wisdom?

Jill Alvarado

DIRECT INVOLVEMENT

Proverbs 26:17

"Like one who grabs a stray dog by the ears is someone
who rushes into a quarrel not their own." (NIV)

During my safety class for becoming a bus driver, I learned that if students get into a fight on the bus, my only option is to say, "Stop fighting, please," and repeat myself two more times with my hands behind my back. If they do not comply, I notify the dispatchers of the situation over the radio. First, the dispatcher will ask if my bus is moving and if the surroundings are safe. Then, they ask several safety questions to make sure the bus is securely stopped before they send law enforcement.

Why am I not to separate the fighting students? The first reason is that I am the only adult there, and the second is that if I become involved, I will be responsible for fighting with a minor. In the event that I am hit or knocked out, who will be responsible for the rest of the children? Using caution in volatile situations, instead of running into them blindly, is wisdom.

Before understanding the whole picture, I used to rush head-long into a situation without assessing what was going on, and sometimes it became unhealthy or unsafe. Since then, I have learned that a story always has two sides, because people have different perspectives.

Now, if I get involved, I assess the situation and ask God for wisdom, guidance, and what He would have me do. The intention to do the right thing may be good, but if the situation is dangerous, I have learned not to rush into an argument because it may be none of my business! Depending on the severity of the situation, instead of our direct and maybe unsafe involvement, helping may look like calling the police or the paramedics—this is why they are there! Use wisdom when approaching situations; not everything calls for our direct involvement.

Alicia Suarez

GOOD WINS!

Proverbs 14:19

*"The evil will bow down before the good,
and the wicked [will bow down] at the gates of the righteous." (AMP)*

I love heroes! Everyone loves a hero who can save the day. The good guy always beats the bad guy. Even when the circumstances seem tough, the "good guy" always wins. That is what we long for in this world. We long for good to prevail over evil. Even though the world is full of sin, we know that good will always win in the end.

Since the beginning of creation, God has always had a plan to defeat evil, sin, and death. It was through the death and resurrection of Jesus Christ, the Son of God. God Himself died that we, His people, would have victory over sin and death. And we know from the book of Revelation, *"He will soon come for His Bride and cast out death, sin, and Satan into 'the lake of fire' forever and ever."* (Rev. 20:14)

The apostle Paul writes, *"But thank God! He gives us victory over sin and death through our Lord Jesus Christ."* (1 Cor. 15:57, NLT) Jesus, who is God Himself, emptied Himself to be born in the likeness of man. He did this so He could be the sacrificial lamb for all our sins. *"For this reason also, God highly exalted Him and bestowed on Him the name which is above every name, so that at the name of Jesus every knee will bow, of those who are in heaven and on earth and under the earth."* (Phil. 2:9-10, NASB) The evil will bow down before the good, who is Jesus, the definition of goodness.

Not only will the evil bow to God and His goodness, but the wicked will also bow to the righteous. The book of Revelation says, *"And watch as I take those who call themselves true believers but are nothing of the kind, pretenders whose true membership is in the club of Satan—watch as I strip off their pretensions and they're forced to acknowledge it's you that I've loved."* (Rev. 3:9, MSG)

Joshua Bauer

FIT FOR THE MASTER'S USE

Proverbs 25:4

*"Take away the dross from the silver, and there comes out [the pure metal for]
a vessel for the silversmith [to shape]." (AMP)*

I learned a lesson many years ago—the Lord is watching to see what we will do in adversity! So not only does He want us to call on Him and trust Him in times of trouble, but also He is watching to see how we will respond.

I worked as the supervisor over two ladies in a previous job. The three of us worked really well together until one evening, while I was not there, I became the subject of judgment and gossip. The following morning when I learned about it, even though it was very hurtful, I consciously decided to forgive them, treat them with kindness, and do my work as unto the Lord.

When I made the decision to forgive them, the Lord, as He often does, put a picture in my mind and the understanding of what it meant. He showed me a picture of an ancient water pot. The water pot was clay on the outside and shiny gold on the inside. I immediately understood that as we allow the Holy Spirit to work in our lives, as we choose to forgive and be obedient to His Word, we allow the Lord to form us into purer vessels.[2]

The Bible tells us that going through trials is like being in the furnace![3] The heat gets turned up, and we start screaming and crying, praying and petitioning (and rightly so)! It is no fun to go through a trial. But in that affliction, as our impurities come to the surface, and we allow the Lord to work His will into us and our circumstances, we will see Him skim the "dross" off the top and make us into purer vessels of honor fit for the Master's use.

I have also learned another lesson over the years…it is a constant process. The Lord is continually "testing our mettle"[4] to develop us into people who, when He looks at us, He sees the image of Himself.

Michelle Glush

---

2   2 Timothy 2:20-21

3   Isaiah 48:10: See, I have refined you, though not as silver; I have tested you in the furnace of affliction.

4   Oxford Dictionary defines mettle as: a person's ability to cope well with difficulties or to face a demanding situation in a spirited and resilient way."

DECISIONS

Proverbs 19:3

*"People ruin their lives by their own foolishness
and then are angry at the Lord." (NLT)*

"But if God is good and all-powerful, why did He let this happen?" This is a common indictment against God that I, and I am sure you, have heard many times. People will say that it is a reason not to believe in God and that prayer, church, and the Bible are all a sham. However, they are missing a huge piece of the puzzle—the human factor.

It comes down to why God created us. He did not make us to be robots but gave us free will and the opportunity to become His children. God created us to share in rulership over His good creation, and He gave us intelligence, stewardship, and ruling capacity over all things.[5] Just because God is all-powerful does not mean that He will subvert the decisions we make. Quite the opposite. He honors our decisions and respects us as the people He created us to be. Many hold the theological idea that God is supreme and can do whatever He chooses whenever He chooses to do it. And that is certainly true; however, God chose to partner with you and me. Our word carries weight. While God does honor our decisions, be they good or bad, we will carry the consequences of the decisions we make. At the end of the day, we will be judged by God for the decisions we made.[6]

Without understanding the Biblical truth of our role in God's creation, God and the devil become easy and convenient scapegoats for our bad decisions. "Why didn't God stop me?" "The devil made me do it." God did not stop you because He gave you a free will, and He gave you his word for guidance. The devil has no capacity to make you do anything. Much of it is on us. It is our responsibility—to take responsibility—for our own actions. Though God does not revoke our decisions, He does work to redeem the harm that many of our choices cause, and in the process, redeem, restore, teach, and grow us to be more like Him.

Kyle Bauer

---

5   See Genesis 1:26-28 and Psalm 115:16
6   See 2 Corinthians 5:9-11

PLANS SUCCEED THROUGH WISE COUNSEL

Proverbs 20:18

"Plans are established by counsel;
by wise counsel wage war." (NKJV)

I have known many people in my life who did not know the difference between a plan and a goal. I have had people tell me, "I plan to make a million dollars." I said to them that is a goal; what is your plan to achieve that? They looked at me with a blank stare.

First, set a realistic goal, and then establish a plan to achieve it. It is wise to ask advice from people you respect and who you know are successful and are willing to help you. It is unwise to seek advice from anyone who cannot do what you need to accomplish. Nor is it wise to seek advice from anyone who does not have your best outcome in mind, such as a competitor or a person who is jealous of you. The more serious the goal, such as waging a successful war where winning is the only acceptable outcome, the more important wise counsel and advanced planning is. Do not even start until you are sure the plan is sound and the outcome is realistic. Vladimir Putin attacked the country of Ukraine based on bad advice and with wrong information about the capabilities of the Ukrainian Army. It has resulted in ongoing disaster and embarrassment for Putin and the Russian people.

As Christians, the goal and the plan should be presented to our Heavenly Father first. Then we should wait upon the Lord to hear from Him before we proceed. Then and only then should we give serious thought to establishing a plan to achieve our stated goal and seeking wise counsel.

I would much rather be known as an example of what to do, rather than what not to do.

Martin Laufer

VICTORY

Proverbs 24:6

"For by wise counsel you will wage your own war,
and in a multitude of counselors there is safety." (NKJV)

According to the Oxford dictionary, one of the definitions of war is "a sustained effort to deal with or end a particular unpleasant or undesirable situation or condition." Another definition from the KJV Dictionary is "to contend; to strive violently; to be in a state of opposition."

My husband and I were going through bankruptcy. (See above Oxford definition.) Hollywood was involved in a writer's strike. There were additional strikes in solidarity, affecting many businesses, including ours. We had an attorney, but we were in such a state of shock that this was happening to us that we were both unable to process the situation. We felt totally brain-dead. We thought we were functioning, but we were just on autopilot. Our attorney was only trying to get us through the legal part of the process, but we had no personal advocates. We talked to no one. We were frozen. We also did not have the Holy Spirit at that time.

Again, years later, after my husband died suddenly, I immediately realized that I was in shock and went into autopilot mode. But this time I made sure I had people in place who would look after my best interests. Proverbs 15:22 confirms, "Plans fail for lack of counsel, but with many advisers, they succeed."

Never let your ego or self-esteem stand in the way of what is the best course of action. As brothers and sisters in Christ, we are called to love one another and to do unto one another as we would have done to us. Do not let false pride, embarrassment, or shame get in the way of healing. Do not be afraid to ask for help. Remember, the enemy wants us to fail, so stand on God's Word and the promises of Jesus, and by wise counsel, have victory—not just over an "undesirable situation"—but through Him.

Pat Nannarello

APRIL

My child,

don't reject the Lord's discipline,

and don't be upset when he corrects you.

For the Lord corrects those he loves,

just as a father corrects a child

in whom he delights.

Joyful is the person who finds wisdom,

the one who gains understanding.

For wisdom is more profitable than silver,

and her wages are better than gold.

—Proverbs 3:11-14

COME TO THE LIGHT OF CHRIST

Proverbs 20:20

*"If you insult your father or mother,
your light will be snuffed out in total darkness." (NLT)*

Many people have testimonies of bad parents who mistreated them. As they came to Christ, they had to surrender their pain and sorrow to God to be able to heal and forgive their parents, the ones who should have loved and cared for them. But I have also met people who never let go of their pain and unconsciously repeat the same mistakes with their own families. It is an unbroken cycle of pain through lack of forgiveness.

This proverb says that whoever curses his parents enters a deep darkness. Cursing is not only with our words, but it also refers to the resentment that remains in our hearts that does not allow us to bless them and wish them well. We can all understand this on a human level, but in the end, resentment leads to obscured vision, and we are unable to see the healing that God wants to bring.

One of the Ten Commandments is, "Honor your father and your mother, so that your days may be long in the land which the Lord your God is giving you." (Ex. 20:12) This order carries a rich reward and allows God's blessing to come into your life! It does not say that we only honor parents who are good and loving. It says to honor our parents—regardless of their being good or bad.

As adults, we should recognize that perhaps we, too, contributed to some of the fractured relationship. Most parents do their best according to the understanding they had at the time. No one is perfect. We cannot continue to blame our mistakes and bad decisions on our parents. They had their chance to make decisions as adults, and now you and I have our chance, don't waste it!

Strive to be the best son or daughter to your parents, and if you are a parent, be the best father and mother for your children. Enough of living in the past! Come to the light of Jesus, and He will allow you to see life in a different way and with purpose. God can redeem your past and use it to bless others with a testimony of redemption!

Teresa Bauer

TRUST IN THE LORD

Proverbs 11:7

*"Hopes placed in mortals die with them;
all the promise of their power comes to nothing." (NIV)*

Ecclesiastes 7:2 says it is better to go to a funeral than a party because it puts life in its proper perspective. Ecclesiastes also gives the accurate assessment that whether you are rich or poor, strong or weak, overlord or slave, death in this life awaits us all the same. Perhaps one of the most stunning examples of the "promise of power" is going to a rich man's funeral. It can be spectacular, with the richest procession, a coffin of solid gold, and even lie in state with great honors. They are like the tombs of the ancient Pharaohs: great pyramids to remember their earthly greatness; and sepulchers filled with the riches of their lives. But at the end of the day, all we are left with is a rotting corpse. Nothing can be taken with us to the other side except the life we lived, which will be judged by the living God.

So often, we live to please other people because they hold emotional or financial power over us or we fear or idolize them. We desire peace and prosperity, but many times this comes with strings attached, because we believe our peace and prosperity are mainly based on the people that can provide it. This becomes an even bigger issue if those people, and the resulting circumstances, conflict with our personal convictions. Many people sacrifice their personal convictions when powerful people promise what they most desire.

When we die and stand before the Lord, where is all that promised power and prosperity we sought during this life? We cannot take it with us. Better yet, where are all the powerful people who tempted you to betray your convictions? They will not stand with you when you are in front of God—you will do that alone. It is compelling that the exact center of our Bibles is Psalm 118:8, which is the heart of everything the Bible instructs us to live by: *"It is better to trust in the Lord than to put confidence in man."* Live by your convictions. Fear the Lord alone and trust Him, for He is your Provider and eternal reward!

Kyle Bauer

HOLD ON TO PEACE

Proverbs 11:12

*"It is foolish to belittle one's neighbor;
a sensible person keeps quiet." (NLT)*

Have you ever witnessed one person belittling another? Have you ever seen someone picking on a person, making fun of them, teasing them, or bullying them? To belittle one's own neighbor only leads to hurt, pain, and damage to all people involved. Instigating problems among people is never a smart idea.

I am sure that, by this point, almost everyone has heard stories of tragedies due to bullying, insults, and further quarreling among individuals. Anyone who willingly chooses to instigate problems among school peers, coworkers, fellow church congregants, or neighbors is not wise. Proverbs 11:12 teaches us that quarreling can develop from any "foolish" individual intent on causing verbal damage, using words to belittle, hurt, insult, anger, and demean. Within our own lives, if we live after this pattern, we are risking serious repercussions to our neighbor's emotional and physical well-being, as well as our own.

In contrast to foolish living, when people use words to hurt others, Proverbs 11:12 also teaches us that "a sensible person keeps quiet." The wise know how to live in harmony among their neighbors by holding their peace. When we choose to hold our peace among our peers, coworkers, or other individuals, we not only save ourselves from harm, but also minister the grace and peace of the Lord into any situation in which we find ourselves. It is wise to refrain from purposely using words to hurt or put down others. The Lord instructs us to use self-control whenever tempted to utilize words in any way He did not intend. Imagine a world where every believer held their peace and positively affected their environment—even on social media.

The Lord's instructions are designed to keep us in peace and free us from the negative consequences of our own words. Therefore, rather than adding to the hateful language and quarreling on this Earth, let us become a people who hold onto peace, so much so that the Lord changes the very environments we inhabit.

Victor Miguel Rivera

STARVING FOR JESUS

Proverbs 14:31

*"Those who oppress the poor insult their Maker,
but helping the poor honors him." (NLT)*

Proverbs 14:31 seems like a pretty straightforward scripture, right? God wants us to help the poor. Period. The end. Plain and simple. But is it, though? As the Body of Christ, we are called to help those in need. However, this verse is not just about providing clothing for the homeless or making monthly donations for starving families around the world. Those are noble actions, even spiritual actions, and are part of our responsibility as believers. Poverty, however, is more than physical; it is also spiritual. So how can we honor the Lord by helping the spiritually poor?

I am not talking about what Jesus calls the poor in spirit, those who recognize their need for God. I am talking about the spiritually impoverished, those who live opposed to the Holy Spirit, or those who are hanging on by a thread. Their disheartening traits may include grumpiness, crabbiness, jealousy, narcissism, antagonism, and/or rudeness. They are the kind of people you do not enjoy being around, because they relish being miserable and are just plain ugly on the inside.

How do we respond to spiritually impoverished people, those who truly just need a big dose of Jesus' love? Do we pass by them with disdain? Or do we offer to hold them in prayer and show unconditional love? Instead of shunning them like lepers, we might consider inviting them over for dinner. Wait, what? Why would we do that? Because they may not realize that their spirit is starving for Jesus. The invitation to the love of Jesus in you has the answer.

In 1 Corinthians 13:3 NLT, Paul states, *"If I gave everything I have to the poor and even sacrificed my body, I could boast about it; but if I didn't love others, I would have gained nothing."* While giving to the poor is honorable to God, providing unmerited love to the spiritually destitute is like extending an invitation to come sit and feast together with the Lord. So, let's be gracious and start inviting others to the table.

Jennifer Shank

SAME OLD POLITICS

Proverbs 28:15

*"Like a roaring lion and a charging bear
is a wicked ruler over poor people." (NKJV)*

Proverbs 29:7

"The godly care about the rights of the poor; the wicked don't care at all." (NLT)

It is amazing to read Proverbs, written around 3,000 years ago, and see their relevance for our times. People's sin nature is the same in every generation. Still today, as 3,000 years ago, politics are dirty, and those who wield power often oppress the weak for their own gain.

The word "poor" does not refer only to the economically poor; it also carries the sense of those powerless to induce change and weak in resources and influence. We see corrupt politics steamroll people of lesser influence who commit minor offenses—or none at all—and are defenseless against the onslaught and lose everything, while powerful and corrupt people get off scot-free. Morality has very little to do with these kinds of politics—whether they are the politics of a corporation, office setting, or the highest offices in the land. It is power that guides these people, not morality. It is the dog-eat-dog world where only the strong survive; the strong form alliances, gather more power for themselves, and exonerate each other with impunity. Power permits them to pass laws favorable to themselves that end up damaging the economy of the weak and poor—the common person—with crushing inflation, taxes, and bureaucratic red tape that makes life unnecessarily expensive and difficult for hardworking people while the wicked benefit.

Those who are guided by godly morals see the world differently. No one is above the rule of law, and all are held accountable to the same criteria, whether rich or poor, man or woman, white or black, powerful or weak. This worldview disallows the powerful to dominate the weak or the important to escape godly justice. Godly people value and care for all people without favoritism and work for the good of others, never themselves.

The Lord commands us to pray for those in authority. Good and bad times ebb and flow in politics, and it is easy to bless when things are good and curse when things are bad. So let's be those who bless at all times and pray for our leaders.

Kyle Bauer

119

LAUGHTER CAN CHANGE YOUR LIFE

Proverbs 17: 22

*"A merry heart does good, like medicine,
but a broken spirit dries the bones." (NKJV)*

A few years after my father passed away, my mother and I, along with a cousin, took a vacation to visit a friend on the big island of Hawaii. My father had passed away a week after Thanksgiving. As a result, this became one of the most difficult holidays to get through.

Growing up, our house was the destination for Thanksgiving. It was not unusual to set the table for 30 or more people for a homemade dinner with all the trimmings, including three kinds of pie.

This particular year we spent Thanksgiving with wildly-growing Hawaiian philo-dendrons, eating a store-prepared turkey dinner, entertaining geckos, watching old movies, and sharing stories of "people long gone and the good old days."

But what we did most was laugh! The friend we went to visit told stories and jokes one right after the other, and we laughed until our sides almost burst. We drove around the island and laughed. We ate mangos and pineapple and laughed. We visited all the usual tourist spots, and we laughed! In the space of a week, we laughed so much that by the time we left, I felt like I was whole again. I had forgotten what it felt like to be free. On that short trip, God restored my joy, so much so that when we returned, I could see such a stark contrast between the joy and freedom I had just experienced versus the stress and oppression in my workplace. As a result, I started making changes in my life to keep that freedom. Stepping outside of my everyday circumstances and experiencing "a merry heart" gave me a fresh perspective and clear vision.

Laughter is one of God's counterbalances to sadness, anger, and other negative emotions that keeps us from falling too hard to one side. Laugh! Change your point of view. Laugh! Change your perspective. Laugh! Change your life.

Michelle Glush

A BEST FRIEND

Proverbs 18:24

*"One who has unreliable friends soon comes to ruin,
but there is a friend who sticks closer than a brother." (NIV)*

William Shakespeare said, "A friend is one that knows you as you are, understands where you have been…and still gently allows you to grow."

In the Bible, we are shown great examples of friendships: Ruth and Naomi, David and Jonathan, and Paul and Timothy, to name a few. Friendship is a beautiful gift from God and, when cared for, can bless your life immeasurably. But a friend you cannot trust or depend on can become stressful, sad, and maybe an emotional rollercoaster. Sticking with that friend can wear you out, and you may become bitter, angry, and want to walk away, and the friendship "comes to ruin."

But my husband (my best friend) and I realized no matter what we want to expect from a friend, we cannot put our hopes on one person, because people can let us down. No one is perfect, and no one can be there for us every moment of every day.

However, there is One in whom you can put your hope, One who would be there for you anytime. In John 15: 12-16, Jesus is speaking and says, *"This is My commandment, that you love one another as I have loved you. Greater love has no one than this than to lay down one's life for his friends. You are My friends if you do whatever I command you. No longer do I call you servants, for a servant, does not know what his master is doing; but I have called you friends, for all things that I heard from My Father I have made known to you."* (NKJV) God will never leave you. He will listen, encourage, and love you even when you are at your worst.

Have you cultivated a friendship with God? Talk to Him, listen to Him daily, and find how powerful a real friendship and relationship with the Almighty can be.

Jill Alvarado

LAZY AND GREEDY VS. GODLY AND GENEROUS

Proverbs 21:25-26

"Despite their desires, the lazy will come to ruin,
for their hands refuse to work.
Some people are always greedy for more,
but the godly love to give!" (NLT)

Our mother could grow anything, and there were over 100 potted plants on the back patio to prove it! My brother and I had to water them regularly. We were also under orders to smash the shells of any snails we found. Snails and slugs may be slow, but they can wreak havoc with all sorts of vegetation.

In the King James Version, verse 25 refers to the lazy person as a "sluggard"—that is, someone who acts like a slug: habitually lazy, idle, and inactive. His lustful cravings will end up killing him, however, for since he refuses to work, he is more likely to turn to lawbreakers to provide for his immoral (and often illegal) fleshly pleasures. The habitually lazy person will eventually starve.

Just as the wind and the waves are always found together, so are laziness and greed, for the desires of the sluggard are impulsive and insatiable. According to Matthew Henry, they cry, *"Give, give;* they expect everybody should do for them, though they will do nothing for themselves, much less for anybody else."

The godly, however, are hard-working and righteous; their desires are satisfied. They are honest and diligent. Unlike the sluggard, they are always full and looking for ways to give to others. They enjoy giving cheerfully and generously. They "give and spare not" (v. 26, KJV). May we, too, live by the words of our Lord Jesus: "It is more blessed to give than to receive." (Acts 20:35b)

Karen Heimbuch

GOD IS PRACTICAL

Proverbs 24:13-14

"My child, eat honey, for it is good,
and the honeycomb is sweet to the taste.
In the same way, wisdom is sweet to your soul.
If you find it, you will have a bright future,
and your hopes will not be cut short." (NLT)

One weekend, many years ago, I was doing some cleaning in all my graphics archives. As an art student in college, I was encouraged to keep magazines and books as examples for reference and inspiration. I decided to rip apart the magazines, keep only what really inspired me, and get rid of the mass amount of paper clutter I had accumulated. So, what I was getting rid of became a mound of paper on one side of my bed. Later that night, I was tired, and when it was time to get on my knees and pray, I looked at the pile I had created and realized it was right in my prayer spot. I fell into my bed and said to the Lord, "But Lord, can I just skip praying tonight? All that "stuff" is in the way, and I am too tired to move it!" As I lay there, I heard the Lord say to me, "What about the other side?" I laughed and rolled out of bed—on the other side—and said my prayers! The sweetness in the way I heard it still brings a smile to my face! God is so practical. I wanted an excuse not to pray, but He wanted time with me!

Wisdom is sweet to the soul. Whether it is in the practical things we need to do every day, in our relationships, multi-million-dollar business ventures, or things having to do with our spiritual life—like where, how, and what to pray—God has practical wisdom for you and me so that we can prosper at what we set our hands to do.

So next time something seems like too much to handle, pray! Ask the Lord for wisdom and knowledge! Listen for the smile in His voice (He is happy you asked!), and remember God will meet you in both the practical and spiritual applications of life to give you a bright future and a lasting hope.

Michelle Glush

PRIDE VERSUS HUMILITY...

Proverbs 29:23

"Pride ends in humiliation,
while humility brings honor." (NLT)

Isn't it ironic that pride often leads to humiliation, and a humble spirit can lead to honor? Jesus spoke of this in His answer to His disciples' question,*"Who is greatest in the kingdom of heaven?"* Jesus answered them in Matthew 18:3-4, *"Assuredly I say to you, unless you are converted and become as little children, you will by no means enter the kingdom of heaven, therefore whoever humbles himself as this little child is the greatest in the kingdom of heaven."* Again, in Luke 14:7-11, Jesus taught that humility is wisdom, *"For whoever exalts himself will be humbled, and he who humbles himself will be exalted."* (NKJV) It could be said that Jesus quoted Solomon's proverb.

In modern terms there is a saying, "Don't believe your own press." In politics and most businesses, actual results are a far better measure of a person's stature than any self-created evaluation. Jesus' advice to us is to humble ourselves before others and let them bring us any deserved honor, rather than trying to honor ourselves with the result of bringing public shame.

Pride is a weapon the enemy has used against humankind since the beginning. Lucifer was ejected from heaven because he equated himself with God. Lucifer used pride to cause Eve to question God about the Tree of the Knowledge of Good and Evil. She, too, wanted to become like God. Don't we often confuse pride with wisdom? Our pride leads to shame and dishonor, but humility before God leads to grace, love, and honor. When we are humble before God, we are aware of the need for a Savior, and only through Christ's death and resurrection can we stand boldly before the throne of God, seeking unearned grace. "Humility brings honor" would be a good motto to live by.

Martin and Bea Laufer

RESTING IN THE ROCK

Proverbs 30:24

"There are four things which are little on the earth, but they are exceedingly wise:
The ants are a people not strong, yet they prepare their food in the summer;
The rock badgers are a feeble folk, yet they make their homes in the crags;
The locusts have no king, yet they all advance in ranks;
The spider skillfully grasps with its hands, and it is in kings' palaces." (NKJV)

I find this Scripture puzzling, but upon reflection, I have come to realize that God can use the humblest of creatures to do extraordinary works and teach great lessons, in particular, the ants! As a child, I remember being astonished at how well-organized and disciplined ants were. They would find a portion of food and somehow communicate with one another, walking single file to and from the supply to their mound until the food was utterly gone. Truly amazing! We can learn a specific point of insight from each of these creatures:

From the ant: Work hard, store up, and do not cease until the work is done, because the season of abundance does not last forever. Far too often, we quit before quitting time, whether at home, at work, or for the Lord.

From the locust: Even an insect with almost no brain can organize and work together. We surely can do the same!

From the badger: While he may not be strong, he knows where to safely dwell by relying on the exceeding strength of the rock.

From the spider: A small creature can still work its way into the king's palace. Work hard, and your skills may land you in a place of honor and greatness!

Let us, therefore, be wise, diligent, and never cease until the task the Lord has given us has been completed. We trust in the strength of the Lord and work hard at the tasks God has given us—there is wisdom in the work and blessing in the end!

Jose Nolasco

THE RIGHT THING TO DO

Proverbs 21:15

*"When justice is done, it brings joy to the righteous
but terror to evildoers." (NIV)*

This verse reminds me of when I was about 6 or 7 and went to the market with my parents. In those days, we walked. I stole a pack of gum, and when we got home, my parents discovered what I had done, and they walked me back to the store (it was a long walk…). They made me apologize to the store manager and give it back. Needless to say, there was terror in my heart.

Proverbs 10:29 says, *"The way of the Lord is a refuge for the blameless, but it is the ruin of those who do evil."* (NIV)

That lesson made such an impression on me that I never stole another thing. In fact, I turned the experience around 180 degrees. Now, one of my favorite things to do is to return incorrect change to a cashier when I find they made an error in my favor or pick up fallen items in a store that everyone else will just step over. I like to do these things because of the incredulous look on people's faces…and it is the right thing to do. These days, no one expects honesty. They expect that everyone is trying to get away with something.

Personally, I love it when I can make someone smile. It makes me smile too. So, try going out of your way to make someone smile, and the blessing will return to you. Plus, it's the right thing to do. It's what Jesus would do.

Pat Nannarello

FEASTING WITH JESUS

Proverbs 19:15

"Go ahead – be lazy and passive.
But you'll go hungry if you live that way." (TPT)

Being a wife, mother, homeschool educator, business owner, and leader in our church is a life filled with a whole lot of busyness! Yet, there are days when all I feel like doing is staying in bed, watching movies, eating my favorite foods, and doing absolutely nothing. Yes, sometimes I simply want to be lazy and disconnect from the world and all of my responsibilities. And you know what? I believe that taking a time out is completely okay and is actually good for our mental, physical, and spiritual health!

But, there are times when we need to discern whether we are taking a day off to be refreshed so that we reconnect to our lives or if we are heading down a path that will completely disconnect us from our purpose. Have you ever faced that cross-road? I have. Thankfully, Jesus helped me recognize that I was heading toward self-destruction by way of laziness.

When my daughter was about 18 months old, I had some health issues. It all started with the flu. The symptoms lingered for a couple of months. I became extremely lethargic. My muscles ached, I felt lazy, and I found it difficult to accomplish daily tasks. I decided to have blood tests done only to discover there were huge nutritional deficiencies that needed immediate correcting. In spite of the sickness, I knew in my spirit this was more than a physical problem. I started seeing a Christian therapist to help me navigate through the deeper issues I was battling.

Reflecting on this season of my life, I now recognize that I allowed my physical ailments to affect my spirit. My walk with the Lord had become lazy and passive. I learned that physical laziness could be a symptom of spiritual passivity. My spirit was starving. Taking the time to feast with Jesus is how my spirit was filled and satisfied. Jesus said that people do not live by bread alone but by the Word of God. So, if you ever find yourself becoming lazy, passive, or spiritually starving, come to the banquet table and dine with Jesus. He is the Bread of Life, and He is always the answer!

Jennifer Shank

IS THE REAL ME RIGHT WITH GOD?

Proverbs 12:2

If your heart is right, favor flows from the Lord,
but a devious heart invites his condemnation. (TPT)

There are times when the scriptures speak literally, and there is no need for deep analysis or extensive pondering. Sometimes, they are so clear it is almost impossible to say you do not understand. This is one of those times! If we are speaking in a spiritual context, what does it mean to have a heart that is right? You almost instantly begin checking your conscience and evaluating yourself by thinking, "Oh man, is my heart right?" Am I doing things with a right motive to honor God and serve other people? Or am I just in this for myself? Okay, so a deep thought: On the inside, deep inside of me, the real me that few folks really know, is that person right with God? Do I truly love Him, or do I just pretend? Am I being honest with myself or just telling myself what I want to hear?

So, is your heart right? Are you in a "good place" with the Lord?

If so, favor flows from Him to you. Favor means God's special provision, Him choosing you in advance, Him "opening doors" for you, Him selecting you perhaps before others to receive His best. Note the word "flows." This indicates a steady stream, not something that is intermittent or uncertain or occasional. It is positional, meaning always in the present tense. The promise is not that someday favor will flow, or favor will flow only for a time. The promise is that God's favor flows, period. What an infinite blessing.

However, there is something that will block the favor of the Lord—a devious heart. We really do not need to explore the word devious. The same conscience we just spoke about is already checking your heart—the real you on the inside—to see if you are the devious person the scripture speaks of. If so, God strongly opposes this heart condition, and it blocks the flow of His favor. So, the question is, how is your heart today?

Lloyd Speese

HONOR MOM AND DAD

Proverbs 30:11-12

"There is a generation that curses its father, and does not bless its mother.
There is a generation that is pure in its own eyes,
yet is not washed from its filthiness." (NKJV)

Honoring our father and mother is one of the most essential commands—important enough for God to make it one of the Ten Commandments! There is a reason for this: Mom and dad are the foundational relationships that orient a child to how life is lived.

There are a few guiding philosophies that Teresa and I have followed in raising our four children. One of these is that there are five sins that are never allowed in our house: 1) Disobedience, 2) rebellion or defiance, 3) lying, 4) hiding, and 5) manipulation. Another one of our guiding philosophies is: *Obedience to God is formed through obedience to mom and dad first.* In our house, obedience was *never* at the count of oooone…twooooo…. threeeeee. We never gave our children even three seconds to disobey or defy us. This is not out of a domineering or spirit-breaking attitude, but our goal was to prepare them for a lifetime of responding to God's voice immediately.

When a growing child is not required to show immediate obedience and receives no consequences for their actions, they learn a very important lesson—they are right and in control. What child is right about their life at so young an age?

We have seen when kids win the showdown of wills with their parents; they start down the path of self-righteousness with no one who can contend with their will. This is not an issue of the child's intelligence; it is a matter of their will, pride, and fallen sin nature that needs to learn to be submitted to authority and ultimately to God.

It is a dangerous place to be where, in the core of a person's being, he believes he is righteous and justified in all he does, yet in comparison with God's Word, he is way off. Salvation happens through Jesus' work on the cross and our repentance from sin. Our job is to prepare a generation to walk in and respond, not to its own righteousness, but to Jesus' righteousness.

Kyle Bauer

REMAIN TEACHABLE

Proverbs 15:12

"Mockers resent correction,
so they avoid the wise." (NIV)

At a church I used to attend, we decided to go out witnessing to share the gospel of Jesus Christ, offer the prayer of salvation, and invite people to come to service on Sunday. We approached a house that I felt in my spirit we should avoid. I shared my thoughts and kept walking, but some in the group decided to knock on the door anyway. They started up the walkway to the door, and a person came out and started yelling at them, calling them names, quoting scriptures, and condemning them! I was still walking past the house, and when I looked back, our group was running off the property as fast as they could! It was a funny sight but a sad situation spiritually, because we knew this person was lost. We have to use wisdom with understanding, which means sometimes we have to use wisdom and respect boundaries.

We all know a know-it-all or two. They do not like to be corrected and do not take instructions well. They can be argumentative, think they are smarter than you, and mock you for disagreeing with them. They are not interested in conversation or any opinion other than their own. If they do not receive your words, then let them follow their own foolishness. This spirit is not of God. Dust off your feet and walk away!

Let's be wise and remain teachable so the Holy Spirit can correct us and show us how to respond in His love to the difficult people we meet. God has given us all we need in His Word to walk according to His Spirit and love people in the same way Jesus did.

Debbie Speese

KEEP SILENT

Proverbs 17:28

"Even fools are thought wise when they keep silent.
With their mouths shut, they seem intelligent." (NLT)

Have you ever tried to stop somebody who starts talking and makes no sense, or you know that someone is being offended by what that person is saying? In referring to the tongue, James 3:5 says, *"Consider what a great forest is set on fire by a small spark."* That small organ can create an immense injury to a lot of people.

Proverbs 17:28 highlights several benefits of keeping quiet: 1) It is the best policy to keep it to yourself, if you have nothing worthwhile or beneficial to say. 2) It allows you the opportunity to listen and learn. The Bible tells us that it is better to listen than to speak. "Listen, my son, and be wise" (Prov. 23:19). 3) Being slower to speak gives you something in common with those who are wiser. Make sure to pause to think and to listen so that when you do speak, you will have something worthwhile to say.

In my lifetime, I have made many mistakes when trying to control my tongue. I regret the words I spoke that hurt family and friends. But if we listen and ask the Lord for self-control over our emotions, the results will be much different. As Paul says, *"For God did not give us a spirit of timidity, but a confidence of power, love, and SELF-CONTROL."* (2 Tim. 1: 7) My prayer is and will continue to be: "Lord Jesus, please help me control my words whenever I open my mouth."

The Apostle Peter spent three years with Jesus and had the same problem regarding taming his words. But through mistakes and corrections, he was used in a mighty way! If God can use Peter, He can use us too!

Ricardo Chaidez

DUMPSTER DIVING

Proverbs 15:14

"A wise person is hungry for knowledge,
while the fool feeds on trash." (NLT)

On average, people spend 2.5 hours per day on social media, which is likely to rise in upcoming years. It is estimated that younger generations will spend 3.4 million minutes on social media during their lifetime.[1] They check their phones an average of 58 times per day, with an average of 48 minutes per day texting.[2] Americans averaged 600 hours on Netflix in 2020.[3] One media outlet claims that in 2022, 13 hours per day will be spent by the American public on digital media.[4] That seems a bit high to me, but maybe not too far from the truth.

So, what do people consume on any media device or outlet? News. Sports. Cat videos. The latest dance craze. The latest music. The newest show. The stupidest TikTok viral video. The hottest Instagram influencer. People's worthless opinions on everything. The list goes on and on. In my opinion, 99% of those 3.4 million minutes (6.5 years!) are spent dumpster diving in pure drivel.

What else could you do with those same 6.5 years? Get a Bachelor's AND Master's degree. Be with your family. Read non-drivel books that actually build you up. Spend time in God's Word, pray, and cultivate a relationship with the Holy Spirit. You could do many things that build your spirit, build your family, build your wealth, build your career or future, build your church and community. What are you hungry for—knowledge or trash?

Kyle Bauer

---

1 "Average Daily Time Spent on Social Media (Latest 2022 Data)" (accessed 10/18/2022)
2 Damjan. "How Much Time Does the Average Person Spend On Their Phone" https://kommandotech.com/statistics (accessed 10/18/2022)
3 John Eggerton. "Analysis: Americans Averaged 600 Hours of Nextflix in 2020." (Broadcasting & Cable) January 27, 2021. (Accessed 10/18/2022)
4 Insider Intelligence. (April 20, 2021) (Accessed 10/18/2022)

LAZINESS KILLS

Proverbs 19:24

"A sluggard buries his hand in the dish;
he will not even bring it back to his mouth!" (NIV)

Laziness is the death of action. It's a state of being in which one drowns in the depth of self-soothing comfort. Some may confuse rest with laziness. For the sake of rest, I want to clarify that rest has the purpose of resetting the body or allowing yourself to recharge in one way or another. It is actually an active thing, because it reinvigorates your life.

I would love to sit here and tell you that I am never lazy, but alas, despite being a hard worker in general, there are still tons of aspects in my life that I approach with severe laziness. Laziness, for me, is like a slide that appears fun. When I give in and go down the fun slide, I end up sliding down into the depths of my now unfinished work. I then become so overwhelmed that I do not know where to start to fix my problems which were preventable.

Scripture often refers to "the sluggard," which is the laziest of lazy persons. This proverb points out that it does not matter what you give to a sluggard, they will not steward it. In this case, it is food. Their laziness will not allow them to satisfy their hunger even with their hand already on the food. Regardless of kind intent, giving a lazy person aid is squandering it on someone who will waste anything you give to them.

Rachael Hopkins

WHO ATE MY FIG NEWTONS?

Proverbs 27:18

*"The one who guards a fig tree will eat its fruit
and whoever protects their master will be honored." (NIV)*

Did you know that figs or fig trees are mentioned 200 times in the Bible? Must be something important about that fruit. You may recall that Jesus had an encounter with a fig tree. Mathew 21:19 says, *"Seeing a fig tree by the road, He went up to it but found nothing on it except leaves. Then He said to it, 'May you never bear fruit again!'" Immediately the tree withered."* Now there is a tree that was not guarded, and no one ever ate from it again.

Why the fig tree? Probably plentiful and grew well in that region. Lots of nutritional value to them as well. And I love me a Fig Newton. But you had to guard it, take care of it. If it were your tree in your yard, would you not want to take care of it so it would keep producing? Do not take care of it, no Fig Newtons!

So, you might ask, "what do fig trees have to do with your master?" Four things I have tried to teach my children about any job they have or any opportunity to serve (church):

1. Always honor your master (Pastor, boss, manager, owner of the company).
2. Always leave things better than how you found them.
3. Always do more than what is asked.
4. Always treat your job as if you owned the business.

In theory, sounds great, but in practice, I have missed the mark on many occasions. But as I matured, the more I saw the fruits of these "rules." I have had three jobs in my entire life. I have seen what happens when I have not protected my "master," but I also have had the pleasure of being honored when I have. The Lord has blessed me with more fig trees than I deserve, because I learned to protect my master. So, guard your fig tree and protect your master because your master wants to bless and honor what you have been given charge over. Now, who wants a Fig Newton?!

Fred Alvarado

ALIGNING WITH GOD

Proverbs 19:8

"Grow a wise heart—you'll do yourself a favor;
keep a clear head—you'll find a good life." (MSG)

The heart: The home of passions, faith, wisdom, beliefs, and dreams.

The mind: The home of goals, knowledge, strategies, skills, and memories.

If you want this summed up in one word, the word is *alignment*. Alignment is when your heart and mind are in line with the Holy Spirit in such a way that He can tend to your soul. Take the heart's passions as an example. Are all of your passions worthy? The Holy Spirit may not only ask this question of us, but also illustrate for us what passions our heart actually contains. The heart and mind are not always clear. Take any one of the traits mentioned above from our hearts and mind. Sometimes they line up with God, and sometimes they do not.

Often, we have not given the Holy Spirit access to our inner self so He may align us with Himself. We put that part of ourselves strictly "off limits." One can only presume why this is. After all, the Holy Spirit knows our motives and intentions in each of these different traits of the heart and mind. Truth hurts, yes, but the truth will also set you free. What part of your heart and mind could you consider offering up for God's review to align with His best for you? It is not as painful if this is done in "bits" that you can volunteer…something you have noticed…something you do not like or appreciate in yourself. Just begin. This "something" can be a more excellent, upstanding quality increasing in measure today.

Juline Bruck

SPEAKING THE TRUTH IN LOVE

Proverbs 12:17

*"He who speaks truth declares righteousness,
but a false witness, deceit." (NKJV)*

Much of this crazy world we live in seems to ignore God's truth—or even despise it—and this same world tells us that we are hateful when we speak biblical truth. Some would call us every phobic name in the book before they even get to know us. But even in a hostile culture, we can live graciously with others, but ultimately, we live to please God.

Speaking the truth declares what is right as defined by God and not by today's culture. God never lies, but people do. God's Word never changes, but our society changes daily. God loves people regardless of who they are, but our society hates those who disagree with them. Our society thinks it knows what is best, that we are evolving, and that God's ways are antiquated. It tells us that we need to throw off these old ideas and follow modern thinking. Our culture has devolved so radically that it has bought the lies that men can be women, that any disagreement is racist, abortion is good, and the list goes on. When we hold these ideas up to the Word of God, they do not hold any semblance of truth and only deceive people into a wrong way of living. God's Word is the measurement of truth. What He says is right and righteous and worthy of listening to. He created humanity, loves people, and desires the best for them.

We are to be people filled with grace and truth. It is the role of the Holy Spirit to convict people of sin (John 16:8). We are to be His mouthpieces speaking the truth with God's heart of love (Eph. 4:15). The world has become a dark place, and as we keep shining the light of Jesus, we will be like streetlamps guiding people on the road towards God.

Stephen Larkin

TRUE TREASURES

Proverbs 15:16

"Better to have little, with fear for the LORD,
than to have great treasure and inner turmoil." (NLT)

Some time ago, I was in the car with my son, and we saw a really nice car go by. He mentioned how nice it would be to be rich and successful. I suspected his comments were based on the thought that success consists of having nice things. So, I followed the conversation and asked him his definition of success. His answer reflected my suspicions. He said success was having a good-paying job, a good car, a nice house, and lots of money.

We began to explore the validity of his claim. I asked him what he would rather have: A family that loves each other or lots of money. As a kid whose best friends are his siblings, he said he would rather have a family that loves each other. I further questioned that if money were the definition of success, then why are not all people with money happy? I went even further. I asked if a person could consider themselves truly successful in life if they had lots of nice things, but their family hated each other, did not serve the Lord, and the person, though rich, did not have peace, love, joy, fulfillment, or happiness. I could see the gears grinding in his head as he processed the conversation. He concluded that perhaps success looked different than he first thought.

Jesus said in Mark 8:36, *"What does it profit a man to gain the whole world and forfeit his soul?"* In other words, godliness, righteousness, and wealth of relationship with God are worth more than owning the whole world without Him. Perhaps the definition of success lies in knowing the difference between transient treasure and eternal treasure.

Kyle Bauer

GENEROSITY

Proverbs 28:27

"He who gives to the poor will not lack,
but he who hides his eyes will have many curses." (NKJV)

Poor doesn't always mean no money, no food, homelessness, or down and out. It could also mean spiritually dry, needing a hug, a helping hand to move a couch, or just someone to listen.

Eons ago, my in-laws were living with my husband and me in Tarzana. One day, my macho, strong-like-bull father-in-law had gone to a morning appointment at the VA Hospital in Westwood. When I got home at 7:00 that evening, he still was not home, and neither my husband nor mother-in-law knew where he was. We were about to go looking for him when he walked in the door downcast. He walked to the dining room table, sat down, and began weeping. His wife left the room, and his son walked to the other side of the room. I was aghast, but went to him, held him, and let him cry. He reported that he had been diagnosed with cancer.

Can you imagine doing that to Jesus? Can you imagine that happening to you? They "hid their eyes." Needless to say, I had a "come-to-Jesus meeting" with both my husband and my mother-in-law! (That was the "cursing" part!)

Matthew 25:40, 45—My translation: That which you do to the least of these your brothers, you do unto Me. And that which you do not do to the least of these your brothers, you do not do unto Me.

Proverbs 19:17 says, "Whoever is kind to the poor lends to the Lord and He will reward them for what they have done."

Proverbs 3:27 says, "Do not withhold good from those to whom it is due, when it is in your power to act."

Remember, everything we do is for and to Jesus! So, please be kind, generous, and respectful of God's commands. HE will bless you a thousand-fold!

Pat Nannarello

WORDS LIKE A FLOOD

Proverbs 17:14

"Starting a quarrel is like opening a floodgate,
so stop before a dispute breaks out." (NLT)

I am sure you have heard the phrase "sticks and stones may break my bones, but words will never hurt me." The meaning of this phrase is that it should not matter what mean things others say about you; although this is true, they still hurt. The Bible talks about the tongue, which can bring life and death. *"The tongue has the power of life and death, and those who love it will eat its fruit."* (Prov. 18:21, NIV) To start a quarrel also means inviting death through your words. The longer the quarrel goes on, like a flood, sinful words will rush out of the mouth and bring only destruction.

What is the reason we argue and say harsh words? Everyone is born with sin in their hearts, and our sinful desires overtake our words, bringing death and destruction. Listen to what James 4:1 says: *"What is causing the quarrels and fights among you? Don't they come from the evil desires at war within you?"* (NLT). Also, Romans 3:10-12 (NLT) says, *"No one is righteous—not even one. No one is truly wise; no one is seeking God. All have turned away; all have become useless. No one does good, not a single one."*

So, how can we avoid quarrels and harsh words? By not answering in anger but answering in gentleness and self-control. *"A gentle answer turns away wrath, but a harsh word stirs up anger."* (Prov. 15:1, NIV) Just as starting a quarrel is like a flood, *"The words of the godly are a life-giving fountain; the words of the wicked conceal violent intentions."* (Prov. 10:11, NLT) Speak life into the lives of others. Speaking life to others will end quarrels, make friends, and build them up instead of tearing them down.

Joshua Bauer

ESTABLISHING THE KINGDOM

Proverbs 20:2

*"A king's wrath strikes terror like the roar of a lion;
those who anger him forfeit their lives." (NIV)*

Haman, second in command to the King and the villain in the book of Esther, thought everything was going his way. He was preparing to destroy all the Jewish people throughout the kingdom, not realizing that the queen was herself Jewish. So, when Queen Esther invited the king and Haman to dinner, he was feeling pretty good. When Esther revealed that Haman's plan was not just against some random rebellious people but the queen's own people, the King was enraged, and Haman became terrified. The king left in anger to think over what he had just heard, and Haman fell on Queen Esther, begging her to plead for his life to the king. The king returned to find Haman begging so fiercely that he mistook it as him assaulting the queen. The King was already angry, but this sealed Haman's fate.

Haman was the antagonist to the Jews, just as the devil is to God's people. The reality is that whether it is Haman, some other murderous tyrant, or the devil himself, they seek to dominate the world and eliminate God's people.

But, we as God's people—the body of Christ—are called as kings and priests to rule and reign and establish God's kingdom on earth. We have full authority over the devil and the demonic realm (Eph. 6:12, Rom. 8:38-39, and Matt. 18:18) by the name of Jesus (Phil. 2:10) and His blood (Rev. 12:11). The devil is terrified that we could walk in and exercise that authority because he knows he will lose his influence over society. As long as the Church is here on earth, it is our job to take ground (Josh. 1:3) for the kingdom of Heaven. The gates of hell shall not prevail against His Church (Matt. 16:18).

Let's be wise not to anger those in authority. But also, let's advance God's kingdom as His priests and kings, praying fervently, declaring God's Word, and believing for His promises to be established on earth.

Stephen Larkin

HELPED BY "THE UPRIGHT"

Proverbs 29:10

"The bloodthirsty hate blameless people,
but the upright seek to help them." (NLT)

Upon first glance at Proverbs 29:10, one may resolve that being a blameless person might not be such a good idea! I mean, who wants to be hated by a bloodthirsty murderer just for pursuing a virtuous lifestyle? On the other hand, there is some comfort in knowing that if you practice living a blameless life, at the very least, those who are upright will seek ways to help you.

But what if we took a little interpretive liberty and saw this verse in a slightly different light? What if the upright weren't necessarily viewed as a group of people? What if the upright was actually a singular proper noun referring to God as being "The Upright"?

In Deuteronomy 32:4 (NLT), Moses recites a song given to him by God. He sings, *"He is the Rock; his deeds are perfect. Everything he does is just and fair. He is a faithful God who does no wrong; how just and upright he is!"* God IS upright; therefore, by definition, wouldn't it qualify Him to be called "The Upright"?

That being said, if we reread the proverb, keeping in mind that God is "The Upright," then the gravitas of receiving help from Almighty God sets aside the fear of being pursued by the bloodthirsty, and it makes the choice to live a blameless life a lot more palatable. For me, knowing God has my back is a lot more settling than trusting in the help of a group of upright people. It reinforces Romans 8:31 (NKJV), *"… if God is for us, who can be against us!"* So press onward, my friend, live blamelessly, and trust "The Upright" to help you along the way!

Jennifer Shank

APPEASING ROYAL WRATH

Proverbs 16:14

"The wrath of a king is like a messenger of death,
but a wise man will appease it." (AMP)

The kings of Israel and Judah were God's representatives. As such, they had the power to judge (16:10), were the guardians of weights and measures (16:11), were advocates of integrity (16:12-13), and had absolute power (16:14-15).

The power of kings in the ancient eastern countries was especially great, where it was not only absolute but arbitrary. Kings would slay or kings would keep alive. Their will was law. In Esther 7, we see that the wrath of King Xerxes was "a messenger of death" to Haman.

Having absolute power means that no one dares to risk execution by angering the king. Only wisdom can appease his anger. "If a ruler's anger rises against you, do not leave your post; calmness can lay great errors to rest." (Eccles. 10:4, NIV)

Matthew Henry comments that a very wise man will know how to pacify the wrath of a king with "a word fitly spoken," as Jonathan once pacified his father's rage against David (1 Sam. 19:6). Of course, we recognize this phrase from another famous proverb: "A word fitly spoken is like apples of gold in settings of silver." (Prov. 25:11, NKJV)

If wisdom cautions us not to provoke our earthly leaders to wrath, then certainly we should be even more vigilant to escape the wrath of the Lamb (Rev. 6:16-17) and obtain His favor instead. His lovingkindness is better than life!

Karen Heimbuch

GIVE HIM THE REINS

Proverbs 29:1

"Whoever remains stiff-necked after many rebukes will suddenly be destroyed—without remedy." (NIV)

If you have ever seen the process of training a wild horse, you know how sporadic and dangerous the horse's movements can be. No matter how hard the rider tries to control the horse, the animal remains stiff-necked. The horse has a mind of its own and refuses to turn its neck and cooperate with the rider's instructions. We too can become stiff-necked if we refuse to accept helpful criticism from God or those who would give us godly counsel. We are without remedy if we do not put to rest our old ways and step into a renewed life.

When David sinned and stubbornly refused to confess his sin and accept correction, his "…body wasted away, and [he] groaned all day long…[his] strength evaporated like water in the summer heat." (Ps. 32:3-4, NLT) There is a physical effect on us when we are stiff-necked and deny God's discipline. We feel shattered because that stubbornness that lingers inside can make us angry and restless. Pushing away what we know is right creates a heavy, inescapable burden of guilt and sin on our shoulders. However, when we confess our sins to God and accept His discipline, we allow Him to take that burden off our shoulders, so we no longer carry that weight that destroys us.

Just as the trainer works with the horse to help it understand that following his direction will lead to life and peace, the Lord wants us to follow the path He has planned for us. If we become stiff-necked and try to follow our own path, it will only lead to destruction. But if we walk God's pathway, leave our old ways behind, and accept God's discipline for our lives, we will walk in the newness of life He has for us.

When we start to feel that stubbornness, remember, *"The Lord says, 'I will guide you along the best pathway for your life. I will advise you and watch over you.'"* (Ps. 32:8, NLT).There is no weight on our shoulders along God's path, only His loving instruction and guidance. Give Him the reins and allow Him to direct our lives and make us new.

Amelia Montantes

AN ELOQUENT FOOL

Proverbs 17:7

*"Eloquent lips are unsuited to a godless fool –
how much worse lying lips to a ruler!" (NLT)*

In the original Hebrew, this proverb refers to speech that is "lofty, excessive, or over-done." Have you ever listened to someone talk or give their commentary on societal issues or their wealth of Biblical knowledge and found yourself saying, "HUH! What did they just say?" Or "they sure like to hear themselves talk." Better yet, "is he ever going to be quiet?" They will use big words that sound grandiose. To be honest, I know I have been that guy.

Eloquent means fluent or persuasive in speaking or writing. A fool may be fluent or persuasive, but they will reveal their true character once they open their mouths. I Timothy 1:5-7 says, *"Now the purpose of the commandment is love from a pure heart, from a good conscience, and from sincere faith, from which some, having strayed, have turned aside to idle talk, desiring to be teachers of the law, understanding neither what they say nor the things they affirm."* (NKJV) It kind of sounds like a fool if you ask me.

As believers, we must be mindful of how and what we speak. Allow the Holy Spirit to speak to you with the knowledge of God's word. What that means is reading your Bible and being a doer of it. Don't be the eloquent fool.

So, what's worse than an eloquent fool? A lying ruler! In whatever position you hold over others, whether employees, volunteers, or children, you have been given authority over someone else. So, to lie to them is to willingly harm them. Your credibility and integrity are ruined. Lying is a deliberate action against others. Proverbs 12:22 says, *"The Lord detests lying lips, but he delights in those who tell the truth."* Wait a minute! Isn't lying one of the TEN?! Go figure. God detests it.

Do you want to be detestable or delightful?

As I see it, if you are a lying ruler, you have pretty much become an eloquent fool.

Fred Alvarado

MAY

My child,

don't lose sight of common sense

and discernment.

Hang on to them,

for they will refresh your soul.

They are like jewels on a necklace.

They keep you safe on your way,

and your feet will not stumble.

You can go to bed without fear;

you will lie down and sleep soundly.

—Proverbs 3:21-24

BEAUTY REFRACTED

Proverbs 17:8

"Receiving a gift is like getting a rare gemstone;
any way you look at it, you see beauty refracted." (MSG)

You cannot escape the concept of giving if you spend any amount of time with God in His Presence. John 3:16 becomes, in essence, "God loved, so God gave." While on earth, Jesus said, "it is more blessed to give than to receive." This is entirely opposed to the attitudes of "dog eat dog," "make things happen," and "get your own way."

A financial drought will occur if you live long enough. My drought struck during an advanced pregnancy. However, two gifts lifted me out of this drought. First, the gift of a position as church secretary allowed my baby to be with me on the job for six months. Secondly, the financial support gifted by family and friends made up for the financial difference. I wept from a deep reservoir of gratitude for all of these gifts, and no matter how many times I remember them, it is like "beauty refracted."

We are coming into a season of increased hardships on a global scale. What will we do? Are we going to be generous with one another or remain focused on ourselves? Money may not be an option for some, but talents and skills can be given to others. When you are the recipient of someone's gift—whether it is currency or one of these other intangibles, you will experience the "beauty refracted" no matter how the gift shows up.

Juline Bruck

WHAT IS YOUR PRICE?

Proverbs 22:5

*"Corrupt people walk a thorny, treacherous road;
whoever values life will avoid it." (NLT)*

We all have a price—even God.

We are all willing to do certain things up to a certain point, and this shows what we truly value. Following Christ has many costs: *"take up your cross and follow," "do not be surprised when you face trials,"* and for many, throughout the centuries and today, this also means a tortuous death.

A believer's cost is their allegiance to the One who paid the ultimate price for their everlasting life. The cost of following Jesus will never equal the price Jesus paid for our lives. We are not even capable of attempting to pay His price. God's price for us was Jesus' death and resurrection. Seriously, sit and think about what that actually means. The Omniscient, eternal sovereign God facing death. This level of faithfulness and this price is incomprehensible, especially when I think of my shortcomings.

At times, I am a ratchety, undisciplined, defiantly-bent backslider. I want my way, often choose foolishness, and fight God on more things than I would ever care to admit. Yet, He remains faithful to me, teaching me, guiding me, loving me, and allowing me to grow under His perfect, holy presence. I would be annihilated if it weren't for Him paying the price for my life. I have nothing to offer Him but to say yes.

The wicked also have their price, and it never leads to anything good.

So, what is your price?

Rachael Hopkins

PRISON OR POTIPHAR'S HOUSE

Proverbs 14:12

"There is a way that seems right to a man,
but its end is the way of death." (NKJV)

"Honey, you thought that was prison; that was only Potiphar's house!" I heard those words in my heart while standing in the graphics department of a small weekly newspaper two months after I had changed jobs. I knew exactly what they meant…I had left Potiphar's house, and I was in prison! For years I had prayed, "Lord, I feel like Joseph in prison; when will you set me free?" Only to realize that my spiritual journey of prison was just beginning.

What you need to know is—I had prayed about changing jobs. But I was not obedient to what the Lord said! What did He say? "

There is a way that seems right to a man, but its end is the way of death." I heard those words when I asked Him for direction about leaving my job and thought, oh no, that cannot be God! I need to get out of this prison!

When we take matters into our own hands (even after praying), we create more problems for ourselves than if we trust that God has a plan, even though we cannot see it.

I learned many lessons of God's faithfulness over the next two years. God used that time to teach me, develop me, humble me, and turn me into the person to fulfill the calling He had for me. At the end of that season, He moved me into the place He had originally intended for me to go.

Are you hearing God's voice but not wanting to follow? Trust someone who has made the mistake of not listening; it is much better to wait on God than to "jump ship" because you are unhappy. God has a plan, and you are a part of it. He has not left you or put you on the shelf. Be patient, praise Him, and allow God to put all the moving pieces in place.

And if you feel like you've missed it? It is just one short step back…humble yourself and confess your sins to the Lord. He's waiting for you with open arms and will make the path straight to get you where you need to go.

Michelle Glush

ABIDING IN THE LORD

Proverbs 16:15

*"When the king smiles, there is life;
his favor refreshes like a spring rain." (NLT)*

Have you ever awakened to see the sparkle of wetness on the grass outside, knowing well that the rain had fallen throughout the night and given life to parched plants? The once-dying plants are now refreshed, and we have joy in seeing them revived. So often we can also feel parched, dehydrated, and in need of the Lord's favor to revive and refresh us. But just as plants have roots to receive the spring rain, we must also cultivate our roots to receive God's refreshing.

Some time ago, I dislocated my kneecap. Before this, I had had several other dislocations, but never as bad as the one that happened in 2022. For seven weeks I was confined to my bed. Then one day the Lord told me that He wanted me to abide in Him even in the mundane areas of my life. So for the next few weeks, I would pray and talk to God throughout my day, trusting Him to strengthen me through recovery.

When I abide in God in every area of my life, including the ordinary, mundane moments, I feel myself becoming more firmly planted in Him and ready to receive even greater favor from the Lord. For example, the Lord wanted to heal my knee completely through a life-changing surgery so I would not have to struggle with dislocations anymore. If I had not abided in God through those weeks of recovery, I would have grown frustrated at the thought of having surgery. But because I trusted in Him, I knew He would strengthen me once again.

The Lord knows that we can become like dehydrated plants when we do not abide in Him and allow Him in every area of our lives. This is why He provides us with verses like Proverbs 16:15 to remind us that His favor will bring new life and refreshment to our lives. He will rejuvenate our roots when we abide in Him, and as a result, we will receive His favor just as plants receive spring rain.

Amelia Montantes

A GENEROUS HEART

Proverbs 28:8

*"Income from charging high interest rates
will end up in the pocket of someone who is kind to the poor." (NLT)*

In the story of Tom Sawyer, we see a pretty cunning kid. He had chores, and as you might expect, none of his friends wanted to help him. So, he made it look like he was having loads of fun doing the chores and told his friends that they were not old enough to do them. Then his friends got jealous. They wanted to have fun and did not like feeling left out. So, he started charging them to do his chores for him, and they lined up down the block to pay him in toys, ice cream, and all manner of things to get the privilege of having fun doing his chores.

Credit card companies market the fun and freedom people can have when they spend someone else's money. They even offer rewards to make it look more appetizing, but they know they will make loads of money off interest from people. Similarly, Proverbs 22:7 tells us that *"the rich rule over the poor, and the borrower is a slave to the lender."* However, this is not God's biblical financial plan—either for us to live off the money we do not have or for exorbitant interest, which financially enslaves people. Instead, God's plan to fix this financial bondage was with a jubilee—the ancient version of a total reset. In the Old Testament Law, every 50 years all property returned to the original owner, and enslaved people were set free.

There is, however, a biblical way to handle our finances that brings blessing to everyone: Generosity. This proverb speaks of kindness to the poor being repaid. The poor benefit from generosity, and God, in turn, trusts His resources to those who properly steward them. A generous heart—and wallet—are blessed by the Lord!

Stephen Larkin

THE GLORY OF GRACE

Proverbs 19:11

*"The discretion of a man makes him slow to anger,
and his glory is to overlook a transgression." (NKJV)*

The Hebrew word used for "glory" in this translation is not the typical Hebrew word used for God's glory throughout the Bible. The typical word is *chabod*. Chabod has to do with the weight of one's position. If it is a position of wealth or power, it is "glory." However, the Hebrew word used here is *tifawraw*. It is the less common word that is interpreted as being adorned or dressed with something that makes you beautiful. When it speaks of glory or honor, it is not of power or position but of being beautiful in the eyes of others, like a woman who is beautifully dressed and glorious on her wedding day.

Proverbs 19:11 speaks to the glory that beautifully adorns the person who is full of grace, goodness, mercy, patience, and forgiveness toward others. I find it interesting that these traits are hallmarks of a person of understanding, knowledge, and wisdom, as indicated by the Hebrew word *sekel*, "discretion." We experience these beautiful traits of God on a daily basis in His goodness toward us.

When Moses asked to see God's glory, God granted his request saying,

> *"I will make all my goodness pass before you, and I will call out my name, Yahweh, before you. For I will show mercy to anyone I choose, and I will show compassion to anyone I choose." (Ex. 33:19 NLT)*

God then made His glory pass in front of Moses, and He announced,

> *"Yahweh! The Lord! The God of compassion and mercy! I am slow to anger and filled with unfailing love and faithfulness. I lavish unfailing love to a thousand generations. I forgive iniquity, rebellion, and sin." (Ex. 34:5-7)*

God's glorious presence is marked by His goodness, mercy, compassion, slowness to anger, faithfulness, unfailing love, and forgiveness. Indeed, it is then our glory— our beauty—to reflect the very traits of God to others. Colossians 3:13 says, *"Make allowance for each other's faults, and forgive anyone who offends you. Remember, the Lord forgave you, so you must forgive others."* (NLT)

Kyle Bauer

152

BLESSED ARE THOSE WHO ARE KIND...

Proverbs 14:21

"It is a sin to despise one's neighbor,
but blessed is the one who is kind to the needy." (NIV)

According to this proverb, it is a sin to despise a neighbor. Most often, neighbors are equal in cultural stature and standing. Therefore the neighbor being despised is not necessarily referring to someone of a lower social status. Solomon was probably familiar with Leviticus 19:18, which states, *"Do not seek revenge or bear a grudge against anyone among your people but love your neighbor as yourself."* There are people around us we do not like, but as disciples of Jesus, we are called to love, not despise, those we do not like. Jesus said in Matthew 5:44-45, *"But I say to you, love your enemies, bless those who curse you, do good to those who hate you, and pray for those who spitefully use you and persecute you, that you may be sons of your Father who is in heaven."* It is truly a difficult task in human terms to live this way, but we have the support of our heavenly Father, and we live to please Him, not only to please ourselves.

The first half of the verse deals with how we treat those we perceive to be our equals. (That in and of itself is an unworthy way to think. Are we not all one in Christ? Does God view us as different classes? Again, that is human thinking.) Without referring to status, the reality is that there are people who are less fortunate than others in economy and opportunity.

The second half of this proverb deals with our attitude to those who are less fortunate. Our attitude is never condescending or dismissive as if one was better than the other. We are to love and care for those in need, and there is blessing that comes with mercy. We are sinning if we hate or despise—regardless of whether it is our next-door neighbor or our homeless neighbor. If we love and are kind, we will be happy and blessed. It should be a simple choice.

Bless others.

Martin and Bea Laufer

REVELATION COMES FROM GOD

Proverbs 14:6

"The intellectually arrogant seek for wisdom,
but they never seem to discover what they claim they're looking for.
For revelation-knowledge flows to the one who hungers for understanding." (TPT)

In most translations of this verse, "revelation-knowledge" is rendered as simply "knowledge." However, in the biblical usage of this term, it means both. It is used as intellect and understanding[1], and it is also used as the knowledge of God and His Word, which happens through God's revelation of Himself.[2] The same may be said for Proverbs 29:18, "without [prophetic] vision, the people run wild."[3] It is not solely that the people need vision or life-trajectory; they need to know what God says and see what God sees through the revelation of His Word.

In my years of higher education studies, I have seen that much scholarly erudition—in all disciplines—is brimming with disdainful pride. In the name of truth, learning, wisdom, and knowledge, there is much contempt for the common-sense knowledge that often sits in front of our faces. "The entire Bible cannot possibly be accurate." "Science will discredit the simpleton whose faith is in God." In essence, the rhetoric is, "We have degrees. We know better. We are the wise. You and your fairytale are dumb." However, God loves the humble, and He loves to use the humble and simple to dismantle the arrogance of the so-called "wise."[4] James 1:5 says that if anyone needs wisdom—or revelation-knowledge—ask, and God will give it generously. Seek, and you will find.

In his book God and the Astronomers, Robert Jastrow writes,

> "For the scientist who has lived by his faith in the power of reason, the story ends like a bad dream. He has scaled the mountains of ignorance, he is about to conquer the highest peak; as he pulls himself over the final rock, he is greeted by a band of theologians who have been sitting there for centuries."

Kyle Bauer

---

1   See Proverbs 1:4. The difference between discerning knowledge and revelation-knowledge

2   See Hosea 4:6, "My people are destroyed for lack of knowledge." This is much more than intellect, it is the knowledge of God and His Word

3   GOD'S WORD Translation (GW) Copyright © 1995, 2003, 2013, 2014, 2019, 2020 by God's Word to the Nations Mission Society. All rights reserved.

4   See 1 Corinthians 1:22-31

GOSSIP DESTROYS

Proverbs 18:8

*"The words of a gossip are like choice morsels;
they go down to the inmost parts." (NIV)*

If you've lived more than a few minutes, I'm sure you have faced a giant heap of the side effects of man's fall into sin. I would argue that the most common one is facing disagreements. Within disagreements quickly comes the gossip of "he said, she said" that grows into "they said, we said." All this does is spread disunity.

Have you ever considered that perhaps the side of the disagreement you are on (or perhaps both sides?) is not how the Lord thinks about the situation? We hate this idea because we love our two cents more than peace, and Heaven help us if we are proven right! Our now-proven "righteousness" is quickly followed up with an "Mmmm! I told you so!" No matter what the issue is, submit it to the Lord, and He will correct it. But if we stoke the flames of dissension, He will correct us!

We will not always have the power to control what side "wins" something, but in all things, we can show graciousness, kindness, and humility, and trust that God, who sees everything, can work it out for good.

When a problem or something someone does not like has become a point of gossip, our mandate for prayer never changes. But when we refuse to engage in gossip, there is no more opportunity for anything else to spread. This allows you both to operate in peace until the next inevitable disagreement comes along.

Rachael Hopkins

PIERCING OR HEALING

Proverbs 12:18

*"The words of the reckless pierce like swords,
but the tongue of the wise brings healing." (NIV)*

As a small child, I remember nonsensical nursery rhymes that our mother would read to me and my brother. When we began attending school, we learned another ridiculous rhyme:

"Sticks and stones may break my bones,
but words will never hurt me."

Of course, nothing could be further from the truth. The tongue can be used as an instrument of life *and* death. Whether spoken intentionally or unintentionally, reckless words can cut and kill, often having devastating consequences. Words spoken thoughtlessly *"pierce like swords."* The edge of the sword was called "its mouth." The mouth of a person can inflict as much damage as a "mouth" of metal.

To speak carelessly, babbling on and on, is to speak like a fool, causing momentary harm or pain. But to speak hastily in uncontrolled anger, with insulting and abusive language, injects poison into the heart of any relationship. Slander runs the risk of burning a bridge permanently.

Thankfully, words spoken from a wise heart can do just the opposite—they can soothe anguish, undo injury, and close wounds. Gentle words can persuade reconciliation, restore peace, and mend the broken heart.

May we learn to walk patiently before the Lord and with others. Let us be "swift to hear, slow to speak, slow to wrath." (James 1:19, KJV) May we weigh our words carefully before we speak, choosing words that console and uplift, encourage and edify; heavenly medicine that brings healing and wholeness.

Karen Heimbuch

May 11   PATHWAY THROUGH THE PROVERBS

FUN AND PLEASURE

Proverbs 10:23

"Doing wrong is fun for a fool,
but living wisely brings pleasure to the sensible." (NLT)

This proverb highlights another aspect of the differences between wisdom and foolishness—the things that bring fun and pleasure to each, respectively.

There are things I see in the world that, frankly, are incomprehensible to me that others find "fun." Allow me to name a few: 1) Spending all day shopping. 2) Scrapbooking. 3) Running a marathon. Of course, there is nothing sinful or foolish about any of these things; they merely reflect one's tastes and activities one finds pleasurable and re energizing. I am sure there are things I do for fun that some might find equally ridiculous, such as backpacking and golfing!

All joking aside, there are sinful things that I don't understand how they bring pleasure to people. I cannot tell you how unappealing certain things are to me that are considered the pinnacle of "a good time." 1) Going clubbing. Can anyone tell me anything really good that happens there? Loud, ear-bleeding, repetitive, and uninteresting music is not personally gratifying. Why do you have to "follow your drink"? On top of that, there is the foolishness of drunkenness, which makes the danger of predators much more real. Then there are people who are seeking, well, what they are seeking, and it usually does not involve the more noble virtues. 2) Wild parties. Again, can anyone tell me anything really good that comes from immorality, drugs, beer-bonging until everyone is fall-down drunk, and people generally making fools of themselves? Let's not forget the vomit-filled aftermath. 3) Watching horror movies. I personally do not consider inviting demonically-inspired and hell-honoring images to have a place in my home a good time. Yet, for some, all this is considered fun—foolishness, all of it.

But to those who live in wisdom—the beginning of which is honoring the Lord—pleasure looks different. It looks like a life well-lived. There is pleasure in healthy relationships, in the enjoyment of activities that inspire us, develop us as people, keep us healthy, and keep our lives in a balance of peace, fun, work, and rest. Growing as a person can be lots of work, but it brings substance, enrichment, and purpose to life, which in the end, is much more gratifying than hanging upside down attached to a beer bong.

Kyle Bauer

UPS AND DOWNS

Proverbs 21:20

"The wise store up choice food and olive oil,
but fools gulp theirs down." (NIV)

Life has its ups and downs, and we do not know when hard times are coming. A wise person plans for hard times and sets aside extra for when he will need it. Joseph was a perfect example of this. He led Egypt to prepare and store food during a prosperous season, because the Lord had revealed to him that a famine was coming. When the famine finally hit Egypt, the people came to Joseph for food, and they were able to eat because of the storehouses of food Joseph had set aside. He saved an entire nation.

We, too, need to be wise and not just "live for today." You can apply this thought not just to food but also to how you handle your finances or your time. Setting aside money for emergencies or retirement, rather than buying the latest electronics or expensive dinners, will serve you better than enjoying that last piece of cheesecake. Setting aside time to spend it with the Lord is also a good choice because you are storing up treasures in Heaven.

The apostle Paul tells us that he learned the secret of being content in the times of plenty and in the times of lack (Phil. 4:11-13). We can also be content, whether we have a lot or a little, because He is with us through it all.

Thank you, Lord, for providing for our family. I want to be wise and a good steward with the resources You have given me. I will be content, for I know you care about me and will always provide.

Stephen Larkin

KINDNESS TO THE POOR
WILL BE REWARDED BY THE LORD

Proverbs 19:17

"He who is gracious and lends a hand to the poor lends to the Lord, and the Lord will repay him for his good deed." (AMP)

We have all heard the expression, "It is more blessed to give than to receive." (Acts 20:35) But, let's be honest. Did we feel a little hesitation as to how ready we were to "give"? Our culture is steeped in getting more for ourselves, and giving is just to get praise and secretly a tax write-off.

But the way God sees it is quite different! He is honored when we care for others. As Jesus showed us, next in importance to loving God is to love our neighbor as we love ourselves (Matt. 22:37-39). There is a challenge there. How much do we honestly love ourselves? Many of us live with guilt or shame or low self-esteem. But God sees us as righteous, because Jesus took our place and gave His life in our place. Think on that!

I now think of another example, not in the Scriptures, but still a sweet story. The Dr. Seuss story of "How The Grinch Stole Christmas" tells that the Grinch's small heart grew three sizes that Christmas day! He had learned about giving (actually giving back what he had taken). That is our story as well. God has given us so much, and we have taken it to hold for ourselves. But, oh, the joy it brings when we give it back! The Grinch's story goes on to say that as he gave back what was not his, "he found the strength of ten Grinches, plus two." When we give from the abundance that God has given us, He grows our hearts, not just ten times but to the size of His heart. God delights to give to and through us when we become givers like Him!

In these days, there are so many needs around us that it is almost overwhelming. But, as we look to the Lord for where He would like to share His blessings through us, He will direct and give the added blessing of giving back to us. What a wonderful opportunity to be the Lord's Hand extended!

Kathleen Stevenson

THE MOCKER AND THE WISE ONE

Proverbs 29:8

"Mockers stir up a city, but the wise turn away anger" (NIV)

All of us remember the summer of 2020. We had cities that were stirred, destroyed, and burned! I noticed a particular type of individual that started to show up. THE MOCKER. One of the best descriptions I have come across to describe a mocker was this: Mockers (also called "scoffers" in Scripture) defy and renounce truth and good things, not only to their own detriment and destruction but that of others. They are provokers of others to wrong, strife, and evil.

People took joy in abandoning *truth* and *good things*, even if it destroyed their own community against their own good. They provoked others to evil just because they could. Strife and evil reigned.

Jump to 2022. We have individuals who renounce truth. Sorry, there are only two genders: Man and Woman. You have those who say, "men can get pregnant!" No thank you. I saw what my wife went through. That is a hard pass for this man.

What causes one to believe these lies? If you try to correct them or have a conversation, it is not received. The Bible says do not bother. Proverbs 9:7-8a says, *"Anyone who rebukes a mocker will get an insult in return. Anyone who corrects the wicked will get hurt. So do not bother correcting mockers; they will only hate you."* Pretty much sums that up.

"But the wise turn away anger." So, the wise one enters the room, and anger leaves. The wise one knows who he is, where he stands, knows the *truth*, and knows what *good things* are. He comes from a place of humility. He says, "I still have much to learn." The wise one avoids the mocker. He does not waste his time. A wise man will do what is right even if it hurts him.

Proverbs 9:8b says, *"But correct the wise, and they will love you."* The difference between the mocker and the wise one is found in Proverbs 9:10a, *"Fear of the Lord is the foundation of wisdom."*

As we stand in awe of God, we learn to fear and love Him, and from there, we gain wisdom. The mocker or the wise one: Who do you choose to be?

Fred Alvarado

PITCH YOUR TENT

Proverbs 14:11

"The house of the wicked will be destroyed,
but the tent of the godly will flourish." (NLT)

A greatly favored pastime for many Americans is camping. Few things seem to attract people more than heading out into the wilderness and camping under the stars. However, in most cases, where the journey is more important than the shelter, those adventurers carry a tent. Now a tent is meant to be a temporary shelter; it is not intended to be a permanent home. This distinction is critical, as it greatly affects your planning and response to your circumstances.

This distinction also differentiates between two groups of people—those in this world and those who are only en route to somewhere more important. The Bible describes us as aliens, or sojourners, here on earth. The worldly make this earth their home, but for those of us who belong to the Lord, we are simply traveling through it. Those of the world build their houses and make themselves comfortable—creating and living by the world's standards, values, and corresponding actions.

Because of this reality, I must ask myself, with all sincerity, am I getting more comfortable as I walk through life? Am I taking on the ideas, values, standards, and actions of this world?

I am constantly bombarded with the "values and actions" of today's culture and fear that if I am not careful, I will stay a little longer, linger just a little more in the ways this world shows me are comfortable. This is a danger of the highest caliber, because it leads to distraction and, ultimately, destruction. It takes me off course and puts me on a path further away from my eternal destination and my loving Savior, who bought me with the highest price possible.

But lest we become too discouraged, there is great hope in this proverb. For those who realize this place is simply our temporary home and who see our season upon this earth as "en route" to the place of promise, we pitch our tent with the Lord and are guaranteed to flourish, grow, and prosper.

Jose Nolasco

REPAY GOOD WITH GOOD

Proverbs 17:13

"Evil will never leave the house
of one who pays back evil for good." (NIV)

When reading this verse, I am reminded of a time when I experienced playing a practical joke on someone. Yes, it can be funny and give a sense of pleasure for a moment, but after the moment, the consequences kick in, and they can last a lifetime.

I learned early when I decided it would be funny to scare my mom when she walked in the door one afternoon with an armful of groceries in paper bags. It was perfect, she was completely unaware, and it was going to be hilarious. As I jumped up from behind a counter and yelled, "Gotcha," she quickly reacted, dropping bags, bags tearing open, and groceries all over the floor while she jumped and screamed out with panic. It was priceless for a second; then, I realized the magnitude of what I had done. Broken eggs, opened packages on the floor, and a mom that was no longer panicked but now very angry at me. My joy for the moment quickly turned into remorse. I did not realize how much my idea would affect both my mom and me in such a negative way.

The rest of the evening let's just say my mom wasn't very happy with me, and years later (over 50), I still remember the pain that I had caused my mom that day. Mom has long forgotten it, but I never will. That memory has kept me from participating or even watching others repay evil for good, even when it seems funny, because my actions have not left my house (my memory).

This is a silly childhood story, but the lesson I learned is just what this verse teaches. Consider all those that have treated you well in your life. Have you honored them? Have you kindly rewarded their goodness?

Do you reward evil for good to those who have treated you kindly and well? A stranger, a friend, or even family? Ask God to help you be more sensitive to others so you can pay good back for good.

Jill Alvarado

INTENTIONAL DISPOSITION

Proverbs 23:12

"Apply your heart to instruction
and your ears to words of knowledge." (NIV)

The book of Proverbs is an instruction manual on wisdom: the nature of wisdom, the rewards of wisdom, living in wisdom, where and how to obtain it, and the disposition necessary to gain and retain it. It can be summed up in one word—intentionality.

For a time, I worked on the facilities crew at a large church. One day I had to go up to the roof of one of the buildings, and I saw a curious sight. A weed was growing in one of the two air conditioning units. There was no soil but just enough moisture to sprout this weed-seed that floated up and found its way into the unit. I marveled that any plant could grow inside a machine. I began to reflect on what I had seen. A weed might be able to germinate in an AC unit, but certainly, a fruit tree never could. There is no light, no soil, and certainly not enough water. As far as I understand, fruit seeds are not spread by the wind as weeds are. They are carefully planted. Even if an orange seed somehow managed to be lodged in the unit and sprout, it certainly could not bear fruit.

Weeds get everywhere and produce nothing of value. Fruit seeds are planted intentionally and give nutritious food. In the same way, foolishness is found everywhere and provides nothing of value. But listen to how The Passion Translation renders this verse, *"Pay close attention to the teaching that corrects you, and open your heart to every word of instruction."* We must have an intentional, disciplined attitude to gain wisdom—applying it to our hearts, paying attention to correction, and having a disposition of openness to instruction and teaching. We can stumble blindly into foolishness as surely as a weed-seed can float into a machine and sprout. But we do not stumble into wisdom, as surely as tomatoes do not accidentally grow in an untended garden. We must intentionally seek out wisdom, listen to, internalize, treasure, cultivate, and think through it with all humility. If we keep our hearts with an intentional disposition toward wisdom, wisdom will grow.

Kyle Bauer

THE GOD KIND OF LOVE

Proverbs 19:18

*"Discipline your children, for in that there is hope;
do not be a willing party to their death." (NIV)*

When I was growing up, I had no idea about the trouble that parents go through to instruct their children and keep them on the right path. I grew up without an adult role model for most of my early life and thought I had to face my future alone. I had no knowledge that my heavenly Father was building His character in me during that time.

I spent seven years telling myself that I was not good enough. On top of that, I fought the terrible feelings of abandonment. I did not know then that the Bible says that even if my mother or father left me, the Lord would never leave me (Ps. 27:10).

I reunited with my mother and her husband when I was a teenager. I was rebellious, the worst of the worst. I was very disrespectful and did not submit to authority. I always wanted to do things my way. As I reflect on this stage of my life, I believe I was coming to a point where it seemed impossible for me to change my bad behavior and low self-esteem. But, by the grace of God, my mom and stepdad did not give up on me. The Lord used my stepdad (dad) to guide me and help me to find my way in life.

My dad was never afraid to correct me when I was wrong (which was most of the time… fine…all the time!). My dad knew that I needed guidance. Even though we do not have the same DNA or last name, he unconditionally loved me, and at the time that was difficult for me to understand.

Today, I am a mother of three boys, and all I can say is, "Thank you, Jesus" and "Thank you, mom and dad"! I thank God for His Word, His mercy, His grace, and His goodness. He directs, corrects, and guides us—He even did that when we were still sinners. This God-kind of unconditional love is what we want to show to our children. We will never give up praying for them and believing that God will bring them to the fullness of His destiny for them.

Alicia Suarez

GET MOVING!

Proverbs 18:9

"One who is slack in his work
is brother to one who destroys." (NIV)

I became very lazy during the two years of the pandemic shutdown. I did not realize it until things started opening back up. All of a sudden, I had to go into the office, catch the bus, and walk farther than from my bed to the front door! It was challenging to get back into the full swing of life, plus I had gained weight! Not only did these physical manifestations of laziness happen, but spiritual laziness crept in as well.

The pandemic encouraged social distancing, which resulted in a lack of fellowship with friends, family, and church. This lack of accountability led to a whole host of bad habits, and these traits of spiritual laziness were even more dangerous than the physical ones. When you are not in fellowship with the Lord, not praying, not reading your Bible, and not holding yourself accountable to a church, you have effectively disconnected yourself from God. Not a good thing!

The enemy wants you to stay spiritually disconnected from God, and he will lull you into thinking you are fine. But you are not—you are lukewarm, and the Bible is very clear about how God feels about being lukewarm. (See Rev. 14:15-16) So, it is time to stop listening to his lies and get up, get on your knees, get in your Bible, get into worship, get in fellowship, and get moving!

Partnering with Jesus daily will put your life back in order. He will give you life, strength, energy, and purpose. He will be your coach and encourage you. He will give promises to stand on to give you hope for tomorrow. He will keep you far from the enemy. So, repent from spiritual laziness, pray without ceasing, read your Bible, and get moving!

Debbie Speese

FATHER KNOWS BEST

Proverbs 15:21

*"Folly brings joy to one who has no sense,
but whoever has understanding keeps a straight course." (NIV)*

In The Passion Translation, it says, *"The senseless fool treats life like a joke, but the one with living understanding makes good choices."*

We can see this mindset in sinful humanity. They take everything as a joke; they lack respect for others, themselves, and even their bodies. They do not realize that they were created by Almighty God and live life as if God does not exist. Living in this manner makes wrong decisions easy.

When I was young and my father would correct me, at the end of our conversation he always said, "I have lived longer than you, and I have seen other people's mistakes, and I have learned not to make those same mistakes. That is why I am trying to teach you to be smart and don't make those same mistakes."

My father was teaching me to keep a straight course by imparting his understanding to me. In the book of Proverbs, Solomon frequently uses "my son" and tells him what to watch out for and how to gain wisdom. We would be wise to heed the voice of our Heavenly Father. He loves us and will help us keep a straight course through the wisdom in His Word.

Gabriel Martinez

LOVE ONE ANOTHER

Proverbs 22:2

"Rich and poor have this in common:
The Lord is the maker of them all." (NIV)

I remember the first time I was in church, and we were asked to hug the people around us. I turned to someone I had not previously noticed and discovered I was about to hug an unlovely, dirty, smelly, homeless man. I gritted my teeth and hugged that man harder than I had ever hugged anybody else. And, no, I did not like it at all, but I did it anyway, because I knew that is what Jesus would have me do. It is what He would do. God loves all people equally.

This verse is not just about being rich or poor in finances. It is also about being rich or poor in spirit. Some people are blessed with riches, and some have just enough. Some people struggle to make ends meet, whereas some are happy because everything is going their way. There are some who feel heavy in their spirit because a loved one died, they lost their job, they got in a fight with their spouse, or they are just having a bad hair day.

Be mindful of the people around you. Do they need a hug? Do they need a dollar? Do they need compassion or encouragement? Do they need a friend? Proverbs 3:27 says, *"Do not withhold good from those to whom it is due, when it is in the power of your hand to do so."* (NKJV) *"A new command I give you: Love one another. As I have loved you, so you must love one another."* (John 13:34 NIV)

Be a friend. Care. Love one another.

Pat Nannarello

BE SMART

Proverbs 12:12

"Whoever loves instruction loves knowledge,
but he who hates correction is stupid." (NKJV)

An immediate understanding of Solomon's proverb is to see the correlation between instruction and knowledge. Knowledge is gained through being taught, given direction, submitting to a process of learning, and loving to do so. Contrarily, an utter inability to learn (stupidity) is the result of not receiving, embracing, or enacting correction.

There is a second correlation. What is the difference between instruction and correction? When one is instructed, they are given information that should be utilized. Correction, in this context, infers that one has elected to utilize or implement the knowledge (information) which was given or shared, but needs to alter, augment, or modify how or why they used the information (knowledge).

A final correlation or conclusion should be drawn. Wherein one loves receiving information or training, they should also love receiving feedback and further instruction (additional information). One should love receiving additional methods by which to improve the use of the knowledge. Otherwise, their stupidity is demonstrated, and the knowledge is willfully wasted. They, in turn, literally become stupid. Solomon says he who hates correction actually is stupid. Harsh words. Harsh truth. Perhaps the wisest man who ever lived was attempting to ensure that we all hate stupidity most of all.

Lloyd Speese

ONE FACE VS. TWO-FACED

Proverbs 28:6

*"Better the poor whose walk is blameless
than the rich whose ways are perverse." (NIV)*

Whether we are rich or poor, God requires integrity from us in every area of our lives. The ways of the rich are only labeled *perverse* (literally, "twisted") if they are "crooked and two-faced" (AMP). In this case, the rich are gaining wealth dishonestly, but pretending to be upright. This means that they are not only guilty of corruption, but also deception as well.

"God is light; in Him there is no darkness at all." (1 John 1:5b, NIV) God is holy, His message is truthful, He is perfect in righteousness; in Him there is no sin, no wickedness, no imperfection (amp). God has only one face, and He has shown (and shone!) that one face through His Son, Jesus Christ.

In Numbers 6:24-26, God gave Moses the priestly blessing with which Aaron and his sons were to bless the Israelites. For the Lord "to make His face shine on them" would mean to be gracious to them. A shining face expresses benevolence and favor, as the beaming face of a father for his child. True, the face of God can, and does, reveal the gamut of His emotions. Yet God is never dishonest or deceptive in His expressions or ways. One always knows where God stands.

God doesn't hate riches; He hates sin. He hates perverse and two-faced ways. We should, too. By the same token, we should also love what God loves; He loves righteousness and those whose walk is morally whole.

Karen Heimbuch

DILIGENCE VERSUS HASTE

Proverbs 21:5

*"Good planning and hard work lead to prosperity,
but hasty shortcuts lead to poverty." (NLT)*

This proverb is at the heart of a whole host of wise sayings, such as: "Failing to plan is a plan to fail," "look before you leap," or "you only have one life to live, so get it right the first time," as well as "measure twice and cut once." There are many more that I was taught as a child and as an adult. The comparison in this proverb is "success versus failure." It is as true today as it was in Solomon's day.

I was encouraged by my parents and my teachers, during 12 years of Christian schooling, to think about who I wanted to be and what I wanted to do with my life. External influences affected my decisions, and life was not a straight road. My life has been more like a mountain road with blind, hairpin turns, and potholes over which I was driving with bad brakes. That is where good planning and hard work came into play.

Proper Christ-centered training and plans are the best start on the road to success and can help you stay there. I thank God for Christian parents and teachers. I took many detours in my life, but God kept me faithful to Him, which has made all the difference. It is very reassuring to know that God will not let go of me. I pray that you have that blessed assurance. Whether you are facing financial poverty or poverty of the soul (which I believe is far worse), God can lead you and direct your path to a secure financial place and a spiritual place of green pastures beside still waters where you can rest your soul.

Proverb 21:5 has a set of choices. It is up to us to choose. What will you choose? Success versus failure, life versus death, wealth versus poverty, and yes, even Heaven versus Hell. If you fail to choose, then by default, you have made the wrong choice!

Martin and Bea Laufer

VALUED AS TREASURE

Proverbs 18:22

"The man who finds a wife finds a treasure,
and he receives favor from the Lord." (NLT)

Woman is a treasure from God, and everything about her is made in God's image. When she honors God, she is a special gift to her husband, family, and the world around her. If a man loves the Lord and chooses a wife who loves the Lord, he will enjoy a blessed marriage and God's favor. The "favor" mentioned here implies that God is "pleased" by the choice of a godly woman. Whether married or single, we are called to glorify God in everything we do (Col. 3:17).

If you do find a wife or husband, it will be a good thing, but even good things can turn into problems when they are out of balance (1 Cor. 6:12). King Solomon, the same man who wrote these wise proverbs, indulged in too much of a "good thing." He had hundreds of wives and concubines who turned his heart away to other gods, and he did not remain faithful to God, as David, his father, was (1 Kings 11:4).

That is why it is important to be wise when you choose the person you want to date and marry. Do not just consider their beauty or physical appearance. There are more important things you should look for. Do they love God with all their heart? Do they have a soft heart and a desire to continue growing in the Lord? Do they seek to improve in the areas of their personal weakness? At the end of the day, their body and pretty face will not create a happy marriage. My husband and I have decided to be each other's treasure in our relationship. We do not allow bad attitudes or bad behaviors to persist, but we challenge each other to change and grow. When we argue, we call a time-out and talk about it as adults. Everything improves when we recognize our faults, apologize, and forgive each other.

Decide that you will be a treasure to your wife, husband, or future spouse by allowing God to change the immature areas in your heart that are not pleasing to Him. Then you will experience a loving, healthy, and fruitful relationship.

Teresa Bauer

SELF-CONTROL

Proverbs 25:27

"It is not good to eat too much honey,
and it is not good to seek honors for yourself." (NLT)

I will never forget one occasion when, for some reason, the preacher that was supposed to come and hold a crusade could not make it. So, our pastor had to contact someone else who was available. All the publicity had been made for the other evangelist. So, the substitute evangelist humbly said, "I am here as an instrument that the Lord chose to preach His Word."

Proverbs 25:27 tells us that pursuing the honors we think we deserve is not helpful for us. It can make us bitter, discouraged, or angry and will not bring us the rewards we think should be ours.

I learned to depend on God when it comes to claiming our rights and what we perceive to be the honors and privileges due us. It happened when my friend and I visited a close friend's church in another state. I wanted to preach that night to show that I was a good preacher. But the Lord showed me that the attitude I had displayed that day was not that of a humble servant. I apologized to my pastor-friend and realized God had His plans for the service that night. Later, when I revisited my friend by myself, the Lord blessed me and gave me the opportunity to preach the Word to his congregation but this time with a very different attitude. I have learned in my experience that when we humble ourselves, He will lift us up in due time (1 Pet. 5:6).

Ricardo Chaidez

HE TOOK OUR PLACE

Proverbs 17:15

"Acquitting the guilty and condemning the innocent,
both are detestable to the Lord." (NLT)

Growing up as at-risk youth in a non-Christian broken family among all forms of criminal life, I often witnessed things that infuriated me. I was angry at how the guilty frequently escaped the consequences of their actions. Not only were the guilty free to go, but many times the innocent took the blame in their place.

I often asked myself, "how could such injustices go on without consequences?" I witnessed weapon-wielding gangs assaulting innocent people, substance abuse, neglected children, senseless street violence, the tragic loss of life, and much more. Yet, not only were they free to practice injustice, but also they taught others to follow in their footsteps. From street crime life to corruption in politics to moral decay within media and popular culture, it often feels as if the guilty are free to do what they want.

Witnessing the innocent become vilified is just as infuriating. I believe there are men and women of God who stand for truth and justice but are constantly attacked by family, co-workers, politicians, and even secular media. Just imagine being innocent yet falsely accused of serious wrongdoing. Also, imagine taking the blame for all those wrongs, even though you never committed them.

Proverbs 17:15 also describes God as One who detests when the guilty are set free and the innocent are condemned. The Lord is a God of justice and a God of mercy. This makes me all the more thankful for His forgiveness for all the injustices I have committed throughout my life. It makes me eternally grateful that even though I was guilty, the Lord acquitted me, and in my place—and in your place—the innocent one was sentenced. Jesus took all of our blame.

When we find ourselves infuriated with the injustice in life, let's also remember to thank the Lord that in our wrongdoings, He forgave us. The Lord is not blind to injustice; we can trust Him to bring answers, and whether in this life or the next, He will execute justice. Jesus knows firsthand what it is like to be condemned even though He was innocent.

Victor Miguel Rivera

THE WISDOM OF LAWS

Proverbs 28:4

*"To reject the law is to praise the wicked;
to obey the law is to fight them." (NLT)*

Since the summer of 2020, we have heard cries from various groups in our country to "defund the police." Ironically, some of the very politicians who called to abolish the police spend significant portions of their budget on private security. The utter absurdity of such a proposition is immediately evident to any rational person. It is a historically time-proven reality that the only real, tangible thing that keeps society from descending into tribalistic, guerrilla-warfare anarchy is the everyday law enforcement that patrols the streets to draw the line between the lawful and the lawless.

We saw the reality of this play out in Portland, Oregon, and Seattle, Washington, in 2020. In Portland, the anarchists were permitted for more than 100 consecutive days to run wildly through the city and destroy anything they wanted to while the mayor continuously pulled back the police. In Seattle, the mayor also pulled back law enforcement while CHAZ—a separate city-state run by anarchists—was formed over a few city blocks. The lawlessness, wanton destruction, disregard for authority, and personal violence we witnessed in both cities was but a taste of what life would be like without police. In other cities that either implemented the defund the police policy, like Minneapolis, Minnesota, or decriminalized many actions, like San Francisco, California, we saw an immediate skyrocketing of crime.

There is a reason the police are called "law enforcement"—they enforce a commonly held code of conduct that keeps the peace and allows people to live in relative safety. When the law is rejected, especially by those in power like the leaders of Portland, Seattle, Minneapolis, and San Francisco, the wicked were practically given free rule, and, unsurprisingly, devastation ensued. The laws of God and man exist for a reason, and to uphold them is to fight injustice, violence, crime, and wickedness. Laws exist because wicked people exist. To curb the effects of wickedness that affect peace and safety, we obey laws.

Kyle Bauer

RIGHTEOUSNESS AND FAVOR

Proverbs 14:9

"Fools mock at sin,
but among the upright there is favor." (NKJV)

The Lord has favor for those who are upright. But what does it mean to be upright? Can we be upright by helping the homeless, giving our tithes and offerings, respecting other people, and doing other good works? Although all these things are good and important, it is not by good works alone that we become upright.

The upright have favor in the Lord's sight because they repent of their sins. The New Living Translation says, *"Fools make fun of guilt, but the godly acknowledge it and seek reconciliation."* They recognize their sins and seek out God's forgiveness to mend the relationship that has been damaged through sin and guilt. The Lord loves it when His people want to make things right with Him, and He will be faithful to forgive. 1 John 1:9 says, "But if we confess our sins to Him, He is faithful and just to forgive us our sins and to cleanse us from all wickedness." (NLT)

God is willing to forgive anyone if they make the decision to repent of their sins. The book of Proverbs says, *"He who conceals his transgressions will not prosper, but whoever confesses and turns away from his sins will find compassion and mercy."* (Prov. 28:13, AMP) The reason why the foolish are not in God's favor is that they mock and reject repentance, and they obey their own fleshly desires rather than His Word. They love their sin too much to let it go because it would mean putting aside their own pride. It takes humility to admit that we are broken and need a Savior.

We, too, can be upright through daily prayer and repentance. When rising in the morning to lying down to rest at night, pray constantly. No one is perfect, and even the godliest person still sins; that is why we ask the Lord for forgiveness, to purify us and make us upright so that His favor will rest upon us.

Joshua Bauer

STICKS AND STONES

Proverbs 25:18

*"Telling lies about others is as harmful as hitting them with an ax,
wounding them with a sword, or shooting them with a sharp arrow." (NLT)*

Sticks and stones may break my bones, but words will never hurt me.

Whoever coined that phrase did not read their Bible! The Bible has a lot to say about words. The power of God's Word formed the Universe. God spoke, and the world was created. He said the words, "Let there be light!" and it dispelled the darkness in an instant. There is much to be said about words.

We are the only creatures on the planet that can speak words that have creative power. Our Father gave us that privilege and responsibility. There is power in the words we speak to do good or to do evil.

If we speak lies about other people, it can do irreparable harm to the most important part of their being—their soul. Being wounded by a sword or shot with an arrow will kill the body, but evil lies can kill the soul.

Some may say, oh, how can words be that bad? Just ask the parents who lost their daughter to suicide because of the relentless bullying on social media. Evil is real, and it comes in all shapes, sizes, ages, and forms. The enemy will use whatever tactics, means, or willing participants he can to destroy us and our families.

But we can use the creative power God gave us to do battle on their behalf. Speak words of faith, affirmation, truth, healing, strength, and life. Be the defender of your family by praying for them. Find the promises of God in Scripture and cover your loved ones by speaking the Word of God. The Lord will show you the strategies of the enemy and how to defeat them as you pray. He will show you how to build up and edify your children so they will grow strong in the Lord and in their faith.

There is power in the words we speak. Speak the truth and defeat the lies. Speak peace. Speak faith. Speak hope. Speak love.

Michelle Glush

DON'T BE A FOOL

Proverbs 16:22

*"Understanding is a wellspring of life to him who has it.
But the correction of fools is folly." (NKJV)*

Proverbs 4:7: *"Wisdom is the principal thing; therefore, get wisdom. And in all your getting, get understanding."*

The word "fool" seems to come up a lot in the Bible. In Proverbs alone it appears 71 times! "Fool" is defined as "one who is deficient in judgment, sense, or understanding," and "one who acts unwisely on a given occasion."

A foolish person who is prideful, ignorant, and stubborn can make smoke come out of my ears! They just don't want to listen. They don't want to learn. Children can be this way, but some adults also fall into that category. You try and try to explain things to them, such as a better way to solve a problem or a better way to communicate, but they just refuse to get it.

My husband (before he knew Christ) used to tell me how he would occasionally have to explain things to some people "differently." This euphemism usually meant a trip out behind the barn. I think he may have taken Proverbs 19:29 too literally: "Penalties are prepared for mockers and beatings for the backs of fools." This method may have gotten their attention, but it never solved the issue.

The Holy Bible is the cookbook with the recipes for life. If you were to make a cake, knowledge would be the ingredients. Wisdom is knowing which ingredients are the best to use, and understanding is knowing how to put the ingredients together so that the cake will be good.

God did not create us to be foolish, so He provides all the information we need in the cookbook, which is His Word. If we follow His recipes, we will have wisdom, knowledge, and understanding to deal with the issues in our lives—and wisdom to let God deal with the fools!

Pat Nannarello

JUNE

My child,

listen when your father corrects you.

Pay attention and learn good judgment,

for I am giving you good guidance.

Don't turn away from my instructions.

For I, too, was once my father's son,

tenderly loved as my mother's only child.

—Proverbs 4:1-3

POTATOES AND FOUNDATIONS

Proverbs 12:7

"The wicked are overthrown and are no more,
but the house of the righteous stands firm." (NKJV)

When we look at life, things do not always seem fair. We can see the wicked prospering and God's people suffering and in lack, but this proverb is a comforting scripture for us to hold on to. We may have to hold on to the Lord and His Word for a long season, but be encouraged, harvest is coming. Keep planting good and doing what is right, and God will reward you. He is bringing in the harvest; those who do good will reap a reward, and the wicked will also reap what they have sown (Gal. 6:7).

The wicked continue to sow evil, and in their arrogance, they think God is not paying attention. I liken it to growing potatoes. The progress of the harvest cannot be seen until the end of the season. It may look like nothing is happening, but the potatoes are developing under the surface. In the same way, the wicked do not see that their harvest of destruction is ripening like the hidden potatoes.

Jesus compares God's Kingdom to both a seed and a foundation. I find a nice similarity in that both are underground! A seed grows, and a foundation is built. Jesus says that if we hear His words and do what He says, we are like a wise man who builds his house on a foundation of rock. But, the unwise or evil man who hears Jesus' words and does not do them is building his house on sand. When the storm hits both, the house of the righteous stands firm, but the house of the evil man is washed away. What are you sowing in your life? What are you building your life on?

Heavenly Father, give us the grace to heed Your words and to trust that You never lie. Our society tells us to follow our ways, but You have good plans for us, and only through You can we withstand the storms of life.

Stephen Larkin

KEEPING UP WITH THE JONESES

Proverbs 29:25

"Fear of man will prove to be a snare,
but whoever trusts in the Lord is kept safe." (NIV)

At its heart, the fear of man is people pleasing. I find it odd that so many people work so hard to impress people they do not know, do not agree with, or maybe do not even like. Many work so hard to "keep up with the Joneses." But for what purpose? The answer is relatively simple, but the root cause is a deadly trap.

The simple answer is to keep a facade so people will think well of you. The deadly trap is idolatry. This is in direct conflict with the first two of the Ten Commandments: 1) You will have no other gods, and 2) you will make no images. The fear of man is reverent awe and worship of what other people think of you. You will end up wasting your emotional and financial resources, and your true heart worship will be given to others rather than God.

I have learned to identify the fear of man in my own life by some tell-tale signs:

1. **If I feel inadequate by not having or doing things other people have or do.** This signals that my worth comes from keeping up with other people. That is an idolatrous fear of man.
2. **If I feel I have to "walk on eggshells" around people.**
   This signals that either a person is in conflict with my leadership, or I fear confronting an issue because of the person's reaction. Either way, there is a problem. The problem may have started with the other person, but in me, it is the fear of man to perhaps not be liked. The problem will not only persist but get worse.
3. **If I feel the need to conform to a certain opinion.** The signal of the problem is not the *pressure* to conform but the *need* to. If I feel a need to be like everyone else, then I am seeking ungodly approval based on personal idolatry.

The fear of the Lord and trust in His ways and goodness will deliver us from wasting our lives in this deadly idolatry. He is our adequacy, not the Joneses.

Kyle Bauer

DON'T WIMP OUT

Proverbs 24:10

"If you faint in the day of adversity,
your strength is small." (NKJV)

My translation: If you wimp out when life goes sideways, you have no backbone, no courage.

This is exactly what the enemy wants. He wants us to wimp out, be thrown off balance, and be scared. He wants to up-end our peace. And, in today's world, if you do not know how to stand on THE ROCK, you need to learn how—NOW—because the enemy is doing just that. He has upended our peace, and we cannot fight him if we are wimps!

The way I learned how to stand on THE ROCK (and, yes, sometimes I trip, but never fall off) was by learning worship choruses. For me, "Praise the Name of Jesus" was the first I learned, and it has saved my fanny more than I would care to share. The first time was by surprise. I found myself walking on the side of the freeway in the middle of the night because I had run out of gas. Suddenly I realized I was singing PRAISE THE NAME OF JESUS, HE'S MY ROCK, HE'S MY FORTRESS, out loud! Just that little expression of my faith helped me focus on the Lord and kept me from panicking.

Maybe a Bible verse will work better for you: Philippians 4:13 *"I can do all things through Christ Who strengthens me."* Or, perhaps, reminding yourself daily that Jesus suffered and died on the cross for us! Hebrews 12:13 says, "Consider Him who endured such hostility, so that you will not grow weary." So, who are we to ever complain!?!

Stand on THE ROCK that gives you balance and ballast and an anchor so you don't get blown over. Hold on to THE ROCK for dear life, so you don't wimp out. Jesus is already there, holding on to you.

Keep saying, singing, shouting PRAISE THE NAME OF JESUS or Philippians 4:13 for Pete's sake.

Pat Nannarello

WISDOM IS PRICELESS

Proverbs 16:16

_"How much better to get wisdom than gold,
to get insight rather than silver!" (NIV)_

The current value of gold in the United States is roughly $1,700.00+ an ounce. Rubies, depending on the vibrancy, quality, cut, and source, also have their set market value. According to The Natural Ruby Company, a ruby is a minimum of $1,000 per carat, and if it is of a better quality, the price increases dramatically—up to one million per carat! Before reaching the public for purchase, any precious metal or gem must go through a series of tests and trade factors that determine how much it will cost. But no matter what, there will always be a cap on how much someone is willing to pay for anything, and a physical item can never surpass the ceiling of a consumer's desire to obtain it.

Knowledge and wisdom cannot be weighed in this manner. These are not tangibles found in the physical realm, nor can they be quantified and controlled in their distribution. They are created through experience, time, and submission to God, who is the only source of truth. Only through continual pursuit and constant refinement can they ever be truly cultivated and used. When people freely and thoughtlessly express their words and disregard the severity of their impact, the currency of the words they use are reduced to "a dime a dozen."

But how many words coming out of billions of people's mouths on a daily basis add value to their lives? Even if we could measure this statistically, this proverb expresses how much more valuable wisdom and understanding are in a world filled with trillions of words void of benefit and worth. It is in God's mercy that He allows all people to receive understanding, knowledge, and wisdom to the level they search for it. This is worth more than gold or rubies. You can have treasure and still be a fool, but have no earthly treasure and be rich in wisdom.

Rachael Hopkins

LEAD BY EXAMPLE

Proverbs 20:7

"The godly walk with integrity;
blessed are their children who follow them." (NLT)

Integrity is formed by imitating the example of others who live in integrity. Our children are the reflection of the example that we as parents give them at home. Several people have asked my husband and me what the recipe is for having children who love and serve God with all their hearts, children who are friendly and polite and know how to talk with children and adults. One of the answers we give is that they follow the example and the standards that we, as parents, demand and teach at home. Raising well-behaved sons and daughters with integrity requires a lot of intentionality on our part to invest in their lives.

We do not let little sins creep into their hearts when they are young. If we do, after they are teenagers, we cannot control what is going on in their lives, because we did not take the time when they were little to correct their tantrums and capriciousness. Do not allow children to throw tantrums! Correct bad attitudes with love and understanding. Ask the Holy Spirit, who is our Helper and Counselor, to show you how you should love your children through correction and discipline. Teach them that actions have consequences—if they do well, they will be rewarded. If they do badly, they will be disciplined. Then follow up with the reward or consequence.

Learn from other parents who have done well with their children and imitate their example. You do not have to do this alone, nor does your past have to be the only experience you draw from. There is so much knowledge and wisdom available to us in the Word of God and through books by Christian authors that can help you be a better parent to your children. You will see a difference in their lives when you begin to instruct them in the Lord and implement wise discipline.

Let's impact our children by being imitators of Jesus, and our children will see that we do not compromise with sin, not even for a second, because our primary desire is to please our Father God with all our heart, soul, and strength (Deut. 6:5).

Teresa Bauer

DEFINING MOMENTS

Proverbs 13:1

"A wise child accepts a parent's discipline;
a mocker refuses to listen to correction." (NLT)

I will never forget when my dad held up a mirror to my face for about four hours at the Denny's on the corner of Van Nuys and Sherman Way. Of course, the mirror was figurative, but his words uncovered me and brought me face-to-face with myself and the immaturity of my actions and mentality. It was a defining moment of correction in my life. I was 19 years old, and my dad's words were designed to bring me out of my adolescence and into manhood. In essence, my dad's words were that men cannot think like boys anymore. To have a full-grown man juggernaut into a teenager in an attempt to knock him into the next stage of his life was painful.

I remember listening to my dad and, at the same time, having a conversation with myself that went something like this:

> "Ok, Bauer. You have a critical choice to make here. It is hard to hear these words from Dad, but you can choose one of two things. Either 1) you can decide the old man is crazy, ignore him, and go do your own thing on your own terms, or 2) decide that he has your best in his mind, he loves you, and he has lived longer than you and knows more. So, what will it be? Will you listen or not?"

This was the second defining moment of that morning. The first was the correction itself; the second was my response. My future literally hung in the balance of this internal decision. I decided to humble myself, accept the correction, and grow from it.

The Passion Translation uses the term "know-it-all" instead of "mocker." The moment someone—whether a child, teen, or adult—decides they know it all, they mock and scorn counsel and discipline, leaving them at the mercy of their own wisdom (or lack thereof). The moment this happens, they reject humility, a docile, teachable spirit, and wisdom, and they stop growing and become the quintessential "fool," as described in Proverbs. Fools mock discipline, reject counsel, rely on themselves, fight, and are prideful. The wise are respectful and able to receive correction and counsel in all humility. What will define you?

Kyle Bauer

A HAPPY HEART

Proverbs 15:13

"A glad heart makes a happy face;
a broken heart crushes the spirit." (NLT)

We see it every Sunday morning at church, throughout the week among co-workers, in school, or even in families; the traditional smile and phrase, "I'm doing good." We ask each other how we feel and quickly respond with, "I'm fine!" Proverbs 15:13, "a glad heart makes a happy face," is true, but how can we look deeper to see if a crushed spirit hides behind the smile? How do we open up and begin to talk about it?

Our hearts can be glad in life's circumstances, and this happiness can manifest in a happy smile. It is almost as if a smile can suggest a happy life. But a smile can also conceal a broken heart and crushed spirit. Many walk among us daily who carry crushed spirits and yet say, "I'm fine." As the Body of Christ, we must be attentive to the Lord to hear how He would have us minister to those who feel they cannot share their pain with others.

I used to work in the emergency room at several hospitals. In this intense environment, glad hearts and broken hearts were easily discernable. It was clear and loud when family members rejoiced at seeing their loved ones defy death. When individuals lost loved ones, their faces also said it all. A hospital is a metaphor for a church. There are incredibly sick people and others who are on their way to getting well.

I encourage us, as members of the Body of Christ, that when we ask someone how they are doing, take the time to really listen. If we encounter glad hearts, let's rejoice with them. If we encounter broken hearts and crushed spirits, let's be available to come alongside and pray for them. If you, or anyone you know, is experiencing heartache and pain, I encourage you to reach out to someone in the Body of Christ and seek prayer or counseling. We are all here to help each. We are one Body in Christ and are called to tend to one another.

Victor Miguel Rivera

GET UP AND GO!

Proverbs 26:13

"The lazy man says, 'There is a lion in the road!
A fierce lion is in the streets!'" (NKJV)

Some people will use any excuse to avoid making an effort. The Bible speaks of the lazy man who, to avoid having to work, says, "There's a lion in the road!" Today, that excuse might sound something like, "The traffic is terrible. There are too many cars on the road!" Sounds like a poor excuse though, doesn't it? The lazy person who does not show up for work will not collect a paycheck at the end of the week and, ultimately, won't be able to feed or clothe himself or provide for his family. There are always consequences for our choices and the decisions we make.

Often times we make decisions based on how we feel. Who hasn't said, "I am too tired to go to work today" or "I do not feel like going to the gym this morning"? But let's go a little deeper. Have you ever said, "I do not feel like praying" or "I do not have time to share the gospel with my neighbor right now"? Or maybe we say to ourselves on Wednesday night, "I am just too busy to go to Bible study tonight." Ultimately, there will be consequences of the choices and decisions we make. We could miss an opportunity to lead someone to Christ, or the breakthrough you desperately need may be delayed.

When we consider that our heavenly Father gives good gifts to His children who ask Him (Matthew 7:11) and He withholds no good thing from those who do what is right (Psalm 84:11), any excuses we make to avoid the effort of seeking God in prayer, or ministering to others, or studying the Word and fellowshipping with our brothers and sisters in Christ start to seem pretty lame, don't they? The only lion in the streets is the devil who is looking for someone to devour (1 Peter 5:8). Don't fall prey to his tactics. Get up and go!

Rachel Corcoran

TIPPING THE SCALES

Proverbs 20:10

"False weights and unequal measures –
the Lord detests double standards of every kind." (NLT)

When you go to the grocery store and weigh your produce, how well do you trust the scale you are using? Or, when the cashier weighs it again at the checkout stand, do you ever wonder when was the last time the scale was accurately calibrated so that consumers aren't being overcharged? I have these thoughts from time to time. It might be a little bizarre, but I don't want to be tricked by an inconsistent scale, and neither does God. For this very reason, He has given us His Word by which all creation can have one standard to live by.

We live in a Christ-rejecting, sin-filled world, and the standards of the current culture are not the ones by which God wants us to measure ourselves. The world chooses favorites; the scales can tip in the balance for those who can afford it. The current rule of law is not always consistent with Christ-centered morality. We have witnessed corruption in the highest levels of government, business, and even within the body of Christ.

Instead of becoming increasingly frustrated with our society's false weights, unequal measures, and double standards, we must continue to rejoice in knowing that Christ leveled the playing field when He died on the cross for us. We must give honor to God because, in His economy, there are no double standards. There is only one standard—Jesus Christ, who is "…the way, the truth and the life" (John 14:6 NLT). Every one of us was created by God, we all have access to salvation, and we all will be judged by the same scale. "For God does not show favoritism" (Romans 2:11 NLT), and His scale will never waiver.

Jennifer Shank

THE RIGHT PATH

Proverbs 16:25

*"There is a path before each person that seems right,
but it ends in death." (NLT)*

At least a couple of times a year, we hear on the news that someone or a group of people have gotten lost in the Angeles National Forest, and occasionally someone falls off a trail and dies. Almost without exception we are told that they took a wrong turn and got lost. Those trails are well-worn and frequented by hikers all the time. It is when someone decides to take a shortcut, or explore an unbeaten path, that disaster occurs. If they had stayed on the right path, they would have been safe.

In the past, I chose the wrong paths when I did not consider the way God wanted me to go. Now I try to make the Bible my "trail map" and the Lord my guide. This proverb states that the path is before us, and it SEEMS RIGHT, but it ends in DEATH. How do I know the correct path? How do I choose? Psalm 23 says that the Lord is my shepherd who can lead me by the still waters and make me lie down in green pastures. The Good Shepherd will also lead me through the valley of the shadow of death. If I stay focused on Him, Jesus is "a lamp unto my feet, and a light unto my path." (Psalm 119:105) We have a Good Shepherd who can lead us through those shadow places in our life. We need to know His voice and then obey it. We must follow Him to avoid paths that seem right but lead to death. You will be glad you did.

Martin and Bea Laufer

YOUR YOUNGER SELF

Proverbs 19:20

*"Listen to advice and accept discipline, and
at the end you will be counted among the wise." (NIV)*

Do you ever wish you could go back to a point in your life where you remember you did not listen to some good advice? Maybe it was your parents, a teacher, or a manager who gave you some life-changing counsel that might have changed the trajectory of your life.

I think we all can relate to that, and when I get too far into that type of thinking, I remember the story of Lot's wife and how she turned into a pillar of salt because she looked back. I try to look back only for correctional moments and to learn the lessons I need to move forward into the future God has planned for me. So, pressing forward is wisdom. Let the Lord teach you how to grow from the past, grow in grace where you are, and learn to grow by faith, knowing that He is using all things to work together for your good.

If we believe God is for us and working for our good, we will listen to sound advice, look at discipline as a healthy correction, and in so doing, I believe we are following the pathway to wisdom. The more we listen to advice, wisdom, and the teaching of God's Word, the more we allow ourselves to grow and mature.

If I could go back and talk to my younger self, I would say, "It's okay, listen and ask as many questions as you can," and don't be mad or agitated when you are corrected. Pray more, and don't be afraid. Ask God to give you more wisdom and be thankful for someone taking the time to provide instruction." You cannot go back and have that conversation with your younger self, but right now, you are the youngest version of yourself that you will be for the rest of your life. So, listen and grow as much as you can.

Debbie Speese

SMART VS. WISE

Proverbs 15:5

"Only a fool despises a parent's discipline;
whoever learns from correction is wise." (NLT)

It has been said that a smart person learns from their mistakes, but a wise person learns from the mistakes of others. There is truth in this, but the Bible actually flips this around. It is intelligent and very valuable to watch and learn from others. But watching someone else does not require anything from us except to take our observations to heart. Watching does not touch our pride, nor does it augment our personal, hands-on experience—and experience *is* the best teacher.

At the same time, there is not one of us who does not make mistakes and needs correction—and no one likes discipline or correction in the moment. Wisdom is different than intelligence. Sinful human intelligence can manipulate a situation in smart and clever ways, but godly wisdom sees the *why* behind what is happening, puts aside sinfulness and pride, and applies godly correction, thereby learning from it, not how to manipulate, but how to live in a way that pleases God.

As parents, it is never wise (or smart!) to simply enforce the house or family rules. Inevitably the child will ask, "Why?" A foolish answer is, "Because I said so!" If we do not answer with the wisdom of the reason behind our actions, lifestyle, and beliefs, those things will not be passed on to the next generation. A harsh and unwise answer has the potential to breed the kind of foolish person we read about in Romans 1:29-31, *"Their lives became full of every kind of wickedness, sin, greed, hate, envy, murder, quarreling, deception, malicious behavior, and gossip. They are backstabbers, haters of God, insolent, proud, and boastful. They invent new ways of sinning, and they disobey their parents. They refuse to understand, break their promises, are heartless, and have no mercy."* (NLT)

Wisdom is found in humility, understanding, and the application of correction and discipline, which only comes after trying and failing. I submit to you that the saying should be, "A smart person learns from the mistakes of others, but a wise person learns from their own mistakes."

Kyle Bauer

192

WHAT MAKES YOUR FRIENDS SEEM LIKE ENEMIES

Proverbs 13:10

"Wisdom opens your heart to receive wise counsel,
but pride closes your ears to advice
and gives birth only to quarrels and strife." (TPT)

So, right in the middle of an argument, in the back of my head, I am asking myself, "Why are you arguing about this? You know you just do not want to admit you are wrong?" Note to self. I was arguing with a close friend regarding an issue that was totally frivolous and frankly misdirected. It was a deflection from what was really bothering me—my hurt pride. He correctly addressed me as being selfish and small. Rather than just admitting it and choosing to believe he was speaking the truth to me because he is truly my friend, I chose to deflect, defend, and quarrel, almost as an automatic defense mechanism. Why?

Solomon answers this question by noting the aftereffects of pride. Pride takes several actions to defend itself. Specifically, you stop hearing and automatically start defending, often when something is indefensible. Our hearing is not closed entirely; we just stop hearing advice. We often still hear anything that suggests we are correct or supports our prideful position. Interesting. We not only stop hearing what will help us most, but this same pride elicits arguing, conflicts, and quarrels. In the Hebrew text, the word used here for quarreling means "to seek revenge." Again, interesting. We automatically seek revenge, even when it is we who are in the wrong. Concurrently, the word strife is translated here to mean "contention with an adversary." In short, my pride made me blindly turn my friend into an enemy upon whom I was seeking revenge. How horrible.

The good news is, wisdom causes me to respect the words of my close friend (not adversary) and choose to listen to the truth he is sharing with me about myself. Wisdom reaches my heart and challenges me to accept its benefits. Wisdom causes the real me (that person talking in my head while I was arguing) to consider and embrace what will help me most!! Final food for thought—the apostle James was inspired to say, *"If any man lacks wisdom, let him ask of God, who gives it to all men liberally, without rebuke or blame."* (James 1:5).

Lloyd Speese

YOU DO NOT HAVE TO DO IT ALONE

Proverbs 16:3

*"Commit to the Lord whatever you do,
and He will establish your plans." (NIV)*

We face making decisions daily. Big decisions come often in life. However, it is not the wisest plan to make these decisions depending solely on our own understanding.

Being self-employed has taught me to seek God's counsel regularly. I do not know what to do sometimes to keep the flow of work coming in, and I need His ideas revealed to me. In 1993, the Lord instructed us to do a specific task and then give it away. We were serving many clients in real estate who spoke only Spanish. The Lord told us to translate the English purchase contract into Spanish using a court translator and to make sure it was worded just like the English one. Then, He instructed us to give it to our clients and give it free to any agent who wanted it. So, we did. We had no idea that God would use it two years later to save our family from financial ruin.

In 1995, after the Northridge earthquake, we had no work for many months. The thought of caring for my disabled mother, our sons, our bills, and putting food on the table seemed insurmountable. We prayed, hoped, and experienced much anxiety to the point that I felt myself getting sick. One morning the Lord spoke to me after I prayed again and gave me the name of an institution that would call and employ us to sell foreclosures.

It was miraculous!!! The call came, and we were hired! The most encouraging part was that God already knew our future when He asked us to translate the contract. It was the translation, we later found out, that opened the door to serve this lender. An agent we had given it to recommended us to them. We not only were able to care for our family but also put our sons through college.

While on earth, Jesus fully committed Himself to His Heavenly Father, which resulted in the fulfillment of God's plan—Salvation—the greatest victory for mankind. We are called to follow Jesus' example of full commitment to God.

Martin and Bea Laufer

POOR IN SPIRIT

Proverbs 19:19

*"Better to be poor and honest
than to be dishonest and a fool." (NLT)*

The Bible seems to infer that being poor is better than being rich. But what does it mean to be poor, and why is there a special place in God's heart for them? There is more to the meaning of poor than just lacking in wealth and possessions. To be poor also means to be humble and meek.

The Lord loves the humble, and He gives them grace and strength (James 4:6). As the Apostle Paul writes, *"That's why I take pleasure in my weaknesses, and in the insults, hardships, persecutions, and troubles that I suffer for Christ. For when I am weak, then I am strong."* (2 Cor. 12:10, NLT) It is the humble who search for God, and He will turn His face toward them. *"But this is the one to whom I will look: he who is humble and contrite in spirit and trembles at my word."* (Isa. 66:2, ESV) To those who are poor in spirit, he gives them the kingdom of heaven. (Matt. 5:3, NIV). It is the poor in spirit who recognize their need for God.

Not so the wicked. God will not give the dishonest and the foolish the kingdom of heaven. Those who are honest and faithful can be trusted with many things, but the dishonest cannot be trusted with anything. They will not even stand in His presence. *"One who is faithful in very little is also faithful in much, and one who is dishonest in very little is also dishonest in much. If you have not been faithful in the unrighteous wealth, who will entrust you with true riches? And if you have not been faithful in that which is another's, who will give you that which is your own?"* (Luke 16:10-12, ESV) *"No one who practices deceit will dwell in my house; no one who speaks falsely will stand in my presence."* (Ps. 101:7, NIV).

It is better to be "poor in spirit" and turn your eyes to the Lord and depend on Him than to be self-sufficient and fall into foolishness.

Joshua Bauer

OPPRESSORS WILL PAY

Proverbs 23:10

*"Don't cheat your neighbor by moving the ancient boundary markers;
don't take the land of defenseless orphans." (NLT)*

The poor and needy are infinitely important to God. All of us are important, but there are multiple differentiations made in scripture regarding those that are genuinely helpless.

To bring a helpless person to further ruin or take advantage of someone in a lesser position than you is literally to place a wrath of God magnet on your back. In a court of law, society attempts to use fair scales to resolve a dispute, but our justice scales are limited to human reason and chance. God promises those with no natural defender that anything foul done to them will be returned to their oppressor.

When you see a person, a government, or any corporate entity/organization taking advantage of people, it is important to understand that God does not take this lightly. He sets a timer on the implementation of justice. He is merciful to give those who are doing evil a chance to repent, but their time is limited. There is a reason God has a final day for the world. If humanity were allowed to continue unbridled, then brutality and corruption would eventually reign, as people become cold and heartless to the actions of their deceitful hearts, giving in to selfish desires.

The oppression of those in genuine need will not last forever, as this world will not last forever. God has not and will never overlook those deemed "worthless" to society. Showing the heart of God in a heartless world is to show kindness and help to those who are helpless. They have a special place in God's heart. When we help them, we are touching God's heart.

God will show those who think they have power what true power really means.

Rachael Hopkins

TURNING FOES INTO FRIENDS

Proverbs 16:7

"When a man's ways please the Lord,
He makes even his enemies to be at peace with him." (NKJV)

The New English Translation renders this verse: "When a person's ways are pleasing to the Lord, He even *reconciles* his enemies to himself." Before our enemies can be reconciled to us, we must first be reconciled to God. Reconciliation begins with God: "…while we were God's enemies, we were *reconciled* to Him through the death of His Son…" (Rom. 5:10a, NIV)

God is the One who initiates friendship with us. All souls belong to Him (Ezek. 18:4), and He can—and does—move upon the hearts of men and kings at will. "In the Lord's hand the king's heart is a stream of water that He channels toward all who please Him." (Prov. 21:1, NIV)

What kind of ways please the Lord?

- Living a holy life according to His Word (Ps. 119:1, 9).
- Keeping yourself in His love, staying "always within the boundaries where God's love can reach and bless you." (Jude 21a, TLB)
- Serving others wholeheartedly as you would in serving the Lord (Eph. 6:7).
- Living in accordance with the Spirit, not the flesh (Rom. 8:5).
- Walking by faith (Heb. 11:6).

Nothing is too hard for God! He caused King Abimelech to be at peace with Isaac, Esau to be at peace with Jacob, and David's enemies to seek his favor. When we incline our hearts to follow our Good Shepherd along the paths of righteousness (Ps. 23:3), He will incline the hearts of our foes to not only cease their opposition, but also even become our friends!

Karen Heimbuch

CREATIVE OR DESTRUCTIVE WORDS

Proverbs 16:10

"Divination is on the lips of the king:
His mouth must not transgress in judgment." (NKJV)

Growing up can be a challenge for some kids. When parents and teachers teach from their own experiences, it can sometimes be detrimental to children.

Proverbs 16:10 is not just about a King. The King is a figure of authority empowered by God. Therefore, his words should come from divine wisdom and authority. We carry that same authority, because God places us in a position of influence. Therefore, we must be careful what comes out of our mouths.

My husband was dyslexic and was always relegated to remedial classes. As a result, he got bad grades. He was frustrated because he was smart, but in those days, he was labeled dumb and stupid. Because he was good at sports, that became his focus.

When we started dating, it never occurred to me that he was anything but an intelligent guy. After we married, I discovered things about his childhood and realized that he had never been diagnosed (dyslexia had not yet been identified). When we went out socially, he would always look to me for approval regarding a particular word he used. I finally suggested he go for testing. The doctor told him that his dyslexia at 35 years old was not hampering his life, so there was no need for therapy. She also told him that he tested borderline genius on the IQ test. Two days later, as he spoke to me, I noticed his vocabulary went from 500 words to 5000! I remember listening to him with my mouth hanging open thinking, "who is this person?" The difference was that people in authority—schoolteachers—had told him he was dumb, and now a Ph.D. had told him he was smart. I have never seen such a profound turnaround like that before or since!

As children of God, created in His image and given His authority, we must be mindful of our speech. Our words carry weight. We can make people smile, frown, laugh, or cry. We can lift them out of a bad day or make them have one. Giving place to the Holy Spirit will help us to be better stewards of our words.

Pat Nannarello

THROW THE DICE

Proverbs 16:33

*"We may throw the dice,
but the Lord determines how they fall." (NLT)*

When this proverb says "throw the dice" (or "cast lots" in other translations), it is not suggesting that we live by luck or have a fatalistic worldview. Only a few verses earlier, in 16:9, Proverbs says that a man plans his way, but the Lord directs his steps. Sometimes in the midst of planning, we do not know what to do. We do our best to plan, take our best guess, take a vote—or "throw the dice" or "toss a coin," as it were—and hope for the best. I am not suggesting that we do whatever we please, and God is somehow obligated to bless the work of our hands. On the contrary, we must keep in mind what Psalm 37:5 says, *"Commit everything you do to the Lord. Trust him, and he will help you."* (NLT)

Looking even deeper into this, Isaiah 55:8-9 gives us wonderful insight into this proverb. Isaiah provides an understanding of God's intimate involvement in our lives and how we can live in full trust and assurance that He is in everything we do.

> *"For My thoughts are not your thoughts, nor are your ways My ways," says the Lord. For as the heavens are higher than the earth, so are My ways higher than your ways, and My thoughts than your thoughts."* (NIV)

There are times when we commit ourselves to the Lord and are still unsure of what to do. In the times we seek His will and still feel very little guidance (we have all had these moments), we can rest assured that God is still at work, no matter the outcome. Even when we do not understand what He is doing, we can believe that God is in the midst of our situation. He sees the end from the beginning, He has your good in mind (see Jeremiah 29:11), and He is working for your redemption, restoration, and blessing. God is intensely interested in every aspect of your life, and whether you know it or not, or whether your feel it or not, He is steering your life into all the goodness He has planned for you.

Kyle Bauer

[NO LONGER]
LIVING AT THE INTERSECTION
OF HOPE DEFERRED AND HEARTSICK

Proverbs 13:12

"Hope deferred makes the heart sick,
but when the desire comes, it is a tree of life." (NKJV)

For years, I said I was living at the "Intersection of Hope Deferred and Heartsick." It seemed that my dream had dried up and shriveled away. I had plans! I wanted to be married by the time I was 24, have 2.5 children, a cute little house with a white picket fence, and a dog (I do have a wonderful dog!). But that did not happen, and for years, I would fall into depression and ask, "why God"...or, "why not!"

We all have dreams. We have all had hopes—desires that have come to pass, and it truly is a joy. And, we have all had dreams that are still unfulfilled, or even worse, have died. But is our dream more important than God's dreams for us? We do not want our dreams to become idols in our lives, becoming more important than God.

How do we deal with hope deferred? We surrender. We say to our loving Heavenly Father, "You are more important to me than any of my hopes, dreams, or plans, and I want to follow you no matter what. I want your will for my life."

Do not be afraid to give it all to Him. You see, God's plans are always better than ours. He has plans and purposes for you that you have not seen yet. Sometimes, they do not look like what you thought you wanted, but they are oh so much better than what you can even imagine. If you surrender, God will turn that hope deferred into a tree of life.

Michelle Glush

CURB YOUR APPETITE

Proverbs 23:23

"When you sit to dine with a ruler, note well what is before you,
and put a knife to your throat if you are given to gluttony.
Do not crave his delicacies, for that food is deceptive." (NIV)

This proverb is not about food; the food is a metaphor. The context is that of being cautious when sitting with influential and rich people, people in governmental positions, CEOs, and anyone who is in a position of authority. They may or may not be trying to use you for their own ends.

A few years ago, a prominent political figure was caught in a "honey trap," a stratagem that uses irresistible bait to lure a victim into a snare. The New York Post reports:

> It is the stuff of a James Bond blockbuster: a young, attractive woman lures a rising political star into a romantic web, all the while collecting critical information to trickle back to her handler or big bosses back home…more than six years ago Rep. Eric Swalwell, D-Calif., began a relationship with a woman suspected of being a Chinese espionage operative. He was alerted by federal investigators in 2015 and given a "defense briefing," which resulted in him breaking off ties to the suspect.[1]

Not all that glitters is gold. If we live our lives without the wisdom of the fear of the Lord, and we have a raging appetite for influence, position, wealth, praise, or lust, we can become easy prey for fakes, tricksters, swindlers, or even the devil himself who seeks to lead people into a honey trap of sin. People with a lustful appetite, who covet the things of this world, cannot be wise. With sin, strings are always attached, and if you thoughtlessly gobble up what is put in front of you, you will find yourself trapped. So, if you know you have a weakness for a certain type of sin, person, or attitude, beware of it and learn to curb that appetite. Live in the fear of the Lord and rely on His Holy Spirit to help you overcome lustful passions.

Kyle Bauer

---

1   Hollie McKay. "China 'honey trap' plot could span thousands of operatives" New York Post, December 11, 2020, https://nypost.com/2020/12/11/chinese-honey-trap-could-hold-thousands-of-operatives/ accessed July 12, 2022.

DILIGENT OVERSIGHT

Proverbs 27:23

*"Know the state of your flocks,
and put your heart into caring for your herds." (NLT)*

As a leader of a project, a parent, a manager, or even a member of a congregation, how many times have we thought about the true state of our people? When asked how they are doing, it is not unusual for people to respond, "I am doing fine," but we as leaders need to discern if that is reality. As we put our hearts into our various roles, we should seek to understand people more than just on a surface level.

Proverbs 27:23 is a profound concept. The "flocks" represent the people we serve. In any leadership role involving people, it is essential to know the state of those we have been given the privilege and responsibility of serving. The Lord has brought these people into our lives for a reason. Our love for Him compels us to love and care for those He has entrusted to us, whether it be in a leadership role or a friendship. We can ask God for His insight and awareness of the struggles people go through.

The second half of Proverbs 27:23 tells us to "put your heart into caring for your herds…." A true shepherd watches over the flock. Putting your heart into something means being committed to caring for, feeding, nurturing, protecting, binding up wounds, and giving guidance. We see the greatest example of a Shepherd in Jesus, who committed to laying down His life for His sheep.

God loves people. The Lord desires that His community of faith lives as brothers and sisters. The Lord created human beings as social creatures, so it is not good when we are alone. With that thought in mind, let's become a closer family—a family that cares for each other with our whole hearts—serving each other in whatever capacity God calls us as unto Him.

Victor Miguel Rivera

PRAY LIKE NO ONE IS LISTENING

Proverbs 14:30

*"A heart at peace gives life to the body,
but envy rots the bones." (NIV)*

Have you ever heard of food envy? You go out to eat with a friend, you place your order, the food comes out, you see your friend's plate, and you are slightly irritated because their food looks better, smells better, and after taking a bite, you realize it even tastes better than yours! That is food envy!

Another form of jealousy is, what I like to call, prayer envy. Instead of comparing food, you compare prayers. You hear someone praying with you, and you clam up because you believe their words sound and flow better than your own. You stop and think, "Man, God must answer those prayers!" You begin to question the quality of your own prayers because they may be shorter, less wordy, or aren't filled with every scripture known to man.

Satan can utilize prayer envy as a catalyst in preventing us from a deeper relationship with the Lord. You may think that being a little envious of someone's prayers is not really that big of a deal. But hear me out. It is like an avalanche. It starts as a harmless reaction, but then it has the potential to evolve into something that will rot your bones!

Comparing prayers is what triggers the avalanche. It begins to grow as we continue to compare our worship, our purpose, our ministry, and our anointing—to the point where we become overtaken by fear, and we no longer want to engage in a relationship with the Lord! And THAT is where the enemy wants us. He wants us to stop trying and to stop communing with Christ. He wants us to become insecure believers, fearful of being unable to fulfill our calling. Envy rolls into comparison, comparison rolls into insecurities, insecurities roll into an ugly competition, and in competition, someone always loses!

We cannot afford to lose out on the peace-filled abundant life awaiting us. So, get back on the spiritual battlefield and pray like no one else is listening – except for Jesus. He is ALWAYS listening!

Jennifer Shank

A REFINED HEART

Proverbs 17:3

*"Fire tests the purity of silver and gold,
but the Lord tests the heart." (NLT)*

Have you ever asked God to make life easier for you? Maybe you have asked Him to remove certain things or people that would lighten the weight of life. Only God knows the trials and tribulations of each of our lives. However, I have learned that God does test our hearts. No, this does not mean that God brings bad things to our lives and that all things that are bad in our life are because God is testing our hearts. I am saying, however, to ask God to show you what is meant to capture your attention through the different circumstances you face.

Proverbs 17:3 illustrates that gold is refined in a furnace. It then goes on to make a connection about how God will test our hearts, and the refining of our character comes through that test. It is in those situations, when the pressure is on, that the truest parts of our hearts are revealed—both good and bad. Going through the testing will refine our character and heart as we become more like Jesus. To understand these refining moments, we need to step into doing life daily with God. In this closeness to God, we will be more inclined to see the rhythms of God's grace.

I can say this now, being on the other side of some difficult seasons in my life. It was in those moments that I learned to depend on God most. He transformed my thinking in such a way that it impacted me and began to show in other parts of my life. Through this refining, my spiritual ears became attuned to God's voice. What appeared to be or felt as though God was silent during a trial or tribulation, I have come to know He was actively working in me and changing my heart.

Cynthia Medrano

SOW GENEROUSLY

Proverbs 28:22

"The stingy are eager to get rich quick
and are unaware that poverty awaits them." (NIV)

Have you ever met a stingy person? Have you ever been a stingy person? Before you answer, let me give you the definition of stingy according to Oxford languages: unwilling to give or spend; ungenerous.

Have you ever felt unwilling to give or spend or ungenerous in some circumstances? I know I have. The proverb says, "eager to get rich quick." They want to make a quick buck but probably have no desire to spend or share it. What a self-centered, selfish way to live. We each have a decision to make to live generously or not.

2 Corinthians 9:6-7 says, *"Remember this: Whoever sows sparingly will also reap sparingly, and whoever sows generously will also reap generously. Each of you should give what you have decided in your heart to give, not reluctantly or under compulsion, for God loves a cheerful giver."* (NIV) Being generous is an active decision we make. Being ungenerous is also an active decision we make. You decide.

The poverty that awaits them is not necessarily a monetary one. An ungenerous person usually lives alone, is withdrawn, fears losing everything, and has a reputation for being a miser. Think of Mr. Scrooge from *A Christmas Carol*. Many stingy people are proud of their stinginess and wear it with pride. Terms like tightwad, miser, curmudgeon, and cheapskate are usually associated with that person. This individual lives in poverty of the spirit, mind, heart, and soul.

Proverbs 11:25 says, *"A generous person will prosper; whoever refreshes others will be refreshed."* (NIV) So, when your stingy self rears its curmudgeonly head, do not be a cheapskate. Allow the Holy Spirit to guide you in what you decide to give, not reluctantly or under compulsion, but cheerfully.

To live a life of generosity is to save yourself from poverty.

Fred Alvarado

FREE FROM GUILT

Proverbs 21:8

*"The way of the guilty is devious,
but the conduct of the innocent is upright." (NIV)*

In 1 Kings 3:16-28, we are told a story of two women and one baby. The women were fighting over who was the real mother and went to King Solomon for a final judgment. Without DNA testing or witnesses available, they had to rely on the wisdom and judgment of the King. King Solomon had asked God for wisdom, and God gave him a wise and discerning mind like none before or after him.

The devious woman was cunning. When she lost her child, she devised a plan to steal the other woman's child and was willing to do what was necessary to get away with it. After the women told their stories, the King said, "Bring me a sword." Once he had the sword in his hand, he said, "Divide the living child in two, and give half to one and a half to the other." The real mother quickly pled with the King to give the child to the other woman to spare the baby's life. She put her desires aside to keep the baby alive, and King Solomon knew instantly who the real mother was.

The world may try to judge and understand a man's heart, but only God knows and sees if we have innocent or devious intentions. (1 Sam. 16:7)

Proverbs 21:8 tells us that the fruit of an innocent or devious person is revealed by their actions. Jesus said that by their fruit, you will know them.

How are you living your life? It may not involve stealing a baby, but even the simplest and smallest sin is still a sin. Are you carrying guilt? Repent and ask God for forgiveness and choose to live an upright life free from guilt.

Jill Alvarado

PARENTAL CARE

Proverbs 28:24

"Whoever robs their father or mother and says,
'It's not wrong,' is partner to one who destroys." (NIV)

I get to talk to the older generations that were born in the 60s, 50s, and even earlier, and their remembrance of their parents is so special when it comes to respecting and honoring them and providing for their needs. Unfortunately, in our present day, many children see their parents as a burden, and they are robbing the parents, not so much financially, but of love and care.

Proverbs 28:24 says that if we rob our parents, we are akin to those who destroy. This is a very serious warning to us as sons and daughters. When we steal from somebody, we are dispossessing that person of something that belongs to them. It could be caring for them financially, physically, or emotionally. One of the Ten Commandments is "Honor your Father and Mother," and it is also the only commandment that carries a promise. This proverb says that those who do not honor their parents will not receive a blessing but will receive destruction.

My mother is now 89, and I can see her need for extra love and care from her children. It is my honor for my family and me to be a blessing to my mother in this last season of her life. May the Lord help us obey the commandment with a promise given to us as sons and daughters.

Ricardo Chaidez

A HOLY SILENCE

Proverbs 13:3

*"He who guards his mouth preserves his life,
but he who opens wide his lips shall have destruction." (NKJV)*

During World War II, in a time of global war, there was a saying amongst those serving in the Navy: "Loose lips sink ships!" It was meant to make clear that carelessness with one's words could lead to calamity, not just for oneself but for an entire ship, affecting hundreds of other souls.

Likewise, those who guard their lips carefully watch what comes out of them. They are cautious not to speak more than what God wants them to say. By setting a guard over their lips, like Daniel, Nehemiah, and Joshua, they guard not only their lives, but also the lives of those around them. Think of the number of times someone desiring to run for public office did not watch their mouth, paid dearly, or even lost the election because of a careless word. In their case, it brought them to ruin.

The Bible tells us that what comes out of our mouths shows what's inside our hearts. That is why it is vital to guard our hearts as well. Unfortunately, in today's society, it is common to espouse an attitude of "I can say anything I want!" That may be true, but it is not necessarily wise. The consequences can be devastating when we do not employ wisdom regarding the words we speak. It is not difficult to imagine how many jobs have been lost or relationships have been broken because of a momentary lack of sound judgment. Seeing the impact upon those who have had to process the devastating effects of hurtful words, we understand the importance of being wise and guarding our mouths. This principle can help preserve life.

A guarded mouth is a wise mouth. We all have an abundance of things to say, but let us be wise and learn what we need to leave unsaid. Let us repent even from the thoughts that cause negative things to come across our lips. The holy silence we hold may bring life into every situation we are a part of.

Jose Nolasco

HARD WORK PRODUCES RESULTS

Proverbs 28:19

"Those who work their land will have abundant food,
but those who chase fantasies will have their fill of poverty." (NIV)

I remember sitting in my parent's living room after graduating from high school, thinking about my future. I wanted to become my own boss, have a successful business, buy a house, get married, and have three children. I realized that I had learned how to accomplish these dreams in high school!

In high school, I was shy and insecure, primarily because I spoke English with an accent. But I was fortunate to have a teacher who believed in me. Ms. Campos encouraged me and knew I had what it took to accomplish anything I put my mind to, but she also realized I needed more than encouragement. So, during my senior year, she put me to work in the school office and assisting teachers to gain practical experience. Ms. Campos was in charge of the plays for Christmas and Cultural Day. She went all out, and they were always beautiful and inspiring productions. I admired her very much, and I said to myself that I wanted to bring joy and happiness to others the way she did. Ms. Campos was a key person in my life and taught me to work hard and excel. I owe much of what I am to her inspiration and hard work.

Proverbs also says, *"Lazy people want much but get little, but those who work hard will prosper."* (Prov. 13:4 NLT). As Ms. Campos' hard work and encouragement inspired me, God can use our lives to inspire a new generation to do the same. Things do not just happen by themselves; hard work produces results!

Alicia Suarez

THE FAMILY RESEMBLANCE

Proverbs 23:15-16

"My child, if your heart is wise, my own heart will rejoice!
Everything in me will celebrate when you speak what is right." (NLT)

Do you wake up in the morning to animated birds singing a happy tune on your windowsill, cartoon crickets in the kitchen washing the dishes, or mice tidying up around your house? No? Me neither. Or does your morning start something like Lucy's, the main character in the movie 50 First Dates, who cannot remember her life from the previous day due to a brain injury?[2]

You may not be an animated cartoon character with everything going your way, and you probably remember the previous day of your life, but do you wake up and forget who you are spiritually? Maybe the cares of life or stress keep a heavy veil over your eyes, and you cannot see the spiritual inheritance you can walk in. Do not get any grandiose ideas that you have a rich uncle who will leave you a pile of money! But you ARE a child of the King, and with that comes family resemblance and an inheritance. So here are some of YOUR family traits to remember:

I am a child of God—1 John 3:1
I am righteous and holy—Ephesians 4:24
I am the light of the world — Matthew 5:14
I am chosen and appointed by Christ to bear fruit—John 15:16
I am grafted into the true vine and abide in Jesus, and He abides in me
　　—John 15:1-5
I am led by the Spirit of God—Romans 8:14
I am the elect of God, holy and beloved—Colossians 3:12
I am an heir of God and joint heir with Christ—Romans 8:17
I am a servant of righteousness—Romans 6:18
I am hidden with Christ in God—Colossians3:3
I am born of God, and the evil one cannot touch Me—1 John 5:18
I live by faith—Romans 1:17

So along with putting on the armor of God every day, remind yourself that you walk in a Kingdom not of this world and resemble your Father the King. Hey! You look like your dad!

Michelle Glush

2　　Disclaimer: I do not recommend the movie because of bad language, crass humor, and sexual innuendo.

JULY

My child,

listen to me and do as I say,

and you will have a long, good life.

I will teach you wisdom's ways

and lead you in straight paths.

When you walk, you won't be held back;

when you run, you won't stumble.

Take hold of my instructions; don't let them go.

Guard them, for they are the key to life.

—Proverbs 4:10-13

ANOTHER ONE BITES THE DUST

Proverbs 29:18

"Where there is no revelation, the people cast off restraint;
but happy is he who keeps the law." (NKJV)

Restraint: a measure or condition that keeps someone under control or within limits.

It was the summer of 1980. My friend and I were on vacation and had brought our roller skates. He had just upgraded the trucks for his skates. I had not. We were dressed for this occasion—Hang Ten shorts, terrycloth shirts, and calf-high tube socks with colored stripes. Most of you get the picture.

A portion of the road where we were staying had a 4-5-mile-long winding downhill grade. We thought it would be awesome to give the hill a try. This is where two teenage boys "cast off restraint!"

Fortunately for my friend, his run was a success. My run, not so much. Certain laws come into effect as you are rolling down a hill at 30-35 MPH on cheap skates. They are called the laws of physics: inertia, gravity, vibration, and "ignorance."

At 25 MPH, I began to have speed wobbles and decided to ride down the hill on one foot. Realizing that was a bad idea, I launched myself off the side of the road at 30-35 MPH. Had I understood the laws of physics, I would have had a much happier outcome.

This proverb also mentions revelation (prophetic vision). In other words, God has given us divine laws to keep us within "the limits" He has placed for us because He loves us. Every time we live outside those limits and set our own limits, we do not end up happy; hence *"happy is he who keeps the law."*

In John 15:10-11 Jesus says, *"If you keep my commandments, you will abide in my love, …that My joy may remain in you, and that your joy may be full."* (NKJV) God places limits on us because of His love for us. How awesome is that! He wants us to be full of love and joy.

Great news, I survived! Flying 20 or 30 feet off the side of the road and landing with a mouthful of dirt, I suddenly understood the term "another one bites the dust!" But do not worry, I have retired my skates and no longer wish to achieve the downhill medal!

Fred Alvarado

THE SCHOOL OF HARD KNOCKS

Proverbs 19:19

"A hot-tempered man has to pay the price for his anger.
If you bail him out once, you'll do it a dozen times." (TPT)

We all know the term "The School of Hard Knocks," and chances are, anyone who has even a shred of wisdom has attended this school with its perpetual unsolicited enrollment and free tuition. We have had the hard knocks of trauma, disappointment, betrayal, and the consequences of our foolishness coming home to roost. None of those things are pleasant, but they have a way of teaching us valuable lessons that we would not have otherwise obtained. This school is teaching us the value of money, choosing the right friends, what is truly important in life, the fear of the Lord, the reality of consequences for our actions, the necessity of humility and teamwork, being a good winner and a good loser, and many other such life-lessons.

As parents, coaches, or teachers, it is difficult to see our children attend this brutal school. Yet, everything within us wants to save them from some of the same heartbreak or consequences we have had to suffer—because it is hard to see them suffer. Sometimes a good conversation is enough to keep someone on the straight and narrow, but the inevitable savagery of The School of Hard Knocks is what makes the lessons stick.

I heard a pastor once say that the worst thing we could do to our children is teach them that there are no consequences to their actions. If we save them from consequences, helicopter-parent them, make excuses for them, blame-shift everything away from them, assume they are right all the time, give them everything they want, and withhold the necessary and painful discipline from them, they will become the very adults who make the same mistakes for their whole lives and are the worse for it. Those who unenroll their children or themselves from The School of Hard Knocks will become the classic "fool" that this proverb warns us about. They will never learn the valuable life lessons that make them a productive person who adds value to other people's lives, and they will spend their lives needing to be bailed out over and over.

Kyle Bauer

WORDS CHANGE LIVES

Proverbs 15:23

"A man has joy by the answer of his mouth,
and a word spoken in due season, how good it is!" (NKJV)

Words are the outpouring of the heart. God began our existence in words, and by those words, He spoke forth creation. We are not God, but we are created in His image, and we are to reflect His character. He gives us the ability to speak words that will pour out His goodness. To speak God's truth is to pour from our mouths into another person's spirit by way of their ears.

Just as we can speak truth into someone, we can also speak words tainted by sin. Words of hatred, sadness, chaos, cruelty, and self-indulgence—the opposite of the fruit of the Spirit—that bring destruction.

For many years growing up, I was told I was ugly, loud, and weird. In this short description, I understood that everything about myself was undesirable. So, I learned to shut up and do everything I could to fix how I looked and avoid being myself.

Decades later, I still struggle with my appearance and eccentric personality. But simple comments from friends saying, "I really like your curly hair," and, "You have great ideas," have allowed me to see that what God has given me naturally is, in fact, something desirable.

Words have the power to dictate an entire script of decisions and beliefs in a person's life. What narratives (internal and external) are you speaking to yourself and others? When we get out of God's way and allow Him to use us as vessels to speak words of life, He is able to take even the simplest words of goodness and use them against the lies of the enemy.

Rachael Hopkins

A SEAT AT THE TABLE

Proverbs 25:6-7

"Do not exalt yourself in the presence of the king,
and do not stand in the place of the great;
for it is better that he say to you, 'Come up here,'
than that you should be put lower in the presence of the prince,
whom your eyes have seen." (NKJV)

Not many of us will stand before kings in our lifetime, but we may stand before leaders, bosses, and others in authority. Most importantly, we will stand before King Jesus when this age comes to an end. What do we all want to hear when we stand in front of Him? Everyone would say, "Well done, good and faithful servant."

One year, in a previous job, a new boss came into the organization, not knowing the strengths or skills of anyone. For some reason, he treated me as if I did not exist, and it really puzzled me. Around the same time, a co-worker gave me a "word" that he believed the Lord was telling me it was time to move on. Wanting to be obedient to the Lord, I tested the word and knocked on doors to see if they would open. They did not. I finally said to the Lord, "If you want me to leave, you will have to bring the job to me." I continued doing my work as unto the Lord and serving the organization and waited to see what God would do.

A few weeks later, in a department meeting with my boss, I spoke up with an idea, and it brought a change in his manner toward me, an acknowledgment of not only my existence, but also of the value that I brought to the table!

God brought a complete turnaround to the situation. Soon after, I was promoted to manager of a department and, even more importantly to me, given the opportunity to do what God had created me to do. This man turned out to be one of the best bosses I ever had.

Be faithful to what God has called you to do and who He has called you to be. Serve Him wholeheartedly in whatever capacity and in whatever job you have. At the right time, the King will bring you to the head of the table.

Michelle Glush

THE LIGHT WITHIN VS. THE LAMP WITHOUT

Proverbs 13:9

"The light of the righteous shines brightly,
but the lamp of the wicked is snuffed out." (NIV)

When the life of God dwells within us, the light of God will shine through us. To *"shine brightly"* is to burn joyfully, just as the sun is "like a champion rejoicing to run his course." (Ps. 19:5, NIV) Proverbs 4:18 states that "the path of the righteous is like the morning sun, shining ever brighter till the full light of day." (NIV) Matthew Henry points out that the light of the sun may be eclipsed or clouded but continues to shine nonetheless. With the Holy Spirit as our light, we are filled with the joy of His presence (Ps. 16:11).

The transfiguration of Jesus is a vivid example of "shining brightly." When He was transfigured before Peter, James, and John, *"His face shone like the sun, and His clothes became as white as the light."* (Matt. 17:2, NIV) What happened? The glory of God was not being reflected from without but was shining from within right through Jesus' body and even His clothes! May the light of God shine more and more through us.

In contrast, *"the lamp of the wicked is snuffed out"*—it is extinguished (CJB), becomes darker and darker (ERV), flickering out (GNT). The lamp of the wicked shines from without; it is a showy light, produced by the "kindling" of human pride and this world (Isa. 50:11). The lamp of the wicked, however, is soon exposed for what it is and is easily extinguished.

May the light of God's truth, and the truth of God's love, radiate continually from kind and joyful hearts through our words and deeds.

Karen Heimbuch

A DEEPER LOOK

Proverbs 10:32

*"The lips of the godly speak helpful words,
but the mouth of the wicked speaks perverse words." (NLT)*

Some individuals cheapen words. God's words and thoughts, rightly spoken through human lips, can provide wise counsel. How do you evaluate speech? What guide or ruler do you use?

In contrast, perverse words can cripple, twist, and distort. One translation uses the old word *froward,* meaning "difficult to deal with, contrary." Just a little talk about politics, and everyone wants to cuddle up with their dog and separate from the world.

To be transparent, there was a sin in my life—and it owned me at the time. This weakness was so influential that I did not believe in my own repentance when it came to my prayer time before God. But I sought and received counsel. The shortened story? God would not ask us to forgive 70 times seven without his doing it Himself. Grace covers our honest effort to be cleansed from a matter. The truth and grace of these two sentences changed my heart's sagging response to sustained failures to this day.

A deeper look reveals that our language can either elevate or drop a bomb on someone. The Holy Spirit's words show God's intentions for and visions of us as we discern these gems in anointed songs and teachings. With anointed hearing, we can receive them as they are always available for the asking. *"If any man lacks wisdom, let him inquire of God."* (James 1:5) May God's touch be on you today.

Juline Bruck

WORDS MATTER

Proverbs 30:5-6

"Every word of God is flawless; he is a shield to those who take refuge in him. Do not add to his words, or he will rebuke you and prove you a liar." (NIV)

One day I was catching up on the phone with my sister in Atlanta. She asked me to tell her about any new adventures I was getting myself into. I started to tell her about this project, but at that moment, I was slightly distracted. I can't recall what distracted me, and I hastily replied, "My pastor asked a group of us leaders in the church to write the Proverbs in the Bible." There was a long pause, and then she gingerly responded with great confusion. "Um, sis, the Proverbs have already been written." I suddenly realized I accidentally left out some key words in my explanation and should have said, "My pastor asked a group of us leaders in the church to write personal devotionals and deeper insight ABOUT the Proverbs in the Bible." We had a good laugh, but for a second there, she was truly concerned about whether we were actually rewriting the Proverbs and altering the Word of God!

You may think her concern is a little odd, but there is a little backstory. Years ago, she was involved in a cult. They came into her life as if they were truly teaching the Word of God. But, as she got more involved in the leadership of the "church," they manipulated the heart and truth of the Bible. They wove an intricate web of lies about the scriptures and tricked her into believing that she did not hear accurately from the Holy Spirit. Praise God because He was a shield around her heart and revealed the lies to her. Eventually, she boldly chose to walk away from the deception.

Moral of the story: God's word is flawless. We don't need to add anything to it, and those who do WILL BE REBUKED and PROVEN TO BE LIARS!

Jennifer Shank

BEING FOOLISH HURTS

Proverbs 26:3

*"Guide a horse with a whip, a donkey with a bridle,
and a fool with a rod to his back!" (NLT)*

I have a lot to learn about equestrianism, horse herding, and farming, but hopefully even less about being a fool. For instance, I would have thought a whip would be used to direct a donkey and a bridle for a horse but apparently not. I am told that a bit is less comfortable than a bridle since the control generated by a bit focuses on pulling the inside of the mouth to one side or the other. A bridle is outside the mouth and addresses the entire outer jaw for control. This is actually more comfortable for either animal.

That said, Solomon directs us to use a whip to guide a horse, perhaps only for maximum performance. Additionally, to guide, not force a donkey, by using a bridle. Clearly, this is to avoid agitating the animal, reputation notwithstanding. However, most interesting is the instruction for guiding a human, the most advanced and intellectually equipped of all of God's creation, is to use a rod or a stick. Well, a stick for certain humans—the foolish ones.

The Hebrew translation of the word "rod" in this context means a literal stick, meant for whipping, beating, instilling correction, and/or control. This also implies that fools are harder to direct than primary beasts of burden, and the impact of foolishness is immense, hence the beating needed. The obvious desire or outcome is to reflect God enough so as not to need to be whipped, bridled, or caned. It is not that God will beat you with a stick, but He desires that we be wise and absorb correction without having to receive harsher correction.

Lloyd Speese

VEGETABLES AND HERBS

Proverbs 15:17

"Better is a dinner of vegetables and herbs where love is present than a fattened ox served with hatred." (AMP)

Imagine going to a dinner party where the host is someone who despises you. It is an undesirable place regardless of the food that will be served. Nevertheless, in Luke 7, Jesus did exactly that—He attended a dinner with the Pharisees. The religious Pharisees thought they had an abundance to offer Jesus, food to eat and a place to sit and rest, but their lack of common courtesy revealed that there was little to no affection for Him: *"'When I entered your home, you did not offer me water to wash the dust from my feet…'"* (Luke 7:44) In contrast, a "sinful" woman approached Jesus at that same dinner, knelt before Him, and started cleaning His feet with her tears and wiping them with her hair. This woman had little to offer Jesus, no towel or water to cleanse His feet, but her service toward Him was fueled by love. This act of love displayed by the woman is a perfect example of how our hearts should be when we come before God in prayer.

When we approach God with the mindset that we have an abundance to offer Him, it is time to pause to consider the condition of our hearts before we spend time with Him in prayer, lest we think our own piety impresses Him. But just like the woman at the feet of Jesus, our prayers toward God should consist of nothing more than "vegetables and herbs" with the awareness that we have little to give except a heart ready to embrace Jesus as we kneel before Him.

Amelia Montantes

TOUGH LOVE

Proverbs 22:15

"Folly is bound up in the heart of a child,
but the rod of discipline will drive it far away." (NIV)

We usually call it tough love, but let me tell you, it works!

When my oldest child was two years old, he and my wife went to Target, and he saw the little decorative cocktail picks used for fruit in drinks or on sandwiches in the form of swords. He really wanted them, but mom said NO. He did not like that answer and threw a tantrum right in the middle of the store. My wife was so embarrassed, but she kept calm and collected. When they got to the car, she explained to our son that what he did inside the store was not right, and because of that, he needed to be corrected. She disciplined him right on the spot, and he never did anything like that ever again.

Until this day, my son remembers the incident and laughs. He has grown up to be a very polite and respectful man, and we are so proud of him. Do not let bad behavior slide or allow your child to take on a rebellious attitude. Discipline them (in private) as soon as an episode happens and help them understand the reason for their correction. You will prepare them for a better life and save yourself a larger headache later in life.

Gabriel Martinez

WHERE YOUR TREASURE IS

Proverbs 21:6

"Wealth created by a lying tongue
is a vanishing mist and a deadly trap." (NLT)

The Lord detests lying lips, and He delights in those who tell the truth (Prov. 12:22, NIV). God is a God of justice. At the end of the day, ill-gotten wealth, though it may last for a season, will not stand the test of time. Those who gain wealth through lying will lose it all in the end. God is a God of justice and will make the truthful prosper. *"The Lord detests dishonest scales, but accurate weights find favor with him."* (Prov. 11:1, NIV)

It is only through truth and honest work that prosperity is lasting. A life is lived well by turning away from evil. For, *"whoever would love life and see good days must keep their tongue from evil and their lips from deceitful speech. They must turn from evil and do good; they must seek peace and pursue it."* (1 Pet. 3:10-11, NIV) But for those who sow seeds of evil, though they may prosper for a season, the deadly trap is that they will eventually reap punishment. *"A false witness will not go unpunished, and a liar will be destroyed."* (Prov. 19:9, NLT).

So why does it seem like the wicked prosper? Why does it seem like the truthful are punished? We have the promise in God's word that He will set everything right in the end. Our difficulty is dealing with what happens in the meantime. The wicked rig the system in their favor, and the honest often bear the consequences. But it is in the meantime, as we trust in God's promises and grow as disciples of Jesus, that we are storing for ourselves treasures in Heaven. The seeds of righteousness will eventually grow into an eternal reward. And the seeds of wickedness will pass away with this life.

"Don't hoard treasure down here where it gets eaten by moths and corroded by rust or—worse! —stolen by burglars. Stockpile treasure in heaven, where it's safe from moth and rust and burglars. It's obvious, isn't it? The place where your treasure is, is the place you will most want to be, and end up being." (Matt. 6:21, MSG)

Joshua Bauer

FAMILY FEUDS...

Proverbs 18:19

"A brother wronged is more unyielding than a fortified city,
disputes are like the barred gates of a citadel." (NIV)

I can totally relate to this proverb. I come from a family of six brothers and one sister. Family relations can cause all kinds of pain. Fortunately, in my family, the slights, pains, and offenses have been mostly minor ones over the past decades, but they still hurt. My sister, the second oldest, was often called upon to assist with cooking, housekeeping, and laundry by my father. He was a very traditional German Lutheran Christian man who considered those things "women's work." My sister's anger and resentment toward my father and her brothers festered in her. She moved all the way to Pennsylvania and stayed there to this day. She never married and never had a family of her own. When my father passed away in 1998, she was the only one absent as the family gathered to mourn his passing.

I have known many people in my life who have family that they have not spoken to in years because of something that was said or done. The anger and resentment are so strong for some that they will not even speak of it, let alone discuss it with the person that wronged them. They are closed off like a citadel with the gate locked and barred.

That citadel is more like a maximum-security prison with them locked inside. Only God can break through those barriers and restore relationships where hurt runs deep. A simple wisdom that underlies Proverbs 18:19 is: Do not allow family slights, hurts, and offenses to stand. The longer before it is fixed, the harder it is to fix. It is ironic that in many of these situations, the person that caused the hurt is either unaware or does not care that the other party is hurt. So, the anger we hold in our hearts only affects and hurts us, not the one who caused the pain. In the Lord's Prayer, Christ instructs us to "Forgive us our sins, as we forgive those who sin against us." I know it is not easy. If it were easy, everyone would do it. But through our relationship with God, we can have the strength to ask for and to offer forgiveness.

Martin and Bea Laufer

DISPOSITION TO LIFE OR DEATH

Proverbs 11:19

"Godly people find life; evil people find death." (NLT)

As true as it is that the godly inherit God's eternal life and the wicked do not, deeper spiritual principles are at work throughout a person's lifetime that ultimately produce the fruits of life or death.

C.S. Lewis said that "…all find what they truly seek."[1] Whether there is an inner disposition to godliness or to wickedness, the person will find it and identify with it. I have often been perplexed by the culture of death that pervades our world. In ancient times, kings were enamored by the grandeur of their tombs, and so many ancient religions revolved around gruesome human sacrifices. In today's culture, abortion is widely celebrated, and the fixation on suicide is ever on the rise. In pop culture, macabre horror films have a big market, clothing, and art commonly employ hell, dragons, skulls, witchcraft, and demon motifs, while many band names, logos, t-shirts, and songs feature death. One case-in-point, "Slipknot" (which is the knot tied in a hangman's rope) is the name of a popular band. Moreover, so much of the culture drinks it all in, having little repulsion to it. The message is clear: Death is cool. What perplexes me further is that when a person dies, there is an incongruence of thought: people spend life glorifying death but are sad at a funeral.

Wait. What?

Just as one can have a disposition toward death, one can also have a disposition toward life, goodness, righteousness, justice, truth, and love. The culture of death is repugnant to those who love righteousness and life. Opposites may attract on a magnet, but in the spiritual realm, opposites repel each other, and like attracts. People who search for life will find it in the Author of life, and those who love death will not find it in God.

The reality is that sin brings death, and Jesus brings life.[2] We are born into sin and death, but Jesus said we must be born again. This culture of hellish death does not have to be our portion. God offers true and abundant life in Jesus Christ.

Kyle Bauer

---

1   C.S. Lewis, *The Last Battle*. (The Folio Society: London, 1996), 173
2   See John 10:10; Romans 3:23, 6:23

FOOLISH TYRANTS VS. WISE RULERS

Proverbs 28:15-16

"Like a roaring lion or a charging bear
is a wicked ruler over a helpless people.
A tyrannical ruler practices extortion,
but one who hates ill-gotten gain will enjoy a long reign." (NIV)

Political tyrants are dangerous and destructive. We have all witnessed the fallout from an oppressive boss or a greedy politician. Morale is destroyed, hopelessness increases, and frustration leads to violence. Tyrants cause great misery by their unjust treatment of helpless people.

In this passage, wicked rulers are compared to vicious animals that are powerful, terrifying, insensitive, and in search of prey. Such rulers lack wisdom, making them cruel and callous to suffering. Driven by greed, they devastate the people under them with excessive, and often unattainable, demands and taxations. Tyrants view their subjects as expendable, to be discarded after exploitation.

A righteous ruler, however, refuses to use his power for personal gain. In Exodus 18:21, Jethro advises his son-in-law Moses to choose rulers who are capable, God-fearing men of truth, those who hate bribes. Such men do not allow their decisions to be swayed by greed. The love of God governs their hearts, not the love of money. Because of this, both a prince and his people will be happy. The righteous ruler will enjoy the blessing of a long life, a prosperous future, and a peaceful reign.

Of course, these precepts pertain to all of us, not just to kings. If we are careful to follow closely after God—so close that we are clinging to Him (Ps. 63:8)—He will count us as "good and faithful servants" (Matt. 25:21) who can be entrusted with the welfare of others.

Karen Heimbuch

WEIGH YOUR WORDS WISELY

Proverbs 12:23

"A prudent man conceals knowledge,
but the heart of fools proclaims foolishness." (NKJV)

Oh, how difficult it is for someone who knows the answer to a question being asked to remain silent! This scripture is only one of many in which God helps us to understand the value of our freedom to speak or not to speak.

Consider Daniel who was a wise man serving under the pagan King Nebuchadnezzar in Babylon. Though Daniel was wise, spiritually focused, and trained in the best schools of the kingdom, it is clear that he would often remain silent and pray, serve, and wait for the moment when God would give him the right words to speak. Because of his patient, quiet preparation, the result was that when he spoke, it would be an impactful word to the benefit of the king and the kingdom.

As difficult as it is to fathom, we can cheapen spiritual truth or make it less effective in people's lives when we walk around trying to be the Bible "answer man" to everyone around us.

One great reason we should hold onto, or conceal knowledge, is that any fool can speak. The second part of this proverb tells us that the fool proclaims or constantly displays foolishness from their heart. The Bible tells us that out of the abundance of the heart, the mouth speaks. It is commonly said in American culture "better to remain silent and be thought a fool than to speak and to remove all doubt."

A wise person considers when and what to say. He weighs his words wisely to have the most significant impact possible. He also considers whether some or all of his words are better left unsaid. Truly, this is wisdom.

Believe me, as a "talker," this is no easy task for me. But time and time again I find that God is most honored when I speak the least.

Jose Nolasco

BE READY

Proverbs 15:3

"The Lord is watching everywhere,
keeping his eye on both the evil and the good." (NLT)

As we look around at the state of the world, it is terribly tempting to believe that God is not watching, because the wicked prosper and goodness is thrown aside.[3] In his crushing prophecy against Jerusalem, the prophet Zephaniah preached these words from God to the people,

> *"I will search with lanterns in Jerusalem's darkest corners to punish those who sit complacent in their sins. They think the Lord will do nothing to them, either good or bad." (NLT)*

I have long thought about people—even people in the Church who have heard God's Word—who lie, cheat, steal, practice immorality, and often seem to get away with it, or, as Zephaniah articulates, *"…think the Lord will do nothing…"* My thought is that, though they have heard God's Word, they either are ignorant of what it says, willfully disregard it completely, or simply do not believe it. Yet we are fully responsible for what we have heard, and God will not allow sin to go unpunished.[4] God is not eager to punish people but to forgive wherever true repentance from the heart is offered.

However, a day of reckoning comes for us all, and we do not know the day. This is why Jesus told the parable of the wicked servant whose Master went away. The servant began to do wickedly ("when the cat's away, the mice will play"), and when the Master suddenly appeared at an unexpected hour, he caught the servant in his wickedness and punished him.[5]

Likewise, it is our responsibility to understand that God means what He says in His Word, and by His Word, He will judge all our actions. Since we do not know when we will see Him face-to-face, we must live ready at all times by living in faithfulness, obedience, truth, and love regardless of the wickedness we see all around us.

Kyle Bauer

---

3   For a fuller treatment of this subject, read and re-read Psalm 73
4   See Zephaniah and the whole of chapter 1
5   Matthew 24:45-51

HUMILITY INSTEAD OF FOOLISHNESS

Proverbs 19:13

"A foolish child is a calamity to a father;
a quarrelsome wife is as annoying as constant dripping." (NLT)

It is beneficial to everyone that all aspects of the family life function in unity. God's way of living works for our good. He tells us that children should honor and obey their parents, which will bring a promising future for the children and their parents. But the child who does not learn to honor and obey will cause heartache. As we learn to obey and respect to our earthly parents, we will also learn to obey and honor God.

King Solomon experienced the calamity that a foolish son brings to a family. Though a great king, David never corrected his children and reaped terrible consequences. Solomon saw his brother, Absalom, betray his father, King David, in an attempt to usurp his throne instead of waiting and allowing God to promote him (2 Sam. 15). It was during this time that King David wrote in the Psalms about the pain he felt at the betrayal of a son so close to his heart (Ps. 55:4-8, 3:1-6). But Absalom's plan was unsuccessful, and his life ended by the spears of the warriors chasing him. Foolishness never has a good ending.

Honor and respect your parents even when they do not do everything right—their perfection is not the caveat for your honor. David was certainly not perfect, and he did many things against God that brought pain and disunity in his family. Doing the will of God, though sometimes difficult, will allow us to live in unity, humility, and respect with our family. Humility and submission to authority is the key to success in our personal, family, and professional lives. We must constantly read His Word, learn, and meditate on it to allow his teachings to transform our thinking and how we act. The examples we see in the Bible of lives that ended well and ended badly are for our benefit. Let's learn from their mistakes, and our mistakes, so as not to repeat them and live in the peace we desire.

Teresa Bauer

CORRECTION BRINGS WISDOM
INSTRUCTION BRINGS KNOWLEDGE

Proverbs 21:11

*"Senseless people learn their lessons the hard way,
but the wise are teachable." (TPT)*

Life's seasons and transitions are challenging. We learn a hard lesson when we realize that we are not in control of our lives, and in the process, we also learn what it means to be teachable. These difficulties often lead us to question everything about our lives. Yet, in those moments, we must believe that the One who knows all about us hears our cries and answers.

For some time, I had been wondering about the meaning of this current season of my life and how all the changes I am experiencing could work together. For example, I have to adapt to the changes in my vision due to cataracts affecting my ability to see details and perspectives.

This change became apparent when working on a puzzle and thinking I had the right piece for the right place, and it refused to cooperate. In my frustration, I began to question how the puzzle fit together. Then at that moment, I could see that I was also asking how the puzzle of this season of my life and all its pieces fit together.

In the ways that God so often answers, I felt Him softly say that His Hand was on my hand, directing how and where the pieces of the puzzle and the pieces of my life's puzzle would fit and come together. How like Him to give an Eternal answer in the midst of an Earthly answer!

Yes, I did finish the puzzle that day and learned that He not only cared and could help with that challenge, but also was ready and ever so able to bring my Life Puzzle together as well!

Friend, do you sometimes have to learn the hard way? You, too, can learn to be teachable and find that loving Hand who cares for you in the puzzles of your life.

Kathleen Stevenson

THOSE WHO HOPE IN GOD

Proverbs 23:17-18

"Do not let your heart envy sinners,
but be zealous for the fear of the Lord all the day;
for surely there is a hereafter,
and your hope will not be cut off." (NKJV)

A child may do their best to behave until Christmas, hoping that Santa will notice their hard work and, in the end, reward them with amazing presents on Christmas morning. In a less childish example, church history tells us that after Jesus' ascension, the apostle Peter endured intense persecution and did not deny Jesus even to his death. He knew that there was a greater reward waiting for him. As this proverb says, *"surely there is a hereafter."*

Just as there are eternal rewards, there are eternal consequences. Sin is not worth the end result. Those who practice sin may have a cushy life here and now, but if they do not turn from their sin, they will face the eternal consequences of their rejection of God. Death. Hell. Eternal separation from their Creator, the source of life. All the good they had in life will quickly be forgotten amid eternal suffering. The Bible tells us that hell was not made for people but for the devil and his angels (Matt. 25:41). God desires that no one would perish, but every person would come to repentance (2 Pet. 3:9) and eternal life (John 3:16). He not only wants us to be with Him forever in heaven, but He has rewards for us as well (Heb. 11:6).

God will not fail those who hope in Him. Hold tightly to Him, and do not let go. The present sufferings we face do not compare with the glory He has in store for us (Rom. 8:18). So, do not grow weary in doing good (Gal. 6:9) but be passionate (zealous) to love and honor the Lord. You will receive your reward, and your hope in Him will be fulfilled.

Stephen Larkin

THE BEST INTENTIONS

Proverbs 25:20

"Like one who takes away a garment on a cold day,
or like vinegar poured on a wound,
is one who sings songs to a heavy heart." (NIV)

Many times in my life I have been sad, unhappy, mad, and just plain not pleasant to be around…and I wanted it that way. There were times when I just needed to brood, and no amount of bubble blowing could change that. Sometimes I just needed space and time to process.

When my husband died, there were many people who could not handle the fact that I was in mourning and depressed, and they insisted on cheering me up. It only irritated me. I recognized that they had the best intentions but were clueless about the pain I was in. I quickly learned to distance myself. Then there were the people who just came to hug me, breathe the same air, and let me be me.

That experience taught me to be more aware of another person's feelings. To look for the signs that tell me whether it is time to laugh or time to cry. To try and be a blessing and not a clanging cymbal.

Ecclesiastes 3:1, 2, 4, 7 says, *"There is a time for everything, and a season for every activity under heaven:*

> *A time to be born and a time to die,*
> *a time to plant and a time to uproot,*
> *a time to weep and a time to laugh,*
> *a time to mourn and a time to dance,*
> *a time to tear and a time to mend,*
> *a time to be silent and a time to speak." (NIV)*

Galatians 5:22-23: *"But the fruit of the Spirit is love, joy, peace, forbearance, kindness, goodness, faithfulness, gentleness, and self-control." (NIV)*

It all comes back to trying to be more like Jesus and to love one another by being kind and gentle. That way, we will be more able to comfort and care for our brothers and sisters in Christ.

Bless someone today with His love.

Pat Nannarello

THE TRUTH SETS YOU FREE

Proverbs 12:13

"The wicked are trapped by their own words,
but the godly escape such trouble." (NLT)

Before I knew the Lord, I was extremely disrespectful and foul-mouthed. I spoke with a graphic and vulgar vocabulary, even at the age of five…in kindergarten! I used my words to hurt and offend people, and from middle school through high school, I often found myself in handcuffs and in the back seat of a police cruiser.

Proverbs 12:13 speaks about how wicked-hearted people will entangle themselves in their own words. Not only can this include rudeness, vulgarity, and insults, but also lies, deception, and manipulation. Have you ever caught anyone in a lie? Have you ever seen it depicted in a movie or television program? Someone bent on fabricating lies will tell a fictitious story, sometimes forget a crucial part in their own fabrication, and tell the story differently the second time. Those who notice this change will usually catch this deception by asking simple questions and watching the person fall into more lies and stumble over their own words.

I experienced this several times. I remember being questioned by my parents or schoolteachers and, as my wickedness grew, eventually interrogated by the police at a police station. I wanted to escape responsibility for my own actions, and I used lies to do it. However, my life was forever changed when I began to tell the truth! When I accepted Jesus as my Lord and Savior, I was heavily convicted about lying and chose to commit to telling only the truth.

Have you ever been caught doing something wrong and chose to confess and tell the truth, and as a reward, were set free for being honest? Proverbs 12:13 states, "…the godly escape such trouble." (NLT) After the Lord changed my heart, and I committed to telling the truth, I have had several encounters with police officers and courtroom judges due to my past; and, to God be the glory, I have had case after case after case dismissed! The Lord is too good!

I would strongly encourage anyone to submit their words to the Lord. Rather than speaking lies and trying to cover them up in more ways than one, the truth really does "set you free."

Victor Miguel Rivera

GOOD NEWS FROM FAR AWAY

Proverbs 25:25

*"As cold waters to a thirsty soul,
so is good news from a far country." (KJV)*

Amelia is an especially beautiful child who is greatly disposed to silliness and flights of fancy about anything that can occupy the mind of a three-year-old. But being our only grandchild and living in a distant and foreign land known as San Francisco, with parents who have very random schedules as they juggle family, school, and work, interactions are few and far between. This makes those rare moments of communication all the more refreshing when they come together, especially for grandma! Every word Amelia utters refreshes her grandmother's heart, and time spent on the phone or video chat is never inconvenient or wasted on her. Whether it is a grandmother with a grandchild in a faraway city, a parent of a child selflessly serving in the military, or even an adult child away at college completing studies, when "good news" comes to us from afar, it truly is a glass of cold water that refreshes a parched soul.

I believe this to be true in the natural as well as in the eternal realm. The greatest news that has ever been given is the news of the life-saving love and sacrifice of Jesus Christ upon the cross. It could not have been an easy message to receive when the angel Gabriel told a humble young teenage girl that her womb was about to miraculously carry the God of Eternity. By the power of the Holy Spirit, Mary would bring forth a baby who would become a man—the Savior of all humanity—and He would be the solution to the dilemma of sin and death. That good news—the Gospel—changed the course of history, not just on that fateful night in Bethlehem but for eternity!

Let us all receive good news from afar like a refreshment to our souls both in the natural and eternal realms. And to Him be the glory in it all!

Jose Nolasco

THE HEART

Proverbs 14:10

"The heart knows its own bitterness,
and a stranger does not share its joy." (NKJV)

I have attended many funerals in my lifetime, and as is customary in a time of loss, my wife and I will give our condolences to the family. Sometimes we tell them "we know how you feel." But can we really know the deep sorrow they feel? Perhaps we can if we have experienced a similar loss. But even so, at that moment that person hurts way worse than we do.

In Proverbs 14:10, the writer tells us that every person has an intimate relationship with himself regarding his emotions. We cannot break into their privacy when it comes to personal feelings. In the book of Jeremiah, God talks about the heart saying: "Who can understand it? 'I, the Lord, search the heart and examine the mind.'" (17:9-10) Let us be sensitive and mindful of people's emotions. The Bible tells us to laugh with those who laugh and weep with those who weep.

I have learned that people experience feelings and emotions differently, and many times, though we have good intentions, instead of comforting a person, we can be imprudent and hurtful through insensitive remarks. Usually, my words to mourning and hurting people have been: "I pray that the One that knows your heart and feelings will comfort you and heal your heart." There is also something called "the ministry of presence," which simply means that your availability and just "being there" for the other person is the best comfort you can give.

God will put us in situations where He wants us to be His ambassadors to represent Him with His loving kindness to the brokenhearted. So let us always ask the Holy Spirit to lead us in every situation we face. He will do it.

Ricardo Chaidez

SIMPLY TREASURED

Proverbs 13:7

"A pretentious, showy life is an empty life;
a plain and simple life is a full life." (MSG

After my mother-in-law passed away, I was at her home helping my father-in-law organize some of her things. Sue was a beautiful woman both inside and out. She had quite an array of collectibles--from tea sets and crystal, to fine China, elegant Christmas decorations, and a vast collection of porcelain dolls. Her home depicted who she was as a woman—charming, classy, dainty, kind, and exquisite.

Through the process of organizing her belongings, I came to realize that Sue was unable to take any of her little treasures with her. Likewise, none of our things can come with us when we enter through the Pearly Gates. Proverbs 13:7 provides insight as to what genuinely matters in living a full life.

Sue understood that treasures on earth could not outweigh the treasure we have in Christ. For Sue, she loved the Lord, and she loved her family. Those were her true treasures. Plain and simple, her relationship with Christ and her loved ones mattered more to her than her things. Woven between all of the tea sets and dolls were books about Jesus and picture frame upon picture frame of her family, filled with memories. She could have lost everything in a fire, and she would have been content knowing that her life was filled with love, light, and laughter from the quality time she spent with each of us. Her life was full. I pray that regardless of the things you have, remember to seize the plain and simple moments you have with Jesus and the people you love. Those are the memories that will enrich your life for eternity.

Jennifer Shank

FOLLOW THE STEPS

Proverbs 16: 9

"A man's heart plans his way,
but the Lord directs his steps." (NKJV)

One, two, three, and…One, two, three, and…One, two, three, and...

These are familiar words when you are learning to dance. You take your dance partner by the hand and learn to follow his steps as he guides you safely around the floor. As you learn to trust your partner, there is a beautiful synergy that happens as you move together. Except when you miss the beat and step on their toes! (Or is that just me!)

Learning to dance (walk) with Jesus is the same way! When we are in concert with the Creator, even our steps are guided by Him. God has given us the ability to think and reason. He has given us a brain, and as one of my friends puts it, "He expects us to use it!" He has also given us the ability to imagine and be creative, just like Him. When you put imagination, thinking, and reasoning together, you come up with an idea. When you want to make that idea happen, you come up with a plan.

Planning is a good thing. Constructing a building would be a disaster without architectural plans. Winning a war against an enemy would be catastrophic if there were no concerted effort and leadership to provide a plan. Even something as simple as baking cookies requires a plan.

The key is inviting the Lord to be a part of the process. Bring your plans to the Lord and allow Him to direct your steps. As you humbly submit your plans to Him, be willing to listen to guidance, direction, and possible change. He is the Master Planner and gives the best directions and advice.

So, plan! Imagine great things! Take the hand of your Creator and dance!

Michelle Glush

EXCUSES, EXCUSES

Proverbs 22:13

"The lazy person claims, 'There's a lion out there!
If I go outside, I might be killed!'" (NLT)

One of the primary themes of Proverbs is laziness. We read that laziness leads to poverty, and so on. However, this particular proverb links (some) people's fears—excuses, really—as having a root of laziness.

If we were to re-write this proverb for today's world, it might read something like this:

"The lazy person says…

> …I can't go to work; if I do, I might get into a car accident!'"
> …I can't go to church, I have family in town, and they might feel hurt!"
> …I can't help you; I might hurt myself!"
> …I can't go to prayer meeting; I'll be too tired for work tomorrow and get fired!"
> …I can't read my Bible, I have too much homework, and I'll fail the class!"
> …I can't serve at church; I am too stressed!"
> …I can't *[whatever it is you don't want to do]*, *[whatever lame excuse]!*"

At the end of the day, this proverb is uncovering what we pass off as fear as nothing more than excuses and self-justifications for not wanting to fulfill obligations or dedicate ourselves to a life of discipline and work—both physical and spiritual.

The reality is that we always make time for the things that are the most important to us, and we make excuses to get out of the things we deem less valuable. This is a great moment for introspection for each of us:

- What do we routinely make excuses for?
- Where do we spend our leisure time?
- How much time per week do we spend in God's presence, prayer, worship, devotion, Bible reading, and church?
- What do we spend our money on the most?
- What do we meditate on or let run through our mind the most?
- Are we aware of God's presence throughout the day?
- Do we repent when we are convicted of sin by the Holy Spirit? Do we just let sinful things slide in our lives and make excuses for them?

Get up! Go outside and tame a Lion!

Kyle Bauer

LIFE-GIVING WORDS

Proverbs 12:25

"Anxiety weighs down the heart,
but a kind word cheers it up." (NIV)

Have you heard the saying "misery loves company"? The expression became popular because there is some truth to it. Our natural human spirit wants to focus on the negative things in life and share them with others. Fear, anxiety, and crises sell, and we are bombarded daily about how bad things are and how they must be fixed. It is hard to go through the day without negative thoughts and words swirling around in our heads. It is much easier to give in to negative thoughts and words, which can lead to tension, worry, and anxiety, affecting us physically with health problems, addictions, and unwanted behaviors.

It is no wonder the Bible contains so many verses that teach us about our thoughts and words. We must remember our hope should not be based on earthly things or pleasures. Looking for peace and comfort in the world is fleeting. Our joy and peace need to come from God and His great love for us.

The second part of the verse tells us, "But a kind word cheers it (the heart) up." How can you speak life to a heavy heart or speak an encouraging word to yourself and others today?

Look at Philippians 4:8: *"Finally, brothers and sisters, whatever is true, whatever is noble, whatever is right, whatever is pure, whatever is lovely, whatever is admirable—if anything is excellent or praiseworthy—think about such things."*

Do not allow the weight of anxiety to pull you down today; instead, focus on things that are praiseworthy and *"be transformed by the renewing of your mind."* (Rom. 12:2)

And remember Proverbs 18:4: *"A person's words can be life-giving water; words of true wisdom are as refreshing as a bubbling brook."* So speak life to others and yourself today. Ask God to put people in your life today that need to hear a friendly word and take the time to share life, hope, and a kind word with them.

Jill Alvarado

WHO IS THIS PERSON?

Proverbs 16:6

"Unfailing love and faithfulness make atonement for sin.
By fearing the Lord, people avoid evil." (NLT)

When I read this verse, it reminded me of how I have recently been aware that sometimes I do not recognize myself. I have been trying really, really hard to be more like Jesus, and somewhere along the way, unbeknownst to me, the Lord has been transforming me.

In my human nature, I was always a bottom-line, take-no-prisoners kind of person. And I had an extensive vocabulary of snarky, sarcastic remarks. My tongue was like a switchblade. Over the years, that part of me has softened. Still, it was not until recently, when I have been in a few challenging circumstances where normally the reading of the riot act would come into play, that I found myself commenting with kindness, calm, and measure. I am thinking, "who IS this person?!" I have also found myself literally having joy in my person (spirit and flesh) when I'm doing things for Jesus. I also find that "out of character" but wildly satisfying. What a gift!

In this verse, I realize that it is HIS unfailing love for me and my faithfulness to Him that have unconsciously transformed me into a new person.[6] (This is what theologians would call the work of the Holy Spirit in us as "sanctification.") Even though I have been repenting daily and asking the Holy Spirit to help me hold my tongue, and I catch myself and revise what I am about to say, I was totally unaware that while I was working on it on the outside, the Holy Spirit was working on the inside! Hallelujah! Who knew? And because of my complete and total respect for and love of Jesus, I have avoided evil…. so far. Praise God!

So for you, my sister or brother in Christ, love Jesus with everything you have got. Then, faithfully, diligently, and with passion, always follow His commandments and do whatever it is the Lord tells you to do. No whining. You will avoid the evil one and will be blessed beyond measure. And you will not recognize yourself either.

Pat Nannarello

---

6   See Mark 4:26-29

HUMBLE, SMART, AND HUNGRY

Proverbs 16:26

*"Life motivation comes from the deep longings of the heart,
and the passion to see them fulfilled urges you onward." (TPT)*

Years ago, I read a book that described the ideal team member. This person is "humble, smart, and hungry."[7]

The definitions for each of the terms describe a person who first walks in humility. I have learned that humility is what really makes life work. A humble person loves others, is friendly, receives correction, makes relationships, is teachable, forgives and receives forgiveness, and grows. On the other hand, a hard, prideful person makes relationships, growth, and team cohesiveness impossible. Over years of pastoring, I have told many people that if they remain humble, I will give everything for them, and we will grow together, but if they are hard-headed and prideful, we cannot walk with each other.

Secondly, the ideal team member is smart but not smart like you are thinking right now—they are socially and relationally smart. Book smarts and sheer intelligence without humility can end up being a detriment. The know-it-all person, who does it all himself and denigrates others who may not know as much, can break the spirit of a team. A good team member is *relationally* smart, even more than book smart. A person who can "play well with others" is ultimately more valuable than one who merely registers high in intelligence or ability. The same attributes of a humble person are found in the attributes of a "smart" person.

Thirdly, hungry brings us to Proverbs 16:26. The hunger is obviously not physical—it is one's passion and drive for fulfillment and achievement. Humility and relational capacity mean very little on a team when there is no hunger and passion for results; all three components are necessary. Proverbs designates hunger as the primary motivator to succeed, but when tempered with relationship and humility, success becomes more than the realization of a dream or goal; others will share your joy with you!

Kyle Bauer

---

7   Patrick Lencioni. *The Ideal Team Player*. Hoboken, NJ: Jossey-Bass, 2016

LAZINESS...

Proverbs 26:14

"As a door turns on its hinges,
so a sluggard turns on his bed." (NIV)

A door hinge swings back and forth but never goes anywhere else. The sluggard swings back and forth but never gets out of bed. This sluggard gives a door hinge a bad name. Various translations call the sluggard lazy, slothful, and lazybones. We are expected, if and when we are able, to get up, get out of bed, and get to work. God created all of humankind to be fruitful. The concept conveyed by King Solomon is that we are expected to be productive and interactive human beings. God said in Genesis 1:28, *"Be fruitful and increase in number; fill the earth and subdue it. Rule over every fish in the sea and the birds in the sky and over every living creature that moves on the ground."* (NIV) That cannot be accomplished lying in bed tossing and turning.

In my life, I had times when I was exhausted and spent time in bed resting, but once refreshed, I got up and got busy. Likewise, a sick bed is for recovery, and something productive happens as we rest and recuperate. Solomon was not speaking of these times, as he clearly called the person lazy, slothful, or lazybones, depending on the Bible translation. We are made for community and to be productive. I believe we are each called by God for a purpose and have an assignment from Him. We need to ask God for our assignment and then go about doing it. May we never be looked on as being a Proverbs 26:14 person.

Martin and Bea Laufer

TRUE RICHES

Proverbs 14:24

"The wealth of the wise is their crown,
but the folly of fools yields folly." (NIV)

"Getting wisdom is the wisest thing you can do! And whatever else you do, develop good judgment." (Prov. 4:7, NLT) King Solomon asked God for wisdom to govern God's people and to discern between right and wrong. Solomon's petition for wisdom pleased God, and as a result, God also blessed him with wealth and honor. While not every wealthy person is wise, the person who follows the Lord will be crowned with wisdom.

However, fools in their folly will only yield more foolishness. Walking in wisdom and knowledge, and especially the fear of the Lord, is far from them. Only a fool will mock at sin, and as they continue to fill their cup with foolishness and sinful deeds, they are only deceiving themselves into believing their own lies. But the Bible gives us some very wise advice—stay away from foolish people.

As disciples of Christ, the Lord wants us to choose to follow Him, believe his Word, and trust in His goodness and faithfulness. Our wealth is not just found in money, although God has promised in His Word that if we are faithful to give to Him, He will be faithful to abundantly provide for us, but also we are rich in our relationship with the Lord—in His mercy, His faithfulness, and His presence! Imagine the God of the universe wants to sit down and meet with YOU and ME every day!

Do you want to wear the crown of the wise? Ask the Lord for wisdom as Solomon did, and diligently pursue it. God is the same yesterday, today, and forever. If He did it for Solomon, He will do it for you.

Debbie Speese

AUGUST

My child,

My child, pay attention to what I say.

Listen carefully to my words.

Don't lose sight of them.

Let them penetrate deep into your heart,

for they bring life to those who find them,

and healing to their whole body.

Guard your heart above all else,

for it determines the course of your life.

—Proverbs 4:20-23

STATELY IN STRIDE

Proverbs 30:29-31

"Three things are stately in their stride, four of stately gait —
the lion, mightiest of beasts, which turns aside for none;
the greyhound, the billy-goat and the king when his army is with him." (CJB)

The writer of this chapter in Proverbs is Agur, son of Jakeh (30:1). The name Agur translates to the word *gathered*. His father's name, Jakeh, means *pious* or *carefully religious*. A distinctive feature of Agur's teaching is his use of the numerical saying, possibly based on riddles in which the audience is required to respond. The observations of Agur serve to illustrate the ways of man versus the wisdom of God.

In contrast with small, humble creatures mentioned in verses 25-28—the ant, the rock badger, the locust, and the lizard—are those that appear noble in their bearing and walk. First, the lion, fearless and mighty. Second, the *zarzir motnayim*—literally, "girt of loins"—which has been identified as a strutting "rooster" or fighting "cock," the greyhound, the war-horse, or zebra. It is impossible to decide with certainty. Third, the male goat, having an arrogant bearing as he marches before the herd, staring down strangers. Fourth, a king walking with majestic stride as he leads an imposing army.

From these four stately examples we can learn:

- courage and strength from *the lion,* not turning away from any difficulty we encounter.
- swift efficiency from *the greyhound*.
- the care of our family and those under our charge from *the male goat*.
- and from *a king,* to so order our lives that we may not only be safe, but also magnificent, as we advance.

Karen Heimbuch

COMMENDED AND BLESSED

Proverbs 24:21-22

"My child, fear the Lord and the king.
Don't associate with rebels, for disaster will hit them suddenly.
Who knows what punishment will come from the Lord?" (NLT)

The Lord calls us to honor Him and our authorities. Fear the Lord, for He deserves all the honor, glory, praise, and obedience. Fear Him for everything that he has done for you. But why must we obey our authorities? Is there no other authority except God?

There is no higher authority than God, but the Bible also says that our earthly authorities have been placed there by Him. *"Let everyone be subject to the governing authorities, for there is no authority except that which God has established. The authorities that exist have been established by God. Consequently, whoever rebels against the authority is rebelling against what God has instituted, and those who do so will bring judgment on themselves. Therefore, it is necessary to submit to the authorities, not only because of possible punishment but also as a matter of conscience."* (Rom. 13:1-2, 5, NIV)

God calls us to obey Him, and disobedience leads to punishment. So, since our leaders have been placed by Him, then disobeying our leaders will also lead to punishment. *"Then the Spirit of God came upon Zechariah, son of Jehoiada, the priest. He stood before the people and said, "this is what God says: 'Why do you disobey the Lord's commands? You will not prosper. Because you have forsaken the Lord, He has forsaken you.'"* (2 Chron. 24:40, NIV)

Even cursing our leaders will lead to punishment. *"Do not blaspheme God or curse the ruler of your people."* (Ex. 22:28, NIV) *"All these curses are going to come on you. They're going to hunt you down and get you until there's nothing left of you because you didn't obediently listen to the Voice of God, your God, and diligently keep His commandments and guidelines that I commanded you. The curses will serve as signposts, warnings to your children ever after."* (Deut. 28:45-46, MSG)

Obey God and the authorities. We will not only avoid punishment, but also we will be commended and blessed by God for obeying His commands.

Joshua Bauer

CAN YOU HEAR WHAT THEY DON'T SAY?

Proverbs 20:5

"The purposes of a person's heart are deep waters,
but one who has insight draws them out." (NIV)

Do you ever literally hear what a person has not said yet, but it still rings in your ears before they say it? I am not being outlandish or just plain nuts. At times, common sense and life experience let you hear what someone is about to say before they say it. When that happens, you say to yourself, or out loud, "I knew you were going to say that." In a spiritual context, the gift of discernment often facilitates a very similar experience, not only hearing what someone might say, but also hearing what is on their mind. This involves knowing the revelation of the intent of their heart. Jeremiah 17:9-10 teaches us that God alone knows our hearts and "tries the reins," investigates, and tests the true intent of our hearts.

In Matthew 9:4, Jesus demonstrates the gift of discernment. Matthew writes, *"But Jesus, knowing their thoughts, said, why do you think evil in your hearts."* Notice, He knew their thoughts and the intent (purpose) of their hearts. He literally heard what they did not say, as the gift of discernment revealed both their thoughts and their intent. Jesus did not have to ask them about their purpose. He knew already. He asked the question to alert them that He already knew. This is why Solomon says the purposes of the heart are deep waters, because it requires divine revelation to truly know them.

Solomon goes on to clarify this as he specifies insight as the requirement for drawing out the depths of one's heart. Where does this insight come from? Divine revelation. With discernment comes great responsibility. As the Holy Spirit reveals the depths of someone to you, surely His intent for you is to pray on their behalf regarding what you are allowed to "draw out" of them.

Lloyd Speese

THE MENTALITY OF HELL

Proverbs 18:1

"Unfriendly people care only about themselves; they lash out at common sense." (NLT)

Setting aside the bad days that everyone has, generally speaking, unfriendly people are selfish. I am sure you have met one—or many—before. They care for no one, are happy for no one, and only help if there is some sort of benefit for themselves. This self-centeredness is an expression of hell itself.

Hell is certainly a real place, but it is also a mentality of selfishness, fear, and pride. We see this mentality first exert itself in the sin of Lucifer. Five times he asserts *"I will…"* against God (Isa. 14:13-14, NKJV):

> *I will ascend into heaven,*
> *I will exalt my throne above the stars of God;*
> *I will also sit on the mount of the congregation…*
> *I will ascend above the heights of the clouds,*
> *I will be like the Most High.*

Selfishness aims for self-satisfaction. There is no room for serving another person or sharing life, joy, happiness, grief, or love with anyone else. There is no joy for another person, because self must always be at the center of everything with no concern for others.

Fear's aim is self-preservation. I fear because there is a threat to me: My status quo, my social interactions, my position, my success, my influence or power, to my image or honor. A threat to *Me*. This is idolatry.

Pride's aim is self-deification. Pride is an exaggeration, a dishonest self-evaluation, and a desire to hide from yourself the ego-deflating truth about yourself. This kind of pride elevates itself above everything and everyone and believes it deserves and is owed every sort of good thing. Pride covets, craves, strives for, and takes anything it can for the pleasure of self.

This mentality of hell is the core of the human sin nature even today. It is argumentative, defiant, closed-minded, prideful, selfish, arrogant, rude, mean, cruel, hateful, angry, and unforgiving. Hell is a real and physical place of torment, but the mentality of hell disallows for any possibility of relationship. This mentality builds a cage that is no bigger than oneself, and there is no room in such a person's heart for anyone else.

Kyle Bauer

250

CORRECTION IS A GIFT

Proverbs 13:18

*"If you ignore criticism, you will end in poverty and disgrace;
if you accept correction, you will be honored." (NLT)*

I would argue that most of our life lessons are learned through mimicry, seeing and doing what others have done before us (maybe with a little extra personal flare). When you see kids re-enacting their parents' goofy quirks and behaviors, it's because imitation is the first step in learning how to do anything. We repeat the world around us to help ourselves walk through the same world others have walked through before us.

We are "conditioned" to repeat what others are doing around us. There are a lot of negative connotations to the word "conditioning" as brainwashing or deception are typically associated with it. BUT, conditioning the mind is similar to an athlete conditioning their body; they lift weights to grow and strengthen their muscles under pressure.

In the case of learning wisdom and heeding instruction, this is our mind and spirit "lifting weights," going under pressure, listening to, and allowing our Instructor (God) to correct us and lead us in the right direction. When we continually allow Him to work into us His perfect knowledge, we grow and improve daily in every way. We find that we are growing up to the next level.

Those who ignore the wisdom of correction do not grow. They stay where they are and often have the most negative things to say about everyone else as they sit in their own mess. But when you find yourself in a mess, watch others closely. Listen to the Lord. Do not be afraid of correction. It will lead you where you are meant to go.

Rachael Hopkins

FREEDOM FROM RELIGION

Proverbs 14:34

"Godliness makes a nation great,
but sin is a disgrace to any people." (NLT)

No nation is perfect, and the United States is certainly not an exception. Our country has had many shameful national sins from its inception, which is undeniable and, to an extent, ongoing. However, as imperfect as our country is, we were founded on religious freedom and established on a Judeo-Christian foundation that sought to honor God and live by the principles in His Word. As a result, America has grown into the strongest, most exceptional, God-fearing, prosperous, generous, and blessed nation.

The Sexual Revolution of the 1960s put America on the road toward embracing a libertine lifestyle and mindset that no longer sought freedom *of* Religion but freedom *from* Religion so man could supplant God and take His place. This is the same sin that started with Lucifer (Isa. 14:12-15), continued with Adam and Eve (Gen. 3:4-7), and continues to fester in the hearts of corrupted humanity today. Today's culture has erased God from just about every public and official venue to where the very mention of God in many places is anathema. This comes with a heavy price.

Freedom from God is not the result of an evolving humanity but of a *de*volving humanity, which inevitably spirals down further into decay, corruption, amorality, perversion, delusion, and, in the end, an utterly degenerate mind. (See Rom. 1:18-32; 1 Tim. 4:1).

Today, we are paying the terrible price for freedom from God. When we want to be free from God, we enslave ourselves to serve other things, and those things that have nothing to do with God are inevitably destructive to us, who are created in God's image. Our nation is disgraced by the furious growth of the LGBTQ+ agenda that is perverting a generation. Our economy is failing. Most politicians are utterly corrupt, and one wonders how long our country can survive. How did it come to this? Sin. Sin is a disgrace to any people.

Yet, no matter what happens, I know that as long as Jesus' Church is intact, we will continue to advance His Kingdom! God still cares about what happens to our country, and we continue to pray for it to fulfill God's purposes. Yet, we must remember that, ultimately, Heaven is our home!

Kyle Bauer

THE PATH OF LIFE

Proverbs 15:24

"The path of life leads upward for the wise;
they leave the grave behind." (NIV)

Is the path you are currently on leading you toward life, or is it leading you farther and farther away from the Lord? There is a path that leads to life, and the wise seek it out. But, there also exists a path that leads to death, and many find themselves on it, usually of their own volition.

The more we base our lives on the Word of God and follow His ways, the more we will find ourselves experiencing abundant life. We will not only have new life, but also walk farther away from the grave. "The grave," in earthly terms, represents all that is death; death in finances, relationships, ministry, careers, or well-being. "The grave" also represents the reality of eternal separation from God and a place of eternal death.

Proverbs 15:24 conveys the Lord's instructions for the wise to seek the path that leads upward to new abundant life. This path is the journey of daily seeking the Lord and His righteousness. Within an everyday context, this proverb reminds me of diet and exercise. What happens to our bodies when we stay on a path of proper diet and exercise? We experience a new life filled with more energy and health benefits. We also say goodbye to possible sicknesses, diseases, and unhealthy trends that could lead to death. The more we stay on this path, the more we see the benefits. Applying that to a spiritual reality, we can compare that staying on the Lord's way of life is a spiritual discipline that produces spiritual health benefits. If exercise and proper dieting sound beneficial, how much more valuable is it for our eternal spirit to stay on the Lord's path?

In His infinite love, the Lord encourages us to seek the path that leads to life. A path of seeking Him, a path of prayer, a path of spiritual discipline and discipleship. On this path, you will see new life! You will experience abundant life!

Victor Miguel Rivera

WHAT IS A NAME WORTH?

Proverbs 22:1

"A good name is more desirable than great riches;
to be esteemed is better than silver or gold." (NIV)

He was a pillar in the community, faithfully served in the church, owned a successful business, and had a beautiful family. He dressed well and lived in the perfect house. My husband and I and our kids were friends with this man and his family—we did BBQs, celebrated all our birthdays, talked for hours on the porch, and even went on vacation together. It was a perfect fit for our families to be connected, but there was one thing that kept nagging at me that didn't seem right.

The more I got to know the husband, the father, and the pillar of our community, the more I became uncomfortable with his views and ideas. The way he treated his wife and kids, the selfishness he showed, and his disrespect for people when they didn't follow his lead. At the time I could not put my finger on it, but I was no longer impressed by his wealth, standing in our community, or generosity toward us.

What had happened? I was close enough to see who this man really was.

In the end, this man I thought was so impressive, on one particular Christmas Day, walked away from his wife and children without any explanation, stating he never loved his wife. He left the community to live in the family condo near the ocean and hardly ever paid child support while his family had to move into a small apartment to make ends meet.

This man was so focused on his business, his needs, and his wants that all that seemed good in their lives was a facade. All that he and his wife built up was torn down.

What is his name worth?

This man who had a loving family placed his silver and gold above them, ended up losing much of what he earned, and is alone.

In our world, it is so easy to be caught up by money, desire, and self, but God calls us in a different direction—integrity, honor, transparency, humility, and selflessness.

What is your name worth? What are your motives? Ask God to show you any area in your life that has been given over to gold and silver instead of Him.

Jill Alvarado

EATING THE FRUIT OF YOUR WORDS

Proverbs 12:14

*"A man will be satisfied with good by the fruit of his mouth,
and the recompense of a man's hands will be rendered to him." (NKJV)*

Have you ever stopped to listen to what you say? Do you bless others? Do you speak truth and righteousness over yourself? Or do you speak the negativity of the world? I am not good enough…I am not strong enough…I am not pretty enough…I am not young enough.

The Bible is very clear about the importance of the words we speak. Words can bring either life or death. In Matthew 21:19, we have a glimpse of Jesus and the fig tree: *"And seeing a fig tree by the road, He came to it and found nothing on it but leaves, and said to it, 'let no fruit grow on you ever again.' Immediately the fig tree withered away." (NKJV)*

In my imagination, I picture the tree listening to its Creator, bowing in reverence to give up its life with honor to serve its king and in obedience to His word.

Some people think the story of the fig tree is out of character for Jesus, but we must remember that Jesus only did what He saw the Father doing. There was a reason why Jesus spoke to the tree during a time when figs were not in season. He was teaching the disciples about faith and belief. In Jesus' explanation of the fig tree to His disciples, He said that if they believed and prayed, they could even SPEAK to a mountain and cast it into the sea.

What mountains do you need to move? Are you fueling the change with your words, or are the words you speak giving fuel for the enemy of your soul to use against you?

Deuteronomy 30:19 says, *"… I have set before you life and death, blessing and cursing; therefore, choose life, that both you and your descendants may live…" (NKJV)*

Remember who you are in Christ: You are a child of God, you are strong in the Lord and the power of His might, you are loved, you are forgiven, you have been set free from the power of the enemy. How do you stay free? Do not give the enemy fuel to use against you.

Therefore, speak life!

Michelle Glush

255

HONOR TO WHOM HONOR IS DUE

Proverbs 26:8

*Like one who binds a stone in a sling
is he who gives honor to a fool. (NKJV)*

One of the best examples of expert marksmanship with a sling can be found in the biblical story of David slaying Goliath. This proverb would likely have elicited laughter from those of that culture, because no one in their right mind would ever bind a stone to the weapon. Had someone in David's circumstances done so, he would have caused great harm to himself and delivered himself into the hands of his foe. Biblical history would undoubtedly be quite different. So it is when we render honor to a fool; nothing but harm can come of it.

But you would probably say that no one would do such a thing, and I would never give honor to a fool. The people I admire must be of the utmost caliber and quality. Is that really true however? If we consider those we watch on television and social media, we will find that we violate this principle more than we know. Often the ones who draw most of our attention tend to mesmerize us with their ability to swing a bat and run quickly across the field with a ball in hand. Or, in the case of music or fashion, we would find there is often very little ability and far more flash involved. Substance and character seem to be rare, and lack of character is often overlooked simply because of their ability to hold our attention. In that sense, are we not rendering honor to a fool?

If our answer to the question above is yes, does that not mean that this proverb correctly warns us that the only result of this is damage and destruction to oneself in our society?

Let us heed the principle shared here, dear reader. Let us always, with the help of the Holy Spirit, be careful never to render honor to a fool lest we reap the promised benefits of that action. Instead, let us honor those like Esther, Daniel, Nehemiah, and Deborah, to name a few. David said in Psalm 16:3 (NLT), "the godly people in the land are my true heroes! I take pleasure in them!"

Jose Nolasco

A REPUGNANT ATTITUDE

Proverbs 24:17-18

"Don't rejoice when your enemies fall; don't be happy when they stumble. For the Lord will be displeased with you and will turn his anger away from them." (NLT)

This proverb reminds me of a story in the book of Obadiah. At the time of the prophet Obadiah, Jerusalem was being sacked by the invading Babylonians, while their cousins, the Edomites, stood by doing nothing to help (v. 11). They were happy at Judah's destruction (v.12). The Edomites looted their cousins while they were being sacked by the Babylonians (v.13). They killed those who were fleeing for their lives instead of showing mercy (v.14). As a result, Edom would lose everything and be treated the same way they had treated their neighbors, and the Israelites would gain everything back (v. 6, 15-18).

Though God was using the Babylonians to punish the kingdom of Judah, God did not rejoice in its punishment. God loves people and looks for ways to redeem them.[1] To adopt an attitude of retribution against those who do not believe as you do, rejoicing in a wicked person going to hell, and being happy at another's misfortune is utterly repugnant to the Lord.

I remember when I heard of someone who, at that moment, was not doing as well as me. Something of joy leaped up in the pit of my stomach. I was on top. I was better than others. I was…I was…disgusted with myself. It was an ugly feeling, and it felt like the Holy Spirit was stepping away from the revolting attitude that was subtly growing in me. This person was a brother in the Lord, but apart from that, this attitude, in whatever manifestation it occurs, is the opposite of God's heart for people. I immediately called a friend and confessed my sin, and repented from it, asking the Lord to change my heart. According to this proverb (and Obadiah), if the Lord sees such an attitude and lack of mercy toward even those who are being punished, and if no one else will show them mercy or compassion, He will. Our job is not to dole out judgment nor carry a judgmental attitude. We are to love our enemies and do good to those who persecute us.[2]

Kyle Bauer

---

1   See 2 Samuel 14:14
2   Matthew 5:43-48

A CORRUPT WITNESS

Proverbs 19:28

*"A corrupt witness makes a mockery of justice,
the mouth of the wicked gulps down evil." (NLT)*

The underlying truth to these two statements is that: Without truth, there can be no justice, and those who choose to do evil indulge in evil as a hungry man gulps food.

Many years ago, persons who had a false claim against us took us to small claims court. We went before the judge, and the other party presented their case. The judge heard their testimony, saw their "evidence," and then asked us just one question. We answered him with a short, clear, truthful statement. The judge never allowed us to present our defense, but he ruled in our favor because the falseness of the other party's claim was evident to the judge. Justice was served because false witness was exposed. The other party proceeded to berate the judge, and he had to call the bailiff to restore order and remove them from the courtroom. Evil can and does affect all of us, but the wicked feed on evil, and it will consume them. We had been friends with the other party, but their choices had pulled us apart, and it was good that they did.

In modern American law, false testimony is called perjury, and it is a felony. Slander is another form of false witness and can have very serious consequences. In the above proverb, Solomon says that those who do such things "gulp down evil." As Christians, can we use slander, gossip, or perjury against anyone and call ourselves a child of God? We are to choose whom we serve. James 4:7 says, "Therefore submit to God. Resist the devil and he will flee from you." Let us resolve to do that which is good and flee that which is evil.

Martin and Bea Laufer

HAPPY FAMILY

Proverbs 21: 9

"It's better to live alone in the corner of an attic
than with a quarrelsome wife in a lovely home.." (NIV)

Have you ever given advice and then been upset when the person did not follow it? In my role as a wife and mother, I understand that letting my husband and children have a voice in the home is a good way to exercise the love of God. Being a perfectionist created chaos in my house, and it became a war zone. When I saw my family doing the opposite of what I thought was right, it kept me bound in a bitter attitude. I realized I was not trusting the Lord as He wanted me to. I brought all my insecurities and anxieties to the Lord (Phil. 4:6). I also treated my husband like my child, which did not go over very well.

Understanding the difference between my expectations and the reality of my family's needs taught me how to maintain a healthy and balanced home environment. I know now that the love of God will always guide us to fulfill our calling. So, instead of being a quarrelsome wife, I am committed to helping my family grow.

Live your life to unite, not to divide. Instead of helping, I was damaging my family's feelings and hearts. (Matt. 12:30) Having good intentions does not mean I must act on every impulse. I was not a wise wife or mother. I cannot live other people's lives or manipulate situations to produce the outcomes I want. God created us to be people that encourage, help, bless, and lift others up. You can find peace and rest in a home with Jesus as the center. When He is the center of your life, everything else around you finds its proper expression and place.

Alicia Suarez

OBEDIENCE PAYS OFF

Proverbs 16:20

*"He who heeds the word wisely will find good,
and whoever trusts in the Lord, happy is he." (NKJV)*

To heed means to pay attention, to listen with purpose. Before I understood much about God's Word, I knew about tithing, but I did not fully understand it until my pastor spelled it out for me! It is God's money, and we trust Him by giving Him the first 10%.

I wanted to "heed the word wisely," but I had no money. My husband and I were in deep financial distress, and I could only see a way to give God 5% instead of 10%. Even that pittance was painful, but somehow it managed to work. When I finally realized I needed to trust God and do it HIS way – still with very limited funds – I started giving the 10%, and it hurt. But God (that is one of my favorite sets of words, "But God") came through! He was faithful and provided month after month after month. When we finally got past the tight money stage, I began giving more than 10% because I wanted to pay back what I owed Him when I was only giving 5%. But, really, how could I ever pay Him back, because He gave His life for me?

Later, a wise friend of the family told me we also needed to tithe our time and not just our money. Again, it was a challenge. My days were packed, so I started trusting the Lord by giving Him 30 minutes. But I found the more time I spent with God and for God, the easier it was to accomplish the chores of the day. Imagine that! When we are obedient to what God calls us to do, it pays off!

Proverbs 3:5: *"Trust in the Lord, and lean not on your own understanding. In all your ways, acknowledge Him and He will direct your path."*

When we put God first in all aspects of our lives, the blessings come on like a flood. They are indescribably delicious.

Thank You, God!

Pat Nannarello

A DIFFERENT CHARACTER

Proverbs 15:18

*"A hot-tempered man stirs up strife,
but he who is slow to anger and patient calms disputes." (AMP)*

We have a choice in every situation where anger is a possible reaction. It is often difficult not to get angry, because we feel justified in light of what the other person said or did. However, we are responsible for our reactions in any situation. Every day, as we interact with people, we must make conscious decisions not to react to other people's anger. Our choices can significantly affect not only our lives, but also the lives of those around us. Whether on a bumper-to-bumper freeway with drivers intent on not letting us get off in time, in a stressful work situation, or even on the ball field, we interact with problems and problematic people every day.

This proverb describes two different types of people. First, the wrathful (hot-tempered) man, described as chemah in Hebrew, carries a connotation of heat, rage, anger, and even poison or venom. It would appear that a person predisposed to such character tends to create strife in the face of conflict or distressing circumstances. One writer describes this as having venom coursing through their veins. Given any provocation, even the slightest verbal puncture, the poison comes rushing out of them like hot lava from the center of an erupting volcano! The results are painful, heated, and devastating to all involved.

Yet, on the other hand, the same proverb describes a person with a different character. One who is slow to anger when it comes to disputes.

To illustrate this, I picture Jesus with the Samaritan woman at the well. Her reputation was so notorious in her town that she would not venture out to get water at the same time as the other women in order to avoid conflicts. Jesus, being God and knowing all of her sins and failures, says to her, "give me a drink." In the ensuing moments, Jesus calmly addresses her questions and her attempts to create religious or cultural conflicts in a loving manner that culminates in her recognizing him as Messiah.

Let us view these possible conflicts as opportunities to honor God by being slow to anger and ending all disputes so God is glorified!

Jose Nolasco

VOCATION AND AVOCATION

Proverbs 12:24

"Work hard and become a leader;
be lazy and become a slave." (NLT)

Ephesians 2:10 gives us a God-given trajectory for each of our lives: *"For we are His workmanship, created in Christ Jesus for good works, which God prepared beforehand that we should walk in them."* This describes each person's vocation, commonly confused with an *avocation*. An *avocation* is the job we do to earn a living, while a *vocation* is our calling, the reason God placed us on this earth. Sometimes one's *avocation* coincides with their *vocation*—they earn a living by working in their calling—for instance, a person may feel called to be a doctor and then works in that field. Many times, however, this is not the case.

I believe that success in this life should not be defined by the status of the avocation but by fidelity to the God-given vocation. This proverb speaks directly to the vocation we have in life. Simply stated, there is no substitute for hard work and preparation in fulfilling God's call on your life. The question is not "what do you do?" It is, "What has God called you to do?" Fulfilled people do not end up where they are by accident. They are diligent and intentional about the course they take, what they say yes or no to, and they actively make themselves experts in their field of study or work. God honors diligence.

I spoke with someone a while ago who desired to work in a particular ministry. I asked if she had any licensing, studies, or even investigated those things this ministry required of her. "No," she answered. I was bewildered at how she thought she would succeed in what she perceived as her calling. Until she applies herself, she will not fully walk in that calling. In the Amplified version, the phrase "be lazy and become a slave" is translated as *"the slacker will end up working to make someone else succeed."* God has a vocation—calling—for each person. If we pursue His calling with diligent preparation, coupled with spiritual formation, we align ourselves with the path He created us to walk and will find that we are leading, not following.

Kyle Bauer

BARBIES OR WISDOM?

Proverbs 20:26

"A wise king scatters the wicked like wheat,
then runs his threshing wheel over them." (NLT)

When I first read Proverbs 20:26, I thought to myself, "I don't know what a threshing wheel is, but it sure doesn't sound like a good time!" (I have since learned that a threshing wheel was used to roll over the grain to crush it—definitely not a good time!) My next thought was, "Man, being a wise king sounds so much better!" Then I remembered the first time I learned about King Solomon.

I was probably around seven years old when my mom told me how Solomon had an opportunity to ask God for anything, and it would be given to him. After the shock settled in learning that Solomon asked for wisdom and not a room full of Barbies, my mother continued to share the story of Solomon in 1 Kings 3 regarding the two women and the baby. I vividly remember freaking out that the king suggested slicing the baby in half! But when the story ended, I realized the wisdom and pure genius that Solomon had used to discover to whom the baby really belonged. The king skillfully used the sharpness of a sword to cut through the wicked heart of one woman, only to reveal the sacrificial love of the true mother who was unwilling to see her child be killed.

Now that right there was a skill I knew I needed in my own life, so I began to pray for wisdom. It has been one of the most valuable gifts God has blessed me with! So let me encourage you to put wisdom on the top of your prayer list. It will provide you with a foundation that will enable you to respond effectively to evil whenever it rears its ugly head. Wisdom will help you to decide which negative influences need to be scattered out of your life and will reveal to you how to decimate the wicked strongholds that need to be trampled by a spiritual threshing wheel which is the wisdom found in God's Word.

Jennifer Shank

POSITIONED ON THE ROCK

Proverbs 22:3

"A prudent person foresees danger and takes precautions.
The simpleton goes blindly on and suffers the consequences." (NLT)

What image comes to mind when you think of a meerkat? For most people, it's the iconic stance that a meerkat utilizes in everyday life—an upright position on two legs. Meerkats have developed a specialized way of keeping their group safe by assuming this stance. One meerkat will climb to the highest rock, position itself on its hind legs, and stand guard while it watches for predators. When a predator is spotted, the meerkat will alert the others so they all can hide in the nearest burrow. The fact that the meerkats are both watchful and have a place for safety is a perfect example of how we should posture ourselves in this world that would try to harm us.

Meerkats know predators are waiting to devour them and take necessary precautions to protect themselves. We understand from God's Word that *"in this world, you will have tribulation and trials,"* and our enemy *"prowls around like a roaring lion, looking for someone to devour."* (John 16:33; 1 Pet. 5:8 NLT) Just as meerkats are alert to the likelihood of roaming predators, we also are to be mindful of enemies that would seek to consume our lives and be aware that as Christians we will face tribulation.

God's Word gives us an understanding of the dangers that try *"to steal and kill and destroy."* (John 10:10) However, with this awareness we can take precautions in our own lives to help us combat the enemy. Meerkats place themselves on a high rock to watch for predators; similarly, the rock on which we can stand tall and firm is the truth that comes from God's Word. Reading the Bible is the best precaution we can take, because when we meditate on God's Word in the morning, we prepare our hearts and minds for what is to come throughout our day.

If meerkats did not position themselves on a high rock, they would not be able to see potential danger. Likewise, God does not intend for us to wander thoughtlessly into the potential danger around us. Rather He wants to spare us from falling prey to consequences by heightening our awareness. This is done by immersing ourselves in the truth found in His Word.

Amelia Montantes

PONDERING FOUR AMAZING THINGS

Proverbs 30:18-19

"There are three things that amaze me—no, four things that I don't understand: how an eagle glides through the sky, how a snake slithers on a rock, how a ship navigates the ocean, how a man loves a woman." (NLT)

Have you ever just sat and pondered certain things out of the blue?

As you "ponder" that question, I am sure a few ideas popped into your mind, as did with the author of this passage. If you read the whole chapter, verses 2-3 state, "I am too stupid to be human and lack common sense, I have not mastered human wisdom, nor do I know the Holy One." Kind of harsh but to the point. He then goes on to ask a string of questions. "Who?" I'll let you look those up yourself, but he finishes the series of questions in verse 5, stating, *"Every word of God proves true. He is a shield to all who come to him for protection,"* adding in verse 6, *"Do not add to his words, or he may rebuke you and expose you as a liar."* (NLT) Mighty strong words coming from a guy who considers himself "stupid."

In verses 18 and 19, it seems that he is all over the place, but it is an observation of a simple, possibly uneducated, yet humble man. There are things he knows as truths, things he observes and validates, but these four perplex him; a flying eagle, a slithering snake, a sailing ship, and I believe the most fascinating, the way a man loves a woman.

There are few things that are more complex, perplexing, or more beautiful than how a man loves a woman. I have found myself not understanding my wife but at the same time so head over heels in love with her. Like the author, I am amazed and lack understanding as to the way I love my wife. Grateful for her. So, perhaps at that moment, the author, as simple as he may have been, was feeling the same way about the woman he loved. You do not have to be a smart man to know you are in love.

Fred Alvarado

SLOW TO SPEAK

Proverbs 29:20

*"There is more hope for a fool
than for someone who speaks without thinking." (NLT)*

I lost a friendship when I spoke too quickly. I was angry and felt taken advantage of, but too late I realized that lashing out in anger was not the right thing to do. Our relationship never recovered. No matter how hard I tried to take the words back, they were still out there.

Even intelligent people can act foolishly. Speaking rashly can cause all kinds of problems that are entirely avoidable by using wisdom and keeping our mouths closed. As it says in James 1:19-20, I want to resolve to be *"quick to listen, slow to speak and slow to become angry, for the wrath of man does not produce the righteousness of God."* Speaking thoughtfully starts by listening to and thinking about what the other person is saying. If we take the time to ask questions to find out what they mean, we can avoid unnecessary conflict.

Potential disagreements arise when we do not listen or make a rash or wrong interpretation of what is being said without hearing the whole conversation. In our haste, we become angry and respond quickly. But if we stop to listen and truly hear the other person, ask questions, think, and pray about how we respond, the problems will usually disappear.

Heavenly Father, I ask that you help me to be fast to listen, take my time to process what I have heard, ask questions to understand the heart of the other person, and be slow to become angry. Let me not be a person who speaks without thinking. In Jesus' name.

Stephen Larkin

HE IS HONESTY

Proverbs 24:26

"An honest answer is like a kiss on the lips." (NIV)

It may seem obvious that living in truth would be God's delight. God IS truth. Since He is truth, anything that opposes God leads us away from His perfect truth. His truth applied to our lives causes us to be like Him and be formed in His character.

I believe God placed such an emphasis on truth and honesty in the Scriptures so many times because of the daily temptation to lie. It is a continual battle to walk and operate in truth. Something as simple as "how do I look" can cause the best of us to lie. More seriously, we face pressure to compromise everywhere. There are even those whose livelihoods or social circles are threatened for not giving in to a culture that is hostile to anything having to do with God's truth.

Walking in the truth must be the core of who we are, or we will quickly deviate from it. To lie is to plant a seed of rebellion against God, and it will not stop growing until we repent from it. Because of the rarity of truth in the world, to actually hear the truth is quite refreshing. This proverb goes as far as to say it is like a kiss on the lips. It is an unexpected gift in a world drowning in continual falsehood.

You gain nothing but truth from perpetuating truth, just as dishonesty attracts dishonesty. Hmm, this sounds like the spiritual principle of sowing and reaping. Spread lies, and more will come; speak truth, and more will come. So, walk in honesty and reflect God's ways, His holiness, and His truth in everything you do. I am reminded of Psalm 119:165, *"Great peace have those who love your law [truth], and nothing can make them stumble." (NIV)*

Rachael Hopkins

HEADS UP!

Proverbs 11:23

"The desire of the righteous is only good:
but the expectation of the wicked is wrath." (KJV)

There are only two Kingdoms. There are only two destinations—Heaven and Hell. When our time on this earth is done, the reality is that our spirit leaves our body and enters into the supernatural realm. The Bible says that Jesus will judge the works we do in this life, both good and bad (2 Cor. 5:10). Have you ever looked at the works of your life through a magnifying glass? Take some time and do this. As evidenced by this proverb, Solomon clearly did.

Anyone who has had a near-death experience is profoundly changed by it. Having had this experience during the Covid outbreak, two things stand out. One is that the eternal is REAL. Oh, is it REAL! The Bible is real. Jesus is real. Heaven is real. And you DO want to go to Heaven. I miss it. The second thing is that evil is real. And so, yes, the wicked experience wrath. The author of Hebrews says that it is a terrible thing to fall into the hands of the living God (Heb. 10:31).

Today's verse leads in with the truth that the righteous are to experience "only good." The Father desires all to repent and to escape ANY wrath. The way has been opened up through Jesus Christ! Ask! Change! Receive help and receive the goodness of God!

Juline Bruck

A SOUND HEART

Proverbs 23:6-8

"Do not eat the food of a begrudging host, do not crave his delicacies;
for he is the kind of person who is always thinking about the cost.
'Eat and drink,' he says to you, but his heart is not with you.
You will vomit up the little you have eaten
and will have wasted your compliments." (NIV)

Have you ever dined at the house of a "begrudger" or someone who is envious? They put on a good show, set out the best china, and put the finest food on the table for you. But that is all it is—a show. They are trying to impress you with their finest and encourage you to "eat, drink, and be merry," but all the while, their heart is seeking after your praise, admiration, and social status, not your fellowship. They may seem to give "grandly," but they do it reluctantly for their own selfish gain.

We have all encountered less than authentic people. The characteristics may be different, but you always leave with a feeling of being used, manipulated, or "slimed." No matter how much they "give," the relationship never feels right, and it is not, because while they are smiling to your face, behind the scenes, they are sucking the life right out of you.

Solomon gives us some very wise advice; be wary of the person with a stingy and envious heart. In Proverbs it says, *"A sound heart is the life of the flesh but envy the rottenness of the bones."* (Prov. 14:30 NLT) Envy drains life from the bones, and an envious person will do the same to all they meet. But what is a sound heart? Being whole, healthy, pure, wholesome, and not burdened with sin or regret.

So, next time you are invited to dine with a stingy or envious person, run, do not walk, as fast as you can in the other direction. Keep your eyes on Jesus and your "sound heart" with an attitude of thankfulness, and let the envious eat at their own table.

Debbie Speese

IT'S TIME TO GET UP

Proverbs 27:14

If you wake your friend in the early morning by shouting
"Rise and shine!" It will sound to him more like a curse than a blessing. (TMB)

I'm told my father-in-law, a lifetime military man, used to haphazardly awaken his family early every morning with clambering pots, radio music, and general house noise. His family hated this. My own father used to awaken us with a solid slap on the leg and a booming "time to get up" early every Sunday morning. My siblings and I still revisit this experience with less than fond memories.

Solomon hides several aspects of human nature within this early morning scenario. My father-in-law raised the same clamor each morning, supposedly from within self-interest, disregarding those at rest, following his routine because he wanted to be at his duty station on time. My father's morning unsettling had two major concerns. First, he refused any excuse for being late to church as perhaps an indicator of a need for greater spiritual maturity and understanding of the call to ministry service. Second, he considered it irreverent to willfully create the challenges related to tardiness. Too often, human nature considers itself first. Whether selfish or obedient, God alone judges one's intent. The takeaway is that we should ensure our intent for creating a morning clamor is the right one and worth the uproar it may cause. Most certainly, there is a value to rising early. King David, Solomon's father, famously wrote, "early will I seek thee" (Ps. 63) and continued to list the multiple blessings in doing so.

Solomon's counsel also highlights human nature in the seemingly universal disdain for rising early, and by inference, the propensity to innately disavow those things which help us the most.

The negative reaction and associated suspicion in being startled awake early is noted as a curse versus a blessing. Specifically, the sound elicits the agitation. Yet, Solomon infers the value of the early morning "rise and shine" is a blessing. It is also human nature to want the best for ourselves. Might Solomon be urging us toward the wisdom of self-discipline and the value of embracing a positive outlook, daily? He did not say don't wake your friend early. Perhaps we are to wake them gently.

Lloyd Speese

TOGETHER, NOT APART

Proverbs 21:9

*"It's better to live alone in the corner of an attic
than with a quarrelsome wife in a lovely home." (NLT)*

A quarrelsome woman is one who gets angry about everything, and every little thing causes an argument. She is difficult to get along with, communicate with, and live with. She is a woman who does not know when to speak or be quiet.

We were only two years married when we started having serious disagreements in our relationship. My husband would say something to me, and I would quickly tell him what he should do, regardless of his words, his feelings, or his entire story. I did not let my husband express himself, and he did not feel like saying anything to me anymore. So, we had to sit down and talk. He helped me see that I was not listening to him or valuing his input. This made him feel like the proverb says—wanting to go to the corner of the roof or the house. Thank God he didn't do that. Instead, we sat in our living room and had a good talk. I needed to be humble and hear it from his point of view.

God has placed your husband in your life to help you become the woman God wants you to be (and vice versa!). If you see your husband preferring to be alone all the time instead of wanting to be by your side, perhaps some introspection is in order. Are you a pleasant woman to be around? Are you always scolding and yelling for everything? Are you good at listening? Do you give words of encouragement, or do you demean him? Perhaps the husband prefers to "live in the corner of the house" because it is too dangerous for him to come out and weather the storm.

I want to encourage you not to let this continue. Do what we did: Sit down, talk together without rolling your eyes or sighing. Let the other person talk before responding. Have a humble heart to receive input and to start making changes. You are meant to be together and not apart. Ask God to help you see your strengths *and* weaknesses and to help you grow in your marriage.

Teresa Bauer

STRENGTH FOR A NEW SEASON

Proverbs 12: 11

*"Those who work their land will have abundant food,
but those who chase fantasies have no sense." (NIV)*

Time is one of those things in life that can be mysterious. We can never get time back, time keeps going, and not even the wealthy can buy themselves more time. How we spend our time is completely dependent on our free will.

Proverbs 12:11 illustrates two types of individuals: The one who works the land *and, therefore,* will have food, while the person who spends his time foolishly will have lack. Passing pleasures, instant gratification, and chasing daydreams are all momentary desires that are not ultimately productive. Hard work produces food, but even further, 2 Timothy 2:15 says that we must work to show ourselves approved for God's service. Faith requires us to have hope in the things that are unseen, and how we spend our time will be visible in due season.

I have found myself pensive about the past, at times disappointed with the present, and then struggling with faith for the future. However, in praising God, He has given me strength to keep working the land, which in my case, is putting in the work at what is in my sphere of influence and my faith journey, which is expanding the Kingdom of God around me. It is far from easy to keep going when our strength is low, but giving up on everything that God has done in our lives can cause all the crops to rot and us to lose the promised harvest. As we continue to work the land, we can be encouraged that the harvest will come in its due season.

God can prepare us in every season in our lives for the new thing He will do in the next season. As we work hard and in faith, we will find God's grace will give us the strength to keep moving forward.

Cynthia Medrano

HONOR YOUR PARENTS

Proverbs 15:20

"A wise son is a joy to his father,
and only a fool despises his mother." (CJB)

My brother and I were blessed beyond measure to be raised in a godly home with loving parents. Life lessons were learned through obedience, discipline, and example. There was a hanging of the Dorothy Law Nolte poem, "Children Learn What They Live," by the table that I read and re-read every time we sat down for a meal. This poem stressed the importance of the example that parents set for their children.

According to an Old Testament lexicon, young people who are *wise* have an intelligent attitude toward *all* experiences of life. (What a tall order for parents to deliver!) This includes matters of general interest, basic morality, forethought in secular affairs, skills in the arts, moral sensitivity, and spiritual experience. Hebrew wisdom believes that there is a personal God who is holy and just. He expects us to live our lives according to His principles that reveal right and wrong. This all applies to daily life.

Of course, any parent would burst with great pride and joy over such an intelligent and sensible child. Only foolish, arrogant, and rebellious children would despise, disrespect, and hate their parents. Such mocking children think nothing of embarrassing their parents, causing them much sorrow and the deepest grief. Adult children who treat their elderly parents with contempt or neglect are ungrateful, hard-hearted, and cruel. *"Anyone who does not provide for his own people, especially for his family, has disowned the faith and is worse than an unbeliever." (1 Tim. 5:8, CJB)*

Let us always look for ways to honor our parents. *"If you honor your father and mother, things will go well for you, and you will have a long life on the earth." (Eph. 6:3, NLT)* When we bring joy to our parents, we bring joy to the heart of God!

Karen Heimbuch

WORDS WORTH LISTENING TO

Proverbs 24:7

"Wisdom is too lofty for fools.
Among leaders at the city gate, they have nothing to say." (NLT)

One of the principle defining traits of fools in Proverbs is that they run their mouths. They are crass, foul, tactless, graceless, sinful, wicked, obtuse, thoughtless, and provoke fights. This by no means indicates a lack of intelligence, rather a lack of wisdom and discretion. Such people may be very wise and shrewd according to the wisdom of this world, but they continue to be fools, nonetheless, because of their lack of what the Bible defines as the beginning of wisdom—the fear of the Lord.

Psalm 1 juxtaposes the wicked and the godly. The wicked are papery chaff blown away by the slightest breeze, while the godly are healthy, weighty, fruit-bearing trees. The wicked's sinful lives are the idols they have created for themselves. For all their words, however shrewd they may be, they lack wisdom. Psalm 115:4-5, 8 says, *"Their idols are silver and gold, the work of men's hands. They have mouths, but they do not speak…Those who make them are like them; so is everyone who trusts in them."* (NKJV) The foolish speak spiritually weightless words which carry none of the traits of Heaven nor the wisdom of God. Those who serve idols and their own interests carry nothing of eternal value in their words.

Contrast this with those who *"delight in the law of the Lord"* and contemplate His Word *"day and night"* (Ps. 1:2 NLT). They will have weighty and substantive things to say, because their words come from the very source of wisdom, prudence, knowledge, and insight—from God Himself. Consider what Jeremiah 15:19 says regarding the weight of our words *"…if you speak noble words, rather than worthless ones, you will be My spokesman."* (CSB) God's voice gives us a voice; His wisdom gives us wisdom, and in time, the voice of His wisdom coming through our mouths will set us among the leaders that shape the future.

Kyle Bauer

GOOD NEWS

Proverbs 15:30

"A cheerful look brings joy to the heart;
good news makes for good health." (NLT)

Have you heard the news lately? These days, we hear from television and social media about all the news and happenings in our world, most of which is tragedy and uncertainty. But do not despair; there is hope, no matter how dark it seems.

Proverbs 15:30 reminds us that our attitude toward others will make a difference for good or bad. When somebody is angry or happy, you can see it on their face, and it plays a significant role in how we impact others. For 21 years, my wife and I pastored Mission Hills Foursquare Church. I will never forget when one of my church members asked me if I could give him some time to talk to me privately, so I set up a meeting in the church office. He was very upfront by telling me that I would not want him to be in the church after this conversation. He began by telling me about his past lifestyle before coming to Christ, and he was not proud of it. He felt very ashamed, had already repented, and he wanted to live a life of purity for God. When we finished our meeting, I said, "Brother, I have very good news. If the Lord Jesus has forgiven you, who am I to judge? He left that meeting so happy and renewed because of the good news, a smile, and a hug from his pastor.

Like this man in my congregation, we have our personal baggage and reasons to believe that God would not want us. However, God loves us and always thinks kindly toward us. Turn to Heaven because God is smiling at you.

Ricardo Chaidez

JUST PRAY

Proverbs 29:16

"When the wicked thrive, so does sin,
but the righteous will see their downfall." (NIV)

We are not of this world. Hallelujah!

In John 17, Jesus tells His disciples that He is not of this world, and by way of Him, they (and we) are not either! I am so happy to know that.

It is hard to watch the overwhelming manifestation of sin everywhere you turn. From A to Z, you could name the evil that has permeated our world. But God has called His disciples (us) to live above it all and to pray.

Ephesians 6:13-14 says, *"Therefore, take up the whole armor of God that you may be able to withstand in the evil day and having done all to stand. Stand, therefore…"* (NKJV)

Paul tells us to gird our waist with truth, put on the breastplate of righteousness, wear the preparation of the gospel of peace on our feet, and take up the shield of faith so we will be able to quench the fiery darts of the wicked. He reminds us to always wear the helmet of Salvation and wield the sword of the Spirit, which is the Word of God, and pray! We are called to pray—to make supplication (appeal, petition, request, exhort) in the Spirit, with all perseverance (persistence, tenacity, determination, resolve) for all the saints.

We are called to stand, covered by truth, righteousness, the Gospel of peace, faith, salvation, and the Word of God. That is some pretty heavy-duty, better-than-Kevlar, protection!

Every piece of armor has an enormous part to play in the battle we fight, but we must put it on every day. We do not fight in the flesh but in the Spirit, and our most effective weapon against the forces of darkness is prayer. When we stand covered in the armor of God and pray, we are able to pray in the authority of God's Word and in the power of the Holy Spirit and in the name of Jesus—the name above every other name, and at that name, EVERY knee will bow. We have hope in Jesus, and we know the end of the story. He wins, and we win.

We are not of this world. Hallelujah!

Pat Nannarello

RETURN TO SENDER

Proverbs 11:6

*"The righteousness of the upright delivers them,
but the unfaithful are trapped by evil desires." (NIV)*

Have you ever experienced the power of the Word of God defending you?

Recently, I had to bring a matter to some people's attention. I knew they would not be happy, and I would be the topic of an unpleasant conversation. I texted them and almost immediately could sense a battle in my spirit. It felt like a jumble of thoughts and voices bombarding me like a bad TV show playing in the background.

The reason I had a spiritual sense of what was going on is that just the week before, I experienced an incredible encounter of freedom. The Lord had met me, and as a friend and mentor prayed for me, I felt, and literally saw, my gray skies turn to blue. It was a mountaintop experience right here in the San Fernando Valley!

So, when I felt the swirl of unkind, hateful words against me, I did what God's Word says to do. Isaiah 54:17 instructs us, *"'No weapon formed against you shall prosper, and every tongue which rises against you in judgment You shall condemn. This is the heritage of the servants of the Lord, and their righteousness is from Me,' says the Lord."* (NKJV)

I prayed this scripture and asked the Lord to return those words back to the sender. Immediately, the swirling stopped, and the air was clear again! It was not just the absence of noise; it was the presence of peace.

I am (oh soooo) human, and I miss the mark continually, but I am beginning to understand that I do not have to be perfect and stand in my own right-ness. I am learning to take refuge in the Lord and understand that my righteousness is from Him. It is His righteousness that we stand in and look to Him not only to be our Savior, but also our Defender and our Deliverer.

As we walk humbly with our God, we can appropriate the power of His Word to defend us. When we allow the Lord to be our shield, we are trusting in His power and committing ourselves and our circumstances to Him. We can trust in the goodness and unchanging character of our Heavenly Father.

Michelle Glush

SEPTEMBER

My son,

pay attention to my wisdom;

listen carefully to my wise counsel.

Then you will show discernment,

and your lips will express what you've learned.

For the lips of an immoral woman

are as sweet as honey,

and her mouth is smoother than oil.

But in the end she is as bitter as poison,

as dangerous as a double-edged sword.

—Proverbs 5:1-4

SELF CONTROL...

Proverbs 29:11

*"A fool vents all his feelings,
but a wise man holds them back." (NKJV)*

Out of eight Bible translations that I read, half of them replaced "feelings" with either "rage" or "anger." I believe the original intent of the verse is more correctly stated by the four versions that used "feelings" because they cover a whole host of situations where a hasty word can bring much destruction. Have you ever told a woman you did not like her dress? You can bring much destruction without ever having felt any anger at all. The saying "engage your brain before you engage your mouth" is probably based on Proverbs 29:11. "Think first" is another common phrase that addresses the fact that words spoken cannot be retrieved. By holding your tongue, you may very well prevent a lot of grief for yourself and those around you. I apply another saying to this verse: "Better to keep quiet and have people think you a fool, than to open your mouth and confirm their suspicions." Words spoken in haste are often words that were better left unsaid. In all the Proverbs, I do not recall one verse about it being foolish to ponder a situation before you speak. Still, any type of haste is often associated with foolishness.

The four other translations address fools who vent either "anger" or "rage." The comparison is that the wise hold back on expressing what they are feeling instead of venting. They may eventually speak, but not until they are under control. This more restrained view of the text limits foolishness to anger only. I have known people I agreed with, but when they lost their temper, my opinion of them changed. I did not think of them as fools, but it diminished my respect for them.

On the other hand, I have known many people that just could not control themselves and often spoke inappropriately, using crude speech, crude behavior, speaking out of turn, and not listening to reprimands. Those people I thought of as fools. So, the question to us is: How shall we act and speak, as the wise or the fool?

Martin and Bea Laufer

THE TRAP OF ALCOHOL

Proverbs 20:1

*"Wine produces mockers; alcohol leads to brawls.
Those led astray by drink cannot be wise." (NLT)*

Only a few weeks ago (at the time of this writing), I met a homeless man on the street. As we spoke, he told me of his rather obvious addiction to alcohol.

"When I was a young man," he said, "I would drink and drink and not get drunk. I thought I was invincible. Though I didn't get very drunk, what I didn't know is that it made me an addict."

The man spoke with tears running down his face as his hands began to tremble at the need for the next drink. His shopping cart was filled with recyclable cans, which he was going to cash in so he could assuage his body's violent reaction to the lack of alcohol. "I hate this," he continued. "I want to detox and never drink again, but I can't. My body needs it."

I was moved with compassion for him. I prayed with him, invited him to church, and gave him the name of a local ministry that was more equipped to help him than I was.

Many people have said to me "drinking is not explicitly forbidden in the Bible." I remember the words my father said: "I have never heard a person tell me that alcohol has helped their marriage, family, or personal life get better, but I have heard scores of people tell me how it ruined them." Nothing of wisdom was ever born of alcohol. Three times in the Bible, alcohol and the Spirit are compared:

1. Leviticus 10:1-11: Nadab and Abihu (sons of Aaron, the first High Priest of Israel) were burned up by God's fire because they offered inappropriate fire on the Lord's altar. They were drunk.
2. Acts 2: On the day the disciples were filled with the Holy Spirit, they were accused of being drunk.
3. Ephesians 5:18: Do not be drunk, but rather be filled with the Spirit

Alcohol makes you less than what God intended you to be and does not even allow you to do normal things properly. The filling of the Holy Spirit makes you more than what you are at this moment and capacitates you to do the works of God. It is your choice.

Kyle Bauer

SET THE EXAMPLE

Proverbs 10:1

*"The proverbs of Solomon: A wise son brings joy to his father
but a foolish son brings grief to his mother." (NIV)*

We have all seen "that child," the child out in public that is acting out. The mother becomes grieved because of the child's behavior. Her grief might come from anger, sarcasm, ignoring the situation, or giving in to the child.

Foolishness is bound up in a child, and we are all born with a sinful nature (Prov. 22:15). A foolish child lacks control, is selfish, does what feels good, and demands his own way by behaving rebelliously to get what he wants.

However, a child with wisdom will bring joy. Wisdom shows in choosing right over wrong, showing responsibility, working hard, respecting others, taking correction, and showing honor and respect to parents while fearing God. This behavior will produce joy in the parents and directs a child in the way he should go (Prov. 22:6).

The Scriptures are full of examples of foolishness; just read Proverbs. But we are encouraged to strive to live in wisdom (Prov. 4:5-13). King Solomon, the principal author of the Book of Proverbs, became the wisest man by asking God for wisdom (1 Kings 4:4-14), and God gave it to him in abundance (1 Kings 4:29-34).

This verse is powerful and practical. It is a true observation that we can see in our world today, but does this only apply to children? It includes all the children of God. (2 Cor. 6:18)

How are you living your life?

Have you ever done or said something that has grieved your Father in heaven? Are you choosing your worldly ways over God's ways?

Just as children are born into a sinful nature (Prov. 22:15), we too can find ourselves living in our old sinful nature (1 John 1:8-10). Ask the Father what is in your life that you are holding on to and ask Him for wisdom as you confront your own foolishness.

We do not only teach the young; we set the example.

Jill Alvarado

A DAREDEVIL FOR JESUS

Proverbs 11:14

"Without wise leadership a nation falls,
there is safety in having many advisers." (NLT)

In 2016, my husband and I worked on a television production entitled Heaven Sent. Luke Aikins, a daredevil of sorts and an accomplished skydiver, made an historic jump out of an airplane at 25,000 feet without wearing a parachute! He survived the jump because he landed in a 100'x 100' safety net. Most of the production crew members thought Luke was slightly crazy to attempt the stunt. However, when talking to Luke, he was extremely confident that he would survive the perilous fall. Let's be clear; he didn't wake up one morning and do the jump blindly. This was a carefully planned production. Luke had a team of strategic advisors, skilled engineers, and highly trained skydivers preparing him for his stunt.

Proverbs 11:14 is a lot like Luke's jump. If wisdom is not a part of your life, you will free fall into death. Surrounding yourself with a team of wise and godly advisors provides a safety net to prevent your demise. Even with extensive planning, Luke took a leap of faith, and often we are called to do the same. I'm not saying jump out of a plane without a parachute, but what I am saying is that God gives us a purpose, and we have to be willing to free fall into it.

As we make a choice to jump, we also need to seek wisdom. Wisdom is a free gift, and God will give it to those who ask. James 1:5 (NLT), states, *"If you need wisdom, ask our generous God, and he will give it to you. He will not rebuke you for asking."* As we are granted this gift, we also need to establish lifelong relationships with people who have cultivated a life of Godly wisdom because they hold us accountable to our purpose and provide safety from falling into destruction.

It's okay to be a daredevil for Jesus. Jump into your purpose with wisdom, and He will catch you.

Jennifer Shank

GOOD JUDGMENT GOOD WORDS

Proverbs 13:15

*"Good understanding gains favor,
but the way of the unfaithful is hard." (NKJV)*

The best way to have good judgment is to always listen to the Holy Spirit. But… we don't always do that, do we?

The old me liked being in control and making things happen. There was one time in my life that I was so set on fixing a problem that I stubbornly kept searching and searching for the fix while ignoring the Holy Spirit. My last effort was going to an appointment with a Ph.D. to have him tell me what to do. That was a waste of time. When I left, I started laughing and said, "Okay, God, I'm done. I know You know that I needed to do this, but now I know I should have listened to You in the first place!" Over my life, I have had to say that way too many times!

"Good understanding gains favor" can be interpreted as "obedience to the Word of God will be blessed." God didn't write the Bible for Himself. He wrote it for us! When we are disobedient to His rules, even unconsciously, God will not bless the work of our hands. You've heard the saying, "My way or the highway." Well, if you insist on doing it your way, God will watch you walk down that frustrating highway!

In Matthew 25:21 Jesus says, "…*well done, good and faithful servant, you have been faithful with a few things, I will put you in charge of many.*" When we use good judgment, with faithfulness and humility, in working with God and the wisdom He gives, it will result in His blessings.

When we consciously make the Word of God part of the fabric of our being (practice, practice, practice), we gain wisdom and understanding, which then translates to good judgment. The more I read the Bible, and Proverbs in particular, I feel that God is ingraining His Word into me. Get wisdom, get understanding, pay attention, do it My way, and be blessed. The path is so much easier when we do it His way.

Pat Nannarello

THE FINISHED WORK OF JESUS CHRIST

Proverbs 11:21

*"Though hand join in hand, the wicked shall not be unpunished,
but the seed of the righteous shall be delivered." (KJV)*

Punishment is something that people do not like to talk about very much. This is because, especially in today's culture, many westernized or "modern" societies have significantly lowered their moral and ethical standards. As a result, there is a desire to make everything "not a crime" and thus eliminate the need to administer punishment.

Proverbs 11:21 starts with "hand-in-hand" referring to how evildoers will partner up. Evil men and women often feel that by joining together, evil will prevail. Evil men conspire to reach a point of spiritual accomplishment while rebelling against God Himself. This joining of hands reminds us of the biblical story of building the tower of Babel. Though their work was organized and their gains were notable to men and God, their project and conspiracy came to ruin, and God's authority prevailed!

There is, however, a second part to the scripture, which is very good news—the righteous descendants will be delivered. Because of God's promises, the righteous will be rescued from the wrath to come. God promises that He will deliver the seed of the righteous. Though God will destroy wickedness, His grace will cause the righteous to be saved from judgment and wrath. The type of righteousness discussed here and throughout the Scriptures is not self-righteousness but righteousness by faith in the Lamb of God who was slain on our behalf. Again, this righteousness is not based on our works but rather on the perfect and finished work of Jesus Christ upon the cross. We are delivered because of that righteousness.

Jose Nolasco

HIS WORD IS ETERNAL AND TRUE

Proverbs 17:4

"A wicked person listens to deceitful lips;
a liar pays attention to a destructive tongue." (NIV)

This verse immediately brings to mind the picture of Jafar in the movie "Aladdin." Jafar, the advisor to the Sultan, was a wicked man obsessed with power. As the Sultan's advisor, he would bring him under his wicked spell of deception to manipulate the circumstances to his benefit.

Deception, like the spell in the story above, is used by evil people for manipulation and their own personal gain. When people are deceived, they do not see things clearly, and can, at best, be taken advantage of and, at worst, end up following a wicked path. Liars give their attention to destructive advice, and they cannot see their own downfall coming. A pathological liar believes his own lies and cannot distinguish it from the truth.

People who lie and deceive do not realize they are contributing to their destruction. Their lies destroy relationships, reputations, and people's lives. Ask the Holy Spirit for discernment and stop listening to those who purposefully lie and deceive, no matter the source. When you look at what they say through the lens of God's Word, you will be able to divide the good from the evil and see their words and intentions for what they truly are. Seek truth, because the truth will set you free.

God will never deceive us. His Word is eternal, true, powerful, and eternally relevant. So, let's make sure we feed our spirit daily. If we fill ourselves with the Word of God, we will recognize the lies coming at us.

Stephen Larkin

WORDS BUILD OR DESTROY LIVES

Proverbs 30:14

*"There is a generation rising that uses their words like swords
to cut and slash those who are different.
They would devour the poor, the needy,
and the afflicted from off the face of the earth!" (TPT)*

Confession: Though personally I would not say I like drama, I know a natural sinful leaning of mine is instigation. Instigation alone is not evil, as instigation can push people to victory, but the sinful version is to push people into anything. In the hype of a throwdown, my temptation is to be the one shock-faced and yelling, "Ohhhh!! HE SAID WHAT!! Aww naw!!! That ain't it!"

So today, I want to push you away from foolish tendencies and to be a resolver, not a revolver. A revolver has a chamber for bullets. When the chamber of a problem clicks into place, be the first person to turn on the safety and stop that problem from firing. I guarantee you that when a "beef" (disunity and strife) starts between two, the moment it gets bigger, friendly fire and hateful shrapnel will go everywhere you did not intend. Fix it immediately.

Sometimes the greatest acts of valor are closing the mouth, waiting, working through the uncomfortable tension of miscommunications, and pressing through the issue until it is resolved. You may have to take breaks. It may take years. You may face ugliness in your own heart. You might cry. Do whatever it takes to be a resolver.

The above, of course, does not apply to abuse. If you are in danger, involve someone immediately for security and do all you can to escape that situation. Otherwise, always be at peace with people where peace can be achieved. If not, remove yourself from those choosing a lifestyle of anger and disruption. Be quick draw resolvers.

Rachael Hopkins

A STURDY FOUNDATION

Proverbs 16:17

"The highway of the upright is to depart from evil;
he who keeps his way preserves his soul." (NKJV)

When you think of a highway, what are some of your initial thoughts? Do you think about driving, going on a road trip, or traffic? Typically, a highway is used as a solid ground for modes of transportation. It is also used to travel from one location to another. However, when put into the context of Proverbs 16:17, God has formed unique highways for each of us. These roads are built on solid ground, so they are sturdy foundations for us to walk on. Our lives are preserved when we depart from evil and travel along the highway God has designed for us.

On my birthday one year, my mom and I decided to go on a hiking trip. We did not realize that the trail we chose would prove to be a rocky and steep decline. As we were stumbling downhill, we saw a smooth paved road that led directly to our destination while the rocky slope treacherously continued downwards. We had the choice of whether we would stay on the hiking path and risk injury or choose a stable road that led us directly to our destination.

God allows us to choose whether or not we want to walk along the highway He has designated for us. We can choose to remain in a place conformed to this world, or we can choose a highway that is God appointed. Another translation of Proverbs 16:17 states, *"The road of right living bypasses evil..."* (MSG) Living right, according to God's Word, is departing from evil and sin and continually seeking God on *the* plans He has for us, plans to prosper us and not to harm us, plans to give us hope and a future. (Jeremiah 29:11) God's direction for our lives is like a GPS. Following and obeying His directions and guidance preserves our lives, because it leads us away from evil and toward a prosperous future that brings us hope.

Amelia Montantes

BE A KING

Proverbs 29:14 (NKJV)

"The king who judges the poor with truth,
His throne will be established forever." (NKJV)

See GOD. GOD – THE CREATOR OF THE UNIVERSE – THE CREATOR OF MANKIND is the perfect example of a king who judges the poor with truth and whose throne is established forever.

See KING. The word KING is equivalent to someone in authority.

The word POOR doesn't just refer to a lack of money. It can mean poor in spirit. Poor in wisdom. Poor in productivity.

The word TRUTH means facts, reality.

See JESUS.

Isaiah prophesies about Jesus in verse 11:3-4: *"…He will not judge by what He sees with His eyes or decide by what He hears with His ears, but with righteousness, He will judge the needy, with justice He will give decisions for the poor of the earth…." (NIV)*

Jesus' life sets the example of how to lead and live for all of us. He was about His Father's business. He treated people equally with respect and compassion. He spoke the truth to every situation. He did unto others the way He expected others to treat Him.

As disciples of Jesus, we have inherited God-given authority. God also places us in positions of leadership. Therefore, we must be like Jesus and be about our Father's business. We must learn to have compassion and understanding, to treat all people with respect, integrity, and recognize their value just as we would have them treat us. This is not easy. Trying to be like Jesus is a daily challenge. A daily commitment. A daily struggle. If you want to be like Jesus, you have to work at it (work, work, work). But the reward is greater than the effort.

When people are treated properly and justly, they are happy to serve under your leadership and will respect you for it.

Pat Nannarello

LET'S ROLL

Proverbs 22:8

*"Those who plant injustice will harvest disaster,
and their reign of terror will come to an end." (NLT)*

The title, famous words spoken by Todd Beamer, is a call to action. On September 11, 2001, he and several other passengers were on United Airlines Flight 93 headed for San Francisco when their plane was hijacked by terrorists intending to fly it into either the White House or The Capitol building.[1] The plane went down in a field near Shanksville, Pennsylvania, killing everyone on board. But these brave souls, who decided not to be pawns in this wicked scheme, had the courage to fight the evil that took over their flight. They gave up their lives to stop the terrorists and saved this country from further destruction and devastation.

We may or may not be called upon to give our lives in such a way, but we are called to be soldiers in the army of God. We do not fight against flesh and blood; we are called to fight on our knees. In 2 Chronicles 20,[2] the armies of Moab and Ammon came to wage war against Judah and King Jehoshaphat. Judah was outnumbered and faced the annihilation of every man, woman, and child. As they all came before the Lord, King Jehoshaphat gave an impassioned prayer for all the people. The Lord heard their prayer and answered them through Jahaziel, saying, *"Do not be afraid or discouraged…For the battle is not yours, but God's."* (NIV) When Judah went to battle, they watched as the Lord set an ambush and defeated their enemy.

Let's pray for the Church to come alive! It is time for us to seek God with all our hearts, plead for righteousness to be restored, and for souls to be saved. Let's be the Bride that Jesus is looking for when He comes again!

So, as we think about and honor the courage of the passengers of Flight 93 and all of the first responders on 9/11 who gave their lives to save others and take down evil, let's get on our knees and ask for victory in the battle against evil. Let's be courageous, and as in Todd's last words, "Are you guys ready? Let's roll…."

Michelle Glush

1　　https://www.thenewportbuzz.com/9-11-the-todd-beamer-story-lets-roll/31886
2　　Read the full chapter—you will be encouraged.

DOES GOD LOVE YOU MORE THAN OTHERS?

Proverbs 24:17

*"Don't rejoice when your enemies fall; don't be happy when they stumble.
For the Lord will be displeased with you
and will turn his anger away from them." (NLT)*

This proverb reveals something very sensitive about God's heart toward us. In our sinfulness and lack of understanding of God's heart, we tend toward an attitude of "I'm good and righteous, and God loves me, and God hates everyone else not like me, so GET 'EM, GOD!"

Years ago, I had been wronged by someone. Long after we parted ways, I heard this person was not doing well. I was startled by my reaction—it was gladness. I was in a good place, and this other person was not—proof of God's favor, I'd say. Something within me liked it, but my gladness quickly turned to shame. I felt dirty and unworthy as a child of God. I knew I was wrong. My woundedness still wanted vengeance and satisfaction. I wanted my pound of flesh; I wanted blood.

I had been wronged, but who was more in the wrong now? This scripture tells us that such an attitude puts us even more at odds with God. His displeasure falls on us, and His anger turns away from the person we are angry with! When someone wrongs us, what makes us believe that God wants our well-being at the expense of someone else's failure? Why do our woundedness, self-righteousness, pride, and blood-lust somehow make it right that another person should fail? Are those God's feelings toward the other person? Does He really love you more than He loves him or her?

Of course not. The Bible says that God does not rejoice in the death of the wicked. He rejoices in the redemption of relationships and when people repent and live.[3] We want our pound of flesh. We want another's blood for our woundedness, but God's heart is the opposite. He was wounded in the flesh for our sins, and He gave His blood for our offenses and to heal us.[4] Should we not adopt the same attitude? What relationship do you need to make right?

Kyle Bauer

---

3   Ezekiel 33:11
4   Isaiah 53:4-5

STEADY DECREASE VS. STEADY INCREASE

Proverbs 13:11

"Wealth gained dishonestly dwindles away,
but he who gathers by hand makes it grow." (WEB)

The Book of Proverbs continually emphasizes the importance of discipline in all things, including the way in which one accumulates wealth. Not only does this verse refer to the diminishing returns of dishonest gain, but also wealth gotten by *"vanity"* (KJV)—literally *a breath* or *nothingness*. This refers to methods that are hasty, effortless, or worthless. Thus, the familiar phrase: "Easy come, easy go." The way one accumulates is typically the way one spends.

However, the person who gathers little by little—literally, *with the hand*—shall increase. Building wealth steadily requires patience, diligence, and long-term saving and investing. It means a daily commitment to cultivating and stewarding one's hard-earned income that not only builds a personal inheritance, but also an abundance to share with others.

"Anyone who has been stealing must steal no longer, but must work, doing something useful with their own hands, that they may have something to share with those in need." (Eph. 4:28, NIV)

As followers of Christ, let us not squander our time and energy in worthless endeavors that only serve to feed pride and luxury. Any such gains would only dwindle away. Instead, let us bring glory to God by making an honest living, working wholeheartedly, as unto the Lord.

"May the favor of the Lord our God rest on us; establish the work of our hands for us—yes, establish the work of our hands." (Ps. 90:17, NIV)

Karen Heimbuch

LET YOUR REPUTATION SPEAK FOR YOU

Proverbs 27:2

*"Let another man praise you, and not your own mouth;
a stranger, and not your own lips." (NKJV)*

It is a healthy thing to have a positive view of yourself. Romans 12:3 says not to think more highly of ourselves than we ought—but we should not think more lowly of ourselves either! If our self-worth is based on God's view of us, then we will live out that confidence and strength. But the words from others about your character are more powerful than anything you could ever say about yourself. Praising yourself is not an unbiased opinion and certainly will not place you in the "humble" category.

If I learned anything from working in television, it is that people will often present a fake persona that puts themselves in the best light—and we often do the same. However, the people who do life with us will know who we really are. This is why, despite social media, where we can find out quite a bit about someone online prior to ever meeting them, recommendations are still king in business because there is no witness like others who have known the real you. It is always wise just to be yourself in every situation, and the best version of yourself is the one who is accurately reflecting the love of Jesus all the time!

Rachael Hopkins

CHECK-IN WITH GOD

Proverbs 14:12

"There is a way that appears to be right,
but in the end it leads to death." (NIV)

Have you ever told yourself, "I really thought I was making the right decision," only after realizing it was clearly not a wise decision? You meant well; you really thought it seemed like the right decision to make.

Proverbs 14:12 conveys how what is perceived as right may not actually be the way to go. Just because it seems right doesn't mean it is right. This verse goes on to say how one course of action can lead to death. This isn't to say that making a wrong decision can lead to instantaneous death. Some decisions, however, can cost us so much that they cause much destruction. This proverb is advising us that often-times the lens from which we see, and through which we make decisions, is not always in focus with what God would want us to do. Asking God, leaning on God, trusting God, surrendering to God, praying to God—all these actions on our part will focus our lens from which we make decisions on a daily basis.

There have been times in my life when I wanted to act on impulse, in current con-text, or from pain and hurt. It has been during those times that surrendering to God's will has been challenging, and yet the peace that comes from that surrender makes it worth choosing His way over what my emotion felt. When I have made the wrong decision, God has always been there to restore, forgive, and lead me for-ward. However, the older I get, the less I want to learn the hard way, and the more I am willing to pause and check in with God to see what I should do. That requires time and patience, but it is always worth it.

Cynthia Medrano

HUNGERING FOR GOD

Proverbs 27:7

*"A person who is full refuses honey,
but even bitter food tastes sweet to the hungry." (NLT)*

Have you ever been to an "all you can eat" buffet? Even if you have not, I am sure you have experienced the feeling of being so full you could not take another bite. What if you applied that to your life and even your spiritual life? Could it be possible that we have become so blind to the blessings we have that we grumble and forget that there are people in the world who would do anything to be in our positions?

My upbringing was not the best, however, my family still had a roof overhead, clothing, food, shoes, and even extras, such as toys, television, video games, bikes, etc. After traveling to Mexico for the first time, I became extremely thankful for all the things we took for granted in America.

Proverbs 27:7 speaks of people who are too full to consume even honey and those so hungry that even bitter food tastes sweet. However, when a person's life is so full of accumulated things, be it physical things or knowledge, those things can be taken for granted, and we end up forsaking meaningful things of value. We can become so full of things to fill our lives that they can take the place of hunger for deeper things in life, like God's presence. Those who are too full will miss out on the sweetness of God, but those who are hungry will not.

Sometimes in life, especially in America, we find our lives full of material things, relationships, and even head knowledge of the Bible. We need to be careful that head knowledge does not take the place of hungering for the things of God. So, let's become people who constantly seek for the things of God!

Victor Miguel Rivera

LOVE FORGIVES

Proverbs 17:9

"Love prospers when a fault is forgiven,
but dwelling on it separates close friends." (NLT)

The God kind of love is not what we see in the world today. The world is fickle in how they show love—they will love you one day and not the next. Or they love you for what you have or what you can do for them. They pretend to love you and forgive you but always remind you of your shortcomings. This is the world's deficient interpretation of love, and it never fully forgives. By continually bringing up your faults, they try to keep you in the chains of their bondage.

But the God-kind of love is different. Romans 5:8 says, *"…God showed his great love for us by sending Christ to die for us while we were still sinners."* (NLT) What a beautiful picture of God's love! Jesus became the sacrificial lamb to take away the sins of the world. It was because of His love for God and His love for us that Jesus gave His life to die on the cross for our sins. His obedience reconciled us back to God our Father even while we were still His enemies (Phil. 2:5-8), and God's love continues to reach out to all people so that He can reconcile all to Himself. God said that when He forgave us, *"He…removed our sins as far from us as the east is from the west."* (Ps. 103:12, NLT) In Hebrews 8:12, He also says, *"…I will forgive their wickedness, and I will never again remember their sins."* (NLT)

God's love abounds towards us, and in that love, He forgives our faults. Should we not also forgive the faults of others so that God's love can abound to them? God's love and forgiveness need to be the foundation of any relationship: marriage, family, or friendship. Who can you prosper by forgiving a fault?

P.S. Read Psalm 103; it will be refreshing to your soul!

Debbie Speese

PAUSE AND TAKE A BREATH

Proverbs 30:33

*"For as churning cream produces butter,
and as twisting the nose produces blood,
so stirring up anger produces strife." (NIV)*

Anger comes and goes. It is often a gut response to pain, unmet expectations, or insults. When someone we love reacts in anger, we have a choice. We can react and do precisely the same by responding with more anger and watching it swirl out of control while building up strife. But it does not have to be that way. Knowing that the results of stirring up anger are as sure as churning cream results in butter can give us insight.

I always have a choice. I have found that I can pause and take a breath before responding when loved ones erupt in anger, whining, or screaming. When I pray and ask the Holy Spirit for help, He always shows up to offer guidance and resolution. Comparing the results of the same situation when I pray and when I do not, I can see a big difference. Stirring up anger never leads us to feel closer or resolves our issues. Everyone leaves feeling hurt, angry, and not heard. Praying leaves room for the Holy Spirit, and His redemptive work and good things always result.

Heavenly Father, help me to see what is happening amid anger and to be quick to turn to You for help. I know You will come through for me and bring about something good I cannot do in my flesh.

Stephen Larkin

A CALL TO ACTION

Proverbs 21:21

"Whoever pursues righteousness and love finds life,
prosperity and honor." (NIV)

This verse is a call to action.

To pursue is a verb—an action word—and we are called to pursue righteousness and love.

Righteousness is not something we can produce in ourselves. We cannot change our behavior enough to produce righteousness. We cannot do enough good works to produce righteousness. We cannot even give enough to produce righteousness in our lives. However, in faith, accepting Christ as God's Son, believing Jesus died on the cross for our sins, and being in a relationship with Christ while following His Word, we can be made righteous in God. (Phil. 3:9)

Daily, we need to walk with Christ. We should always be in communion with Christ, day by day, hour by hour, moment by moment. Turning away from our natural, sinful desires and turning to Christ and His perfect and righteous ways is a constant work we should cultivate in ourselves. This requires a life of intentional discipline.

Through our consistent pursuit of righteousness and practicing righteousness in our daily lives, we will be blessed as promised in Matthew 5:6: *"Blessed are those who hunger and thirst for righteousness, for they shall be filled." (NKJV)*

Love is also a verb—an action word—and our pursuit of love should be just as engaging in us as our pursuit of righteousness. 1 Corinthians 13:13b tells us, "But the greatest of these is love." Therefore, we must work at loving those around us and showing God our love by putting Him first in our lives through prayer and intimacy with Him, worshiping and honoring Him daily.

Practicing these disciplines daily brings life, prosperity, and honor into our lives through the blessings and power of God.

Consider this verse as you go about your day. Are you walking in righteousness and love, or are other things being allowed to take center stage in your life? Ask the Lord where you can walk closer with Him and see how much more your life overflows with His blessings.

Jill Alvarado

299

GOD'S MATH

Proverbs 11:24

*"There is one who scatters, yet increases more;
and there is one who withholds more than is right,
but it leads to poverty." (NKJV)*

God's math does not work like our math does. That sounds strange because doesn't 2+2 equal 4 in Heaven too? It is not that addition and multiplication are different; there are spiritual principles that release or withhold God's blessing in our lives. These principles do not change the math; they *allow* Heaven's multiplication to happen.

We have been taught to save our money (addition), invest, and earn interest over our lifetime (multiply) to be secure in our old age. There is, however, a spiritual principle hidden in nature that helps us understand how Heaven's money and math work: Giving.

It is counter-intuitive to give a tithe (10%) to the Lord, give an offering on top of the tithe, and expect to be financially viable in this inflation-ridden world we live in. Most people view the tithe as God getting His share of the apple: We think of it as cutting the apple into 10 slices. Nine for me, and one for Him (and sometimes a missionary comes to church, and we will occasionally give a second slice to God, because, well, I guess He needs it.)

Not exactly.

Some of the best tithers are farmers. They understand Heaven's math principles better than most. If they harvest their crops, eat some of them and sell all the rest, what will they have to sow for the next season? Nothing! They *must* give a portion for seed. This is the same as in Heaven's math. God cuts the apple differently. The fruit is for us to eat, and He wants the core that contains the seed. It is in the seed that you sow (give to God) that you will reap in multiplication. You can count the number of seeds in an apple, but you cannot count the number of apples in a seed!

In its simplicity, this proverb is very profound: if we give, life will multiply. If we keep everything for ourselves, there will never be multiplication. An easy maxim to remember is this: Do not sow your bread (what God gives you to live on), and don't eat your seed (the tithe)!

Kyle Bauer

A HANDFUL OF THORNS

Proverbs 26:9

"Like a thornbush in a drunkard's hand
is a proverb in the mouth of a fool." (NIV)

That's not going to end well. Thornbush + drunkard = failure. I do not know about you, but I have seen a few drunkards in my time. So, picture this! You have a highly inebriated individual, and they are holding a thornbush. That doesn't make any sense. Neither does a proverb from a fool.

A drunkard has little to no sensitivity to what they are doing or the damage they are causing to themselves, let alone others. They go around with the thornbush thinking it is a bouquet of flowers. So it goes with the fool interpreting a proverb. In their mind, they possess all the knowledge to interpret said proverb. But what comes out of their mouth is complete nonsense.

Romans 12:3 says, *"…do not think of yourself more highly than you ought, but rather think of yourself with sober judgment, in accordance with the faith that God has distributed to each of you."* (NIV) Unfortunately, too many times in my life, I have become drunk on myself. In other words, I think I'm all that and then some. In those times, I have had the Holy Spirit say to me, "Hey bro, you're not that important or wise," which caused me to begin using sober judgment.

It's like people waking up with a hangover. They wake up with a bad headache, feel sick, smell of vomit, and are left wondering, "what did I do?" They have no recollection of the past 24 hours. It looks like they walked around with a thornbush. They did not use sober judgment.

Interpreting a proverb takes sound judgment and knowledge of God's word. Therefore, we must take the time to understand and apply it to our lives. 2 Timothy 2:15 says, *"Do your best to present yourself to God as one approved, a worker who is not ashamed and who correctly handles the word of truth."* (NIV)

In closing, soberness + God's Word = success. Do not be the drunk fool with the thornbush. Instead, be the sober individual coming into a full understanding of God's Word and correctly handling the word of truth.

Drinks are not served here, nor do we keep thornbushes, just a tall refreshing glass of God's Word.

Fred Alvarado

301

BUILD NOT DESTROY

Proverbs 14:1

"A wise woman builds a house
and the foolish woman destroys it with her hands."
(Aramaic Bible in Plain English)

How can a woman destroy her own house? That seems to be an unimaginable thought that someone would deliberately destroy her own home, but it happens more often than we think. We, as women, can become so busy that we stop attending to our relationship with God. The Bible calls wives and mothers to be stewards of their homes on behalf of their husbands, who are the "head." How we do that has many implications. We must be wise like the woman of Proverbs 31. She applied wisdom in the construction of her house, her family prospered, her husband was respected in the community, and her family loved and praised her for everything she did. She lovingly raised her children with her husband and handled the details in her own home with gentleness and godliness (1 Peter 3:4). This, in turn, made her family prosperous, healthy, and filled with love.

But instead, a foolish woman allows her family to fall apart, and her own hands will be to blame. She does not take responsibility for her shortcomings but blames her husband and children. She does not work hard to provide for her family's needs but attends to herself above anything else. She scolds her husband for not earning enough money, nags at him for the things he does not do, and complains about him and the children. All this will bring discord and destruction. This does not mean that she is solely responsible for the problems in the home. The husband does also hold responsibility for the health of the family.

As women, we need to appropriate the wisdom of God's Word to obey and fulfill everything He calls us to do, just as the woman of Proverbs 31. Godly women do not give credence to the current feminist culture that disparages women who submit to God and their husbands. Instead, they choose God's Word and draw close to Him. Then we will find that applying His Word and wisdom will bring about the fulfillment of a healthy and fruitful home, our primary God-given responsibility.

Teresa Bauer

NO WORK, NO LIFE

Proverbs 21:25

"The craving of a sluggard will be the death of him,
because his hands refuse to work." (NIV)

Why do we crave the things that hurt us or even kill us? Why are we self-destructive? One answer is that without Christ as our Savior, we have no life. We are dead anyway. Ephesians 2:1 refers to man as dead in trespasses and sins without Christ. Contrarily, the Apostle Paul, in his dissertation to the church at Rome, notes that by participating in (believing in) the death of Christ, we now walk in "newness of life." (Rom. 6:4).

Solomon counsels us to be aware that the sluggard, the one who is innately lazy, dispassionate, and lacking initiative, craves what will kill him. Another translation notes that lazy people finally die of hunger, because they will not get up and go to work (Prov. 21:25, TMB). What does a sluggard crave? To do nothing. To be passionate about nothing. Sluggards sleep too much, are repulsed by work, and/or the constructive use of time. Some have said they find literal movement repulsive. Surely this is eventually deadly. Essentially and functionally, in the end, sluggards crave death.

Furthermore, Solomon speaks in a context of the sluggard being completely devoid of self-control. He speaks of the hands of a sluggard as though they are not attached to their body, or for certain, the sluggard has no control of his hands since they (their hands) "refuse to work." It is almost as if their hands have a mind of their own. Theoretically, a sluggard could suddenly desire to eat, but his hands may refuse to feed him. Interesting. In context, the sluggard lacks the self-discipline, intestinal fortitude, and gumption to get going and keep going in order to do what needs to be done—including eating (Prov. 26:15). They lack it so much as to cause their own death. Perhaps this is why Solomon also wrote, *"Whatever your hands find to do, do it with all of your might."* (Eccl. 9:10) Let's choose to be strong in the Lord and in the power of His might! (Eph. 6:10)

Lloyd Speese

303

OUR PLANS VERSUS GOD'S PLANS...

Proverbs 19:21

"Many are the plans in a person's heart,
but it is the Lord's purpose that prevails." (NIV)

What then? Should we not even try to plan? Trust me; King Solomon did not look down on planning! He understood that our Almighty and Omniscient God has a purpose for our lives. So, the underlying concept of this Proverb is that when we plan, we should understand that we are called according to His purpose. If we have godly plans that make room for God's adjustments, then planning is not in vain.

One of Solomon's brothers (Adonijah) wanted to become king before his father relinquished the throne. He created elaborate plans that, in human terms, sound wise and sure. However, he did not factor in that God has a purpose, and God's purpose will always prevail.

Adonijah's plan was exposed and stopped. Solomon was crowned king. Even then, Adonijah did not stop and plotted further to become king instead of Solomon. The result was that he was executed. Surely that was not the outcome that Adonijah expected.

Eons ago, when I was a young newlywed in college, I had plans for my life. I was an art major and expected to go into commercial art as an illustrator and marketing designer. I was good at what I did and saw a clear path ahead of me. I did not invite God into my planning and assumed He would bless whatever I chose to do. Two things happened in the world that changed my plans permanently: 1) Computers became smaller in size, faster, and able to pump out design work faster, cheaper, and as good as humans could. 2) Much of the work went to Taiwan because they could do it cheaper, and by using computers, the file could be sent to the U.S. in a flash. Unfortunately, I was not trained in computers or computer art. I was a dinosaur. I know now that God's purpose for my life was not based on what I do but on who I am. The more I look to His purpose in the way I live my life, the less I butt heads with the Almighty. Proverbs 19:21 would have been great to use as a guide early on in my life, but I have found out that it is never too late.

Martin and Bea Laufer

WITHOUT VISION THE PEOPLE PERISH

Proverbs 29:18

"Where there is no vision, the people perish:
but he that keepeth the law, happy is he." (KJV)

In our American way of thinking, this famous passage would seem to indicate that it is a specific life trajectory that people need, or in other words to have a "vision" for your life. We ask questions such as, "What is your vision of the future?" or "What is your vision for you for the next ten years?" Many will quote this verse. However, this is not what this is speaking of.

The Hebrew word here is Châtzōn, which means revelation or vision from God. The root word (Châzâh) is literally the insights of a seer or prophet.[5] For instance, David uses this same word in Psalm 27:4, saying that the one thing he desires is to "gaze" upon the Lord or to "have revelation" of God. David was the greatest king of Israel. Yet for the man who had *everything,* the *only* thing he wanted was revelation of God. Perhaps that is why he was the greatest king.

It is interesting to note that what keeps a nation at peace is when there is understanding of who God is. When people lose sight of this, the moral and spiritual fiber of the nation deteriorates rapidly. One translation puts it this way. *"If a nation is not guided by God, the people will lose self-control, but the nation that obeys God's law will be happy."*[6] We are seeing this happen to our country at this moment. We suffer not for a lack of desire to advance but for a lack of revelation of who God is.

Moses understood this principle. In Exodus 33:13 and 18, he says these words to God, *"let me know your ways so I may understand you more fully and continue to enjoy your favor….show me Your glory."* (NLT) He asked God to show him more of Himself so he can understand Him better, serve Him better, and continue to find greater favor in His eyes. In an even more spectacular revelation, John 1:14, in talking about God revealing Himself in Jesus Christ, says, *"…and we beheld His glory, the glory as of the only begotten of the Father, full of grace and truth."* (NKJV) The revelation of Jesus is what every person needs.

Kyle Bauer

---

5   Blue Letter Bible, Genesis' Hebrew-Chaldee Lexicon (part (2)) under Strongs 2372 "châzâh"
     https://www.blueletterbible.org/lexicon/h2372/kjv/wlc/0-1/ (Accessed 8/26/2022)
6   Easy-to-Read Version (ERV) Copyright © 2006 by Bible League International

GOD PROTECTS THE RIGHTEOUS

Proverbs 12:21

"No harm overtakes the righteous,
but the wicked have their fill of trouble." (NIV)

To be honest with you, when I read this proverb, I had a hard time believing it.

I have seen plenty of people who walk in the "right" way go through troubles and harm, and those walking in a "perverse" way doing well for themselves. But it is important to understand that God's scales of justice and definition of blamelessness are not the same as ours.

The term blameless, at its face value, means "not responsible for." The term perverse essentially means something that is twisted against God's will. So, in the most practical sense, if you stay out of trouble, you won't be harmed by the consequences of it. If you are not hanging out where trouble is, or with people who perpetuate trouble, you will not have to worry about trouble's consequences.

We do not always know the "behind-the-scenes" story of most situations. The closest information we typically have is soundbites and video clips. For example, you can watch a performer on stage who seems perfectly happy, but backstage is suicidally miserable—you do not always know the whole story. You can see godless people gaining traction and what appears to be blessings and favor in their lives, while godly people seem to suffer. However, behind the scenes, God is working with character issues, even in the midst of the suffering. But the ease of wickedness never produces godliness. In the end, godliness is what will last forever.

So, no matter what happens in this world, trust that the righteous will ultimately be saved from this life filled with evil and that no one walking against God's ways will carry on forever. Be unshakeable in God's truth.

Rachael Hopkins

HEAVENLY TREASURE HUNT

Proverbs 25:2

"It is the glory of God to conceal a matter,
but the glory of kings is to search out a matter." (NKJV)

"Your Word is a lamp unto my feet, and a light to my path."—Psalm 119:105

When I was young, I used to love movies about finding buried treasure…go here…follow the dotted line…x marks the spot! We all know that in real life it is not that easy. (Anyone who has watched an Indiana Jones movie knows that x never marks the spot!)

But God has hidden treasure in His Word for us to search out and find. There are some matters he has concealed in Scripture that require us to dig a little deeper to understand. Scriptures that do not seem to make sense suddenly come alive when we find the key that unlocks the mystery. That key is always found somewhere else in the Bible. Scripture is best explained by scripture itself.

So how do you find buried treasure?

First, you need a map. In this adventure, you do not have to look far, because the map is the Word of God! And even more importantly, you have the Mapmaker to guide you. Ask God to meet you in His Word, and He will be delighted to open the treasure of heaven to you. Ask Him questions, seek out His hidden gems, and watch as He opens your eyes to the wisdom of His Word.

Second, the proverb says that it is the glory of *kings* to search out a matter. In days of old, it was usually a king or queen who directed the explorer to search for new worlds or the treasures of other lands. In Revelation 5:10, the Mapmaker, our Heavenly Father, has made us to be *"kings and priests to our God…"* and He is directing us, His Kings and Priests, to dig deep to find the treasures He has buried there for us to find.

And what will you unearth when you find "x marks the spot"? Will you find silver or gold? Something even better. You will find life, wisdom, knowledge, understanding, health, peace, joy, His unfailing love, and the most important treasure of all, a relationship with your Heavenly Father.

Wisdom is far greater than treasure and more valuable than rubies. Proverbs 8:11

Michelle Glush

307

LOVING DISCIPLINES

Proverbs 11:2

"Pride leads to disgrace, but with humility comes wisdom." (NLT)

I am sure you remember being disciplined as a child. So do I. Of course, no one likes being disciplined, but it is necessary to keep you humble before the Lord and others.

To be humble is to give your life to God and let Him transform it through correction. Through His correction, we become humble, and with humility comes wisdom.

King David, in Psalms 19:7, writes, *"The instructions of the Lord are perfect, reviving the soul. The decrees of the Lord are trustworthy, making wise the simple."* (NIV)

The proud reject God and His discipline, refusing to put their life in God's hands because of their arrogance, and preferring to live in sin and disgrace. But just as a father disciplines his child, so will the Lord to whoever wants to give their lives to Him.

The author writes in Hebrews 12:7-9, *"As you endure this divine discipline, remember that God is treating you as His own children. Whoever heard of a child who is never disciplined by his or her father? If God does not discipline you as He does all of His children, it means that you are illegitimate and are not His children at all. Since we respected our earthly fathers who disciplined us, shouldn't we submit even more to the discipline of the Father of our spirits and live forever?"* (NLT)

It is through the Father's discipline that the humble become wise. If my father did not discipline me as a child, I would not be the man I am today. I remember feeling angry at him after some hard discipline, but he would always tell me afterward that he did not do it out of anger, but he did it out of love—the love that teaches right from wrong and repentance and restoration. The Lord does the same with all His children. But it all depends on us. Are we willing to accept discipline or reject God's dealing with us?

Joshua Bauer

TWO WELLS

Proverbs 14:27

*"The fear of the Lord is a fountain of life,
turning a person from the snares of death." (NIV)*

In high school, I had the opportunity, just like everyone else, to get in trouble, make wrong decisions, and do dumb things. I suppose doing dumb things is inevitable in High School, and wrong decisions are part of growing up and maturing. Getting into trouble, however, involves a level of intentionality that simply doing wrong things may not exhibit. I specifically remember making certain decisions not to do certain things that most certainly would have gotten me in trouble with perhaps some far-reaching consequences. The reason I chose not to participate in those things was simple: fear of my parents. I am not talking about the fear of them beating me, but the fear of losing their trust, the fear of disappointing the very people who had given me so much, and the fear of being an ingrate who, by my wrong actions, would shove all their godly upbringing back in their faces. I decided I did not want to be that person.

The fear of the Lord does the same for us, and it keeps us from the traps of death that would jeopardize our future and our relationship with Him. The Message Translation renders the second part of this verse as, *"so you won't go off drinking from poisoned wells."* Fearing the Lord and living by His Word and Spirit promises that we will have a "fountain of living water" bubbling up from our innermost being (John 7:37-39).

We have the choice of which fountain we will drink from: living wells or poisoned wells. One promises life and the other death. The choices of which of these fountains we will drink from are found in our daily decisions. Cultivate a friendship with the Lord and know His Word. As we do, the fear of the Lord grows, and we will desire to please Him in all we do, resulting in decisions that flow from a fountain of life and blessing.

Kyle Bauer

HIDING VS. THRIVING

Proverbs 28:28

"When the wicked rise to power, people go into hiding;
but when the wicked perish, the righteous thrive." (NIV)

During the Nazi Regime of World War II, a wicked leader—Adolph Hitler—had risen to power. His satanic agenda to rid the earth of all Jews had caused the Jews living in Europe to either flee their countries or go into hiding.

In this verse, however, *"go into hiding"* is a hyperbole; the populace would not go into hiding literally, but they would tread softly and move about cautiously. We have seen this in our own country in recent years. Ungodly leaders impose their ungodly agendas on the common man, and the country suffers destruction.

This proverb is remarkably like 28:12, as well as 11:10, 29:2, and 29:16. Essentially, when the wicked increase (that is, come to power), oppression follows, and transgressions increase. The people groan because of the physical and emotional distress caused by evil rulers.

"But the righteous will see their downfall." (29:16, NET) The righteous will gaze with satisfaction; they will look on the downfall of the wicked triumphantly. *"No matter how widespread evil may be, the righteous will someday see its destruction."* (NET notes)

This blessed truth dovetails with our featured verse: *"…but when the wicked perish, the righteous thrive."* The righteous will flourish, multiply, increase, abound, do well, and become great. They will use their authority to promote righteousness and punish wickedness.

May this verse be more than a political commentary; may it be personal as well. Living righteously will cause us to thrive!

Karen Heimbuch

OCTOBER

My child,

if you have put up security for a friend's debt

or agreed to guarantee the debt of a stranger—

if you have trapped yourself by your agreement

and are caught by what you said—

follow my advice and save yourself,

for you have placed yourself at your friend's mercy.

Now swallow your pride;

go and beg to have your name erased.

Don't put it off; do it now!

Don't rest until you do.

—Proverbs 6:1-4

BOAST ABOUT GOD

Proverbs 27:27

"Don't brag about tomorrow,
since you don't know what a day will bring." (NLT)

This gem of wisdom is almost self-explanatory. Every translation says the same thing: If you brag or boast about yourself, you are setting yourself up to be a fool. You are also relying on yourself and not on God, and therein lies the rub.

In Luke 12:19-20, Jesus tells a parable of a rich man who has an abundance of food, which he decides he will store up and live on, but God says to him, *"You fool! This very night your life will be demanded from you. Then who will get what you have prepared for yourself?"*

In my case of being a fool, fortunately I only needed to be burned once to get the message. In 1983, my husband was getting close to selling a lot of motion picture equipment that would have made us a healthy profit. This would have been really good since we were going through bankruptcy at the time and were about to lose our house. I was so excited about this deal that I told everyone I knew. The deal fell through. People looked at us with pity. I was more upset about what a fool I had made of myself than the fact we had lost this revenue. Even so, since we were not able to bail ourselves out with the equipment sale, I threw up my hands and told God that if it was His will, I was prepared to lose the house. In true-to-form God fashion, He bailed us out at the eleventh hour, and we did not lose our home! I have never forgotten that lesson. I also have never been big on being a fool. But more importantly, I learned to trust God with everything.

Proverbs 16:9 says, *"A man's heart plans his way, but the Lord directs his steps."* We can make our plans, but all things come from Him, so who are we to boast? But if you really need to boast, read Psalm 103 and boast about our awesome almighty God.

Pat Nannarello

WHAT'S NOT IN YOUR WALLET?

Proverbs 22:9

*"He who has a generous eye will be blessed.
For he gives of his bread to the poor." (NKJV)*

Do you have an eye for something? You know, a knack for seeing something that other people may not. It may be a knack for finance, investing, sports, parenting, or humor. Can generosity be something that one can be gifted at? I believe so. Romans 12:8 lists it as one of the gifts of Father God, *"…if it is giving, then give generously."* (NIV) So, it is a gift. But, let's face it, you have probably seen someone who is not as generous as you are and those who are more generous than you. Generosity will vary from person to person. The key is to have "a generous eye."

You will notice that the writer of this proverb does not mention money. He mentions bread. The one with the bread may have been a baker, so he gave. Or it could have been one who only had one loaf of bread for their whole family but still gave of what they had. Or someone who was in between the baker and the one-loaf person. One thing they have in common is "a generous eye." They had, so they gave.

Too many times I have found myself looking in my wallet and basing my generosity on what was or was not in it. However, generosity is beyond your wallet or bank account; generosity is in the heart. It is not a measure of what you have; it is a measure of what you are willing to give away freely. Generosity is a measure of your trust in God in.

Over the years I have grown in my generosity. It has not entirely been monetarily. Often it has been in time, resources, my vehicles, our home, as well as financially. What a blessing it has been for Jill and me to give. Proverbs 11:25 says, *"A generous person will prosper; whoever refreshes others will be refreshed."* (NIV) We have been blessed beyond measure, and it has not always been financially, but it has been refreshing.

So, keep an "eye" out for opportunities to be generous. Ask the Lord how you can be generous. Do not always look in your wallet.

Fred Alvarado

LOVE'S REBUKE

Proverbs 27:5

"Better is open rebuke
than hidden love." (NIV)

God makes it clear to us that open rebuke is necessary at times. When David sinned with Bathsheba, Nathan, the prophet, came to him with an open rebuke. It was a correction that David badly needed, because he needed to repent from that sin. There are times when a person is doing something dangerous and harmful to themselves or others, and they must be confronted. Even a lost world recognizes this and, at times, stages an intervention to help the person trapped in their vice. Done correctly, and at the right time, an open rebuke can help one to turn from a destructive path before things go too far. As this proverb describes, in such a circumstance, an open rebuke is even better than love that is concealed.

Often times people are hesitant to confront, because they feel it is unloving to cause anyone pain or discomfort. But this cannot be love if we leave that person in a situation where they continue to hurt themselves or others. Our love is insufficient and weak if we simply allow people to do what they do, knowing it is hurting them, and we refuse to gently confront the situation. This "love" is based on little more than feelings, and if feelings are all that sustain the relationship, then there will always be an unwillingness to challenge the other person for their benefit. Such feelings may cause us to be concerned for the person, but our "friend" never ends up benefiting from our concern…unless an open rebuke is given.

Love always benefits the other person. An open rebuke must be done in a spirit of humility, love, and grace. That kind of love can save a soul.

Jose Nolasco

TIME TOGETHER

Proverbs 15:8

"The sacrifice of the wicked is an abomination to the Lord: but the prayer of the upright is his delight." (AMP)

Have you ever received a gift or someone made a commitment to you, but you knew that the person gave it solely out of obligation? What did it feel like to receive that gift, time, or action knowing it was simply done out of duty or as if it were a chore? I do not personally enjoy being the recipient of those types of obligations. Why would God be any different?

Proverbs 15:8 states that the action of a sacrifice coming from a perverse heart is literally an abomination to God. On the outside, the gift can be seen as something to admire. However, God sees through to the heart of each human being. He will not delight in an action rooted in darkness and deceit. This verse does, however, convey that God delights in the prayers of an honest person who means what they say and does it wholeheartedly. What a person thinks he can hide from the world he cannot hide from God. He seeks a relationship with us rather than an empty sacrifice.

In a season when I was very busy, I would read the Bible in the morning and essentially check mark it and move on about my day. That was until the Holy Spirit stopped me and reminded me about how it felt when I received time or a gift and knew that the person did not mean it. They were just check marking the box. I preferred to receive nothing. I was reminded about how God wants me, loves me, and can be found when I seek Him with authenticity. Spending time with Him in a relationship is far more fulfilling than an empty sacrifice from a distorted understanding. God delights in the time we spend together with Him in prayer.

Cynthia Medrano

HEALTHY WORDS

Proverbs 13:2

"From the fruit of his mouth a [wise] man enjoys good,
but the desire of the treacherous is for violence." (AMP)

Have you ever heard the expression "you are good for nothing, and you will never amount to anything in life"? These words are very damaging to people. But wise, kind, loving, edifying words do much good to a person's soul.

Proverbs 13: 2 teaches us that our words should be edifying and encouraging to others. If we speak the right words at the right time, let me assure you that the person listening will receive a sweet flavor from your words. When the right and wise words leave our mouths, we will enjoy them, and so will others who are listening to us.

On a recent trip to Durango, Mexico, I experienced what the text says about speaking wise words. The home we visited belonged to my cousin, and she has been battling a terrible disease. The Lord put it on our hearts to spend time with her, to bless her, and pray for her. As we prayed at the table, I led the prayer for the meal. Her daughter heard the prayer and exclaimed, "What a beautiful prayer! I had never heard that prayer before." Knowing that we could bring life and peace to this family who has been hurting and struggling made me feel good.

Let our words be sweet in this bitter world. You will be surprised what a kind and encouraging word will do to somebody who is hurting.

Ricardo Chaidez

A CLEAR CONSCIENCE

Proverbs 16:8

*"Better to have little, with godliness,
than to be rich and dishonest." (NIV)*

I believe that the temptation to do evil to gain material possessions, money, fame, and favor is all around us. However, the Lord says that having little, gained through godliness, is better than riches obtained through dishonesty.

Proverbs 16:8 reminds me of the first time that I ever stole anything. I was four years old, and my mother took my sister and me to visit a friend of hers. This friend's children had many toys, and I stole one; it was the first time I experienced guilt, paranoia, and shame. My mother never found out. However, I knew, even at that age, that I would have felt better without the toy but with a clear conscience.

Temptation comes in many forms—kids who cheat on papers to gain recognition at school; adults who steal or commit fraud; or manipulate people to gain prestige or position. Unfortunately, there is no shortage of ways to be dishonest.

I have learned that, even if in this life we never experience the consequences of our actions, and even if we never feel an ounce of remorse, one day we will still have to answer to the Lord for everything we did.

Having little with godliness will always be better than gaining the entire world with dishonesty, deception, and losing your soul. Momentary earthly pleasures attained through lies and greed will never compare to the riches that await us in heaven. So likewise, things obtained through ungodly means will never benefit us, not in this world and especially not on the day we meet our Maker.

But with godliness, even if we never obtain riches here on Earth, we will receive eternal treasure. On Earth, godliness will reap great rewards: A clear conscience, peace of mind, freedom from condemnation, and favor with the Lord.

Victor Miguel Rivera

JEALOUSY AND IDOLATRY

Proverbs 27:4

"Anger is cruel, and wrath is like a flood,
but jealousy is even more dangerous." (NLT)

Anger and wrath are dangerous, to be sure. These vices that lack self-control are part of Proverbs' definition of foolishness. They are impulsive and rash, easily stoked, like gasoline on a fire, and lead to bad and often damaging decisions.

Jealousy, however, is even more dangerous. Whereas anger is impulsive and domineering, jealousy is based in something more insidious and even idolatrous—fear. Jealousy is envious of what it does not have and afraid to lose what it does have.

Jealousy and envy, driven by the fear of not having, are described in the Bible in terms of covetousness and idolatry. This can push people to live beyond their means, devolve into self-pity, and begin to seek possessions or acceptance as the primary and idolatrous motive of their entire existence. This is dangerous to the soul.

Jealousy also fears losing what it does have and seeks exclusive access to and control over another person. Anyone who has ever lived in such a hellish relationship can testify to its damaging effects. At the heart of such possessiveness is the fear that this person will betray or abandon the other, and that fear drives such a person to extraordinary lengths of persistent control. This jealousy is more than intimidation through anger; it is control over another person's life and decisions. Anger is dangerous, but jealousy is a soul-destroying cage with bars made of another person's fear and insecurity.

When people are deficient of love and meaning in their lives, they grasp onto anything or anyone they perceive will give them this love and meaning. If they have identified what they believe will be the source of their love and meaning, they will make that thing or person their idol, and the fear of loss is not just of that thing or person but of their own identity, which is why jealousy maintains its death grip.

However, when our identities are found in God, the only Source who can actually fill the deficiency in our souls, we will live from the abundance of His life and love in us to the point we no longer need to take from people, but we can live to give!

Kyle Bauer

FEAR OF THE LORD – A SECURE REFUGE

Provers 14:26

"In the fear of the Lord is strong confidence;
and his children shall have a place of refuge." (KJV)

Troubles are a Christ-follower's challenge! Contrast this with the world's way—they do not bat an eye at cheating, lying, or lowering their standards. The question we ought to consider is, when things do get hard, how do we respond? Here is the deeper meaning of this verse: Where do you find a place of refuge?

Some context helps. There was a point when I did not believe God could actually deliver on His incredible promises. At that time, there was someone in my life who absolutely hated me. This relentless pursuer was at my job; office politics were an arena of spite. I had to work. A job hunt was not going to immediately rescue me. The assassination of my character lurked behind every misstep I took. Of course, I tried to address the situation as anyone else might. In the end, this issue became a point of frequent prayer. These prayers became a refuge for my heart and a place for the surrender of my own ways to fix the problem. God came to my aid. I did my best to respond to every attack in a righteous way and as one who lives in the fear of the Lord. And my coworkers saw it. *One* day finally became *the* day the attacker (and not me) had to find other employment.

Trusting in the Lord in the face of pain is often difficult, and we ask ourselves if God really cares. However, we do not always see things from God's perspective. Our need to understand everything on our terms can block a deeper and more joyful relationship with God. We need to rest in the knowledge that God will fulfill everything in His time. My fondest prayer is that you come to know and have confidence in this place of refuge. The confidence in the fear of the Lord truly changes everything in terms of JOY.

Juline Bruck

PLAN FOR HARVEST, BUILD YOUR HOUSE

Proverbs 24:27

*"Do your planning and prepare your
fields before building your house." (NLT)*

I bought furniture from IKEA, which is pretty simple to put together. Anyone can do it. They give you a few simple tools and a whole lot of parts, and it is not rocket science. I knew how to build this type of furniture from previous experience. I have confidence when I begin assembly, but then I reach a point where something is not right. When I pull out the instructions (which I should have done at the beginning), I realized I had skipped a vital step, and now I had to take several pieces apart and almost start over from scratch.

There is a correct order in life. We need to start working and earning an income before spending and building a house. It will not do to run out of funds and have to stop part way. When farming, there is a specific season for every step. If the fields are not prepared in time, you will miss the time to plant. If you do not plant in time, there will be nothing to harvest. Doing the work needs to be the first step, then you can build your home while the crops grow.

Life in God's kingdom, as a disciple of Jesus, also has a pattern of growth. As in farming, sowing and reaping have an order that leads to harvest, and so does growing in the Lord. The Holy Spirit leads us in a purposeful process of spiritual formation to make us more like Jesus. Read your Bible, pray, fellowship with other believers, grow in wisdom and understanding, and learn to hear God's voice. As you grow, you will learn to yield to God's plan for building your life. As Psalm 127:1 says, *"Unless the Lord builds the house, those who build it labor in vain."* (ESV)

Stephen Larkin

ENTITLED TO A BLESSING

Proverbs 10:22

"The blessing of the LORD brings wealth,
without painful toil for it." (NLT)

I have been a believer since I was five years old, but during my senior year of college, I was angry with Jesus. So I thought that by not going to church for a year, He would see just how ticked off I was at Him.

I didn't realize how idiotic I was being until I sat down and talked to an older, wiser neighbor of ours. He asked me, "Why are you so mad at God?" After searching my own heart, I replied, "I'm 22 years old. I have done everything right. I don't have sex, I don't drink, I don't do drugs, I've worked hard in school, I go to church, I am a kind person, and I still haven't found true love! Why haven't I been blessed with a husband yet?" I felt because I was doing all the right things, and I had toiled so hard to be a good Christian girl, that in return, I was entitled to be blessed with the riches of a happily ever after. Boy, was I wrong! My young, immature self was more interested in finding the love of a man instead of seeking the unconditional love of Jesus.

As I have grown in my walk with the Lord, I have come to realize that being a believer is more about building a relationship with the Lord than it is about being good in order to receive blessings. Jesus IS THE BLESSING! He is the gift! A relationship with Him brings indescribable riches. We are given an incredible opportunity to fall in love with Him at no cost to ourselves – no demands, no strings attached. The love He wants to shower us with expands so far and wide that He chose to die for us. Christ is the one who did the toiling for us so that we didn't have to. Now, who wouldn't want to be in love with someone like that?

Jennifer Shank

RIGHTEOUSNESS IS PROTECTION

Proverbs 13:6

"Righteousness is like a shield of protection,
guarding those who keep their integrity,
but sin is the downfall of the wicked." (TPT)

A person's downfall can be caused by the exposure of their weakness due to a lack of protection. Every person has struggles, weaknesses, temptations, and propensities to sin, yet these things in and of themselves are not sin—sin occurs when one gives themselves over to the temptation.

This proverb bears a striking resemblance to the Armor of God that protects us from the spiritual attacks that seek to cause our downfall through outright sin or through other pathways such as slander, gossip, lies, accusations, or even misunderstandings the devil can exploit to our detriment. One of the principal pieces of the Armor is the breastplate of righteousness, which guards our hearts.

An intact heart is essential in our relationship with God. The word for integrity in Hebrew *(tōm)* means something that is whole, complete, full, and innocent. The same word is used for the chest piece that covered the High Priest's heart, called the "Urim and the Thummim,"[1] when he entered the Lord's presence.[2] The entry point was through innocence and integrity before God—a heart undivided, loyal, and pure. Such a heart disallows chinks in the armor by which the devil can find a way in to break us and damage our ability to enter into God's presence.

Living according to God's ways is protection against accusations, lies, gossip, slander, and misunderstandings. However, when we give into sin, we open up our lives for the devil to steal, kill, and destroy, to set us up for a great downfall. Why? Because he now has ammunition to use against us, and there are cracks in a divided, disloyal heart that can be manipulated. Staying away from sin is not the simplistic "don't do bad things." Living right according to God's Word and in the innocence of heart is safety for our lives, families, reputation, testimony, God's ability to use our lives effectively, and the cultivation of our personal relationship with God. Essential to righteous living is to recover our integrity and innocence through confession and repentance of sin (1 John 1:9).

Kyle Bauer

---

1 Thummim is a derivative of the Hebrew tōm
2 See Exodus Deuteronomy 33:8; Numbers 27:21; 1 Samuel 28:6

DETESTABLE VS. DELIGHTFUL

Proverbs 15:8

"The Lord detests the sacrifice of the wicked,
but He delights in the prayers of the upright." (NLT)

When the Lord sent the Prophet Samuel to anoint a king from among the sons of Jesse, He cautioned Samuel as he was looking over Jesse's impressive sons saying: "Don't be impressed by [their] appearance or [their] height, for I have rejected him. God does not view things the way people do. People look on the outward appearance, but the Lord looks at the heart." (1 Sam. 16:7, NET) So it is with our (public) sacrifices and (private) prayers.

God hates sacrifices offered by wicked people, because their offerings are given hypocritically. The wicked merely attempt to fulfill ceremonial obligations to keep up appearances before men. But what does God think of their insincerity? His holy nature is repulsed, because their sacrifices are mingled with their wicked ways. Sacrifice without obedience is worthless (1 Sam. 15:22).

In happy contrast, however, are *"the prayers of the upright"*—intercessors who are godly, righteous, moral, and just. The upright consider all God's precepts to be right, and they hate every false way (Ps. 119:128, ESV), therefore God delights in them.

The Hebrew word for *"delight"* is *râtsôwn*, meaning goodwill, grace, favor, and kindness. It is what a king can do (i.e., show favor) if he chooses to do so (Prov. 14:35). When Moses recounted the nine blessings that God spoke over Joseph, it culminated "with the favor of Him who appeared in the burning bush." (Deut. 33:16, CSB) May our prayers culminate as well with the favor of our Holy God!

Karen Heimbuch

EXPERIENCE AND CARE

Proverbs 13:16

*"Every prudent man acts with knowledge,
but a fool lays open his folly." (NKJV)*

"Use common sense" is a saying we often hear growing up. The expression basically means to use good judgment and to give just a little thought to things when making decisions. However, this seems easier said than done. A wise person thinks and analyzes before considering making any decision.

It is so important to have all the facts and information before making decisions that could affect us for the rest of our lives. I have made many decisions that I regretted later in my life. One of my greatest regrets was the years I waited so long to accept the Lord Jesus Christ as my Savior. As a 10-year-old child, I heard the word of the Lord, but I did not respond. The years went by, and I kept avoiding the call of the Lord in favor of doing my own thing. It was not until the age of 20 that I finally gave my life to Christ. I could have lived an extra decade of my life serving the Lord, but as Romans 1:31 says, I "refused to understand."

My prayer to the Lord is that I become a prudent and self-disciplined person with an open mind to listen to wisdom, receive knowledge, and make the best decisions in my life, marriage, family, and ministry. Our God makes us wise and knowledgeable through reading and obedience to His Word—which is full of common sense! So, let us be wise and think before we act.

Ricardo Chaidez

JUST SCALES REVEAL TRUTH

Proverbs 14:25

"A true witness delivers souls,
but a deceitful witness speaks lies." (NKJV)

Discerning what is true in a courtroom can be difficult. There is so much at stake when deciding on a case where two sides have presented their "facts." The jury is a third party that attempts to discern whose account is most accurate and then renders a verdict.

In America in the last few years, we have seen quite a few major, culture-affecting court cases. Issues as serious as someone being chased down and murdered to things as bizarre as the evidence of a dog being stung by a bee in a domestic abuse case.

Because of the difficulty of finding the truth in a case, witnesses are brought in to state anything they have seen or know about the matter. A witness' account is often the winning or losing leverage. Unfortunately, courts have become societal entertainment, and the public court of opinion makes rash decisions on incomplete information. They also offer their opinions on something they were never involved in.

Regardless of the direction of society, however, it is our responsibility to be truthful witnesses. We are to witness what Christ has done in our lives and are not to add or subtract anything from it; a literal "the truth and nothing but the truth, so help me God." The Bible tells us not to bear false witness or to take up the Lord's name in vain. We are also people who are "called by His name" (2 Chron. 7:14). As we witness to the truth, we are doing so as His representatives walking under His name, testifying to His truth. We are under the oath of the One who sent us, and others will be witnesses to the power of the truth we share.

Rachael Hopkins

LITTLE BIRDIES ARE EVERYWHERE

Proverbs 14:35

*"A king rejoices in wise servants
but is angry with those who disgrace him." (NLT)*

It is horrible to be misunderstood or flat out misrepresented in what you say, and it is especially frustrating when your heart, motive, and attitudes are misrepresented. Such misrepresentation causes your name to be maligned and your reputation soiled.

The "king" refers to any person in leadership or authority. When we are in charge of anything, not one of us desires to do a poor job. When we have people working with us who represent us in their various areas of work and communication, we want to be represented well by a cohesive team. Our jobs and reputations are also at stake!

What position do you find yourself in? Are you the foreman, coordinator, or team lead (the king)? Then lead well, honor your team, and confront misunderstandings head-on with graciousness, understanding, mercy, and firmness.

Are you in a position under authority, answering to the "king"? Then represent them well with honor, wisdom, hard work, and submission—even if you may not agree with everything they do or say, their position is deserving of your honor! Solomon's wisdom gives advice regarding our work:—promotion comes with wisdom, and wisdom serves the "king" well. Also found in Solomon's wisdom is Ecclesiastes 10:20, to keep your mouth shut about your employer and not to dishonor them. *"Never make light of the king, even in your thoughts. And don't make fun of the powerful, even in your own bedroom. For a little bird might deliver your message and tell them what you said." (NLT)*

I have been in the position of both being the one who spoke stupidly about one in power and then had to bear the brunt of the consequences and being the one in authority who had little birds tell me what others said that could potentially bring disastrous results to me or the ministry I lead. Having experienced this from both sides, I am reminded of a line from the Disney movie, "Bambi," in which, Thumper, the rabbit and Bambi's friend, quotes his father saying, "If you can't say something nice, don't say nothing at all." Because little birdies are everywhere!

Kyle Bauer

A FLICKERING CANDLE

Proverbs 18:21

*"Death and life are in the power of the tongue,
and those who love it will eat its fruit." (NKJV)*

What is wrong with you? Can't you do anything right? Shame on you!

Has someone ever spoken words like these to you? Or worse, have you ever spoken these words to someone else? These words do nothing but harm and can kill the soul.

This proverb reminds me of a true story. A young mother went outside in the front yard and saw her child hitting the ground with a hammer. When she walked closer, she could see him smashing snails every time he swung the tool. "Son," she said, "what are you doing? You are killing those snails!" He looked up at her and said, "I am only hitting them; if they die, it is their fault."

That is how some people treat the weight of what they say. In anger, they spew hurtful words— hitting you with their verbal hammer—and leave you decimated to deal with the aftermath.

Words have power. You have been given an instrument that can bless and bring life or curse and bring death. Your tongue does not work independently from your brain and your heart. It will bring forth the fruit of whatever lives inside of you. So, cultivate the soil of your soul with good fruit, fill yourself up on the Word of God, and speak life.

Have you spoken words that have hurt others? Ask the Lord for forgiveness and to put a guard over your mouth to make you aware of the words you say.

Have you been wounded by hurtful words? You can be free of them through the power of forgiveness. When you forgive, you are submitting this offense to God and allowing Him to be not only your defender, but also your healer. By forgiving and letting the offense go, you set yourself free from bitterness, hate, or anger that, in the long run, will only affect you, your health, and your relationship with God. Isaiah 42:3 says, "He will not crush the weakest reed or put out a flickering candle. He will bring justice to all who have been wronged." (NLT)

Michelle Glush

THE BIG YELLOW BUS

Proverbs 22:6

"Start children off on the way they should go,
and even when they are old they will not turn from it." (NIV)

Our children belong to the Lord, and it is our job as parents to guide them on the right path. God gives us knowledge and wisdom, and He wants us to show our kids the fear of the Lord, which is the key to unlocking the treasure of God's purposes in them (Is. 33:6).

I became a school bus driver right after I graduated from High School. I had no idea that the paint color of a school bus was specially formulated in 1939. The color is "National School Bus Glossy." I remember my dad making me go to the DMV to get my H6 (Driving Record) and take it to the recruiting office. I went through extensive training and had to learn the laws, which involved classroom knowledge and driving the actual bus. In training, they gave me the option to drive the big bus that seats 48 adults or 72 children.

It took a lot of dedication to learn a new skill. After three months of intensive training, I passed the test and became one of the youngest bus drivers in the company. The lessons I learned in my training can be applied to our children as well. The trainers are the parents, the trainees are our children, the training classroom is our home, and the action of driving the bus is when our kids grow up and have to navigate the world.

Imagine if I went to the recruiting office with my driving record and the recruiter said, "Oh, very good, here is the key, drive the bus." In the same way, it is equally unwise to send our kids out into the world without proper training.

As parents, we must model for our children how a real follower and disciple of Jesus lives. We cannot expect them to respect us when we are not modeling respect to them or others.

Every moment in life is a good opportunity to show our children about kindness, love, and self-control. When we do that, we are not training our children just for a moment but for a lifetime of happiness.

Alicia Suarez

LOVE AND FAITHFULNESS

Proverbs 16:6

*"Through love and faithfulness sin is atoned for;
through the fear of the Lord evil is avoided." (NIV)*

How can love and faithfulness atone for sin? How can fearing the Lord help believers avoid evil?

Because of the death and resurrection of Jesus Christ, love and faithfulness have atoned for sin. It is because God so loved the world *"that he gave his one and only Son, that whoever believes in him shall not perish but have eternal life."* (John 3:16, NIV) He became the sacrificial lamb to atone for our sins, and we can come to Him whenever we sin. As we confess our sins, He will cleanse and forgive us. *"My dear children, I write this to you so that you will not sin. But if anybody does sin, we have the advocate with the Father—Jesus Christ, the Righteous One. He is the atoning sacrifice for our sins, and not only for ours but also for the sins of the whole world."* (1 John 2:1-2, NIV)

His love shown on the cross for us did the work of Salvation, but we also need to choose to put our faith in Him. The Bible says, *"If you declare with your mouth, 'Jesus is Lord,' and believe in your heart that God raised Him from the dead, you will be saved."* (Rom. 10:9, NIV)

When we put our faith in the Lord, we will grow in the fear of the Lord and devotion to God. Much of our devotion to God is in obedience and meditating on His Word. Those who devote themselves to God learn how to lead a Holy life, and they will prosper. *"Blessed is the man who walks not in the counsel of the ungodly, nor stands in the path of sinners, nor sits in the seat of the scornful, but his delight is in the law of the Lord, and in His law, he meditates day and night. He shall be like a tree planted by the rivers of water, that brings forth its fruit in its season, whose leaf also shall not wither; and whatever he does shall prosper."* (Ps. 1:1-3, NKJV)

Joshua Bauer

TRUSTING IN GOD'S PROVISION

Proverbs 11:28

"Those who trust in their riches will fall,
but the righteous will thrive like a green leaf." (NIV)

Having been a stay-at-home wife in an area with a very high cost of living, while living on only one income, was extremely challenging. I like to describe this as "being voluntarily poor!" This verse really hit home for me!

What does trusting in riches mean during periods of unemployment? Is money life? What happens when illness takes the breadwinner offline? Were we going to die? Though there were times when windfalls came to sustain us, there was a period when we moved in with my husband's parents. I was six months pregnant, and sleeping on a conventional bed became more and more difficult. Oh, how I longed for a recliner, but recliners were very expensive! One day I was surprised when my mother-in-law suggested we hit up some garage sales. As there was no known money available to spend, I was again surprised to find a crusty and still spendable five-dollar bill in my green tote. And then what did I come across? A recliner! As I waddled over to ask about it, the seller said, "Five dollars." It was now mine! The seller's sons placed the recliner in the SUV. The relief provided by the much-needed recliner continued far beyond the first pregnancy and was used later for the next pregnancy. That moment of discovery and provision continues to put a song in my heart.

Just as this beautiful moment is real, so are the dead-end, bottom-of-the-ninth-inning moments when the check bounced, the job ended badly, and there was no comeback in sight. There is a need to tell both sides of the matter. God does not leave His own down and out. He shows Himself faithful in the worst times and the tough experiences life can dish out. Come to Him! Tell Him the whole story. As He listens and considers these things with you, you will know you are not alone! He loves you so very, very much!

Juline Bruck

SNAKE OIL AND DIET PILLS

Proverbs 14:15

"Only simpletons believe everything they're told!
The prudent carefully consider their steps." (NLT)

"All that glitters is not gold." "If it's too good to be true, then it probably is." These two maxims are true about 99.9% of the time. When I was in the third grade, I had a friend who was a storyteller, and at nine years old, I was too naïve to know the difference between reality and this kid's stories. We were on a basketball team together, and during practice, he told me of a cave he discovered, which was the size of the gymnasium we were in. I was captivated. He went on to say that the cave was filled with gold and gems, and nobody knew about it except him. I was utterly entranced and astonished by his fortuitous discovery and the possibility of both of us becoming extremely wealthy. You can smell the cow manure from 1990 all the way to 2023.

Later, in my early 20s, I worked with a guy who was always trying to develop get-rich-quick schemes. One day at work, he told me of a fool-proof investment plan of owning a diamond mine. Fortunately for me, I had grown up, and I just rolled my eyes and kept working. Unfortunately for him, he was not kidding. The diamond mine never panned out. But gullible people continue to chase after silly fables, tales, get-rich-quick ideas, gossip, and fall for slick snake oil sales pitches or the next diet pill that will help you "safely" lose 25 pounds per week.

Nothing can replace hard work, experience, and critical thinking. One cannot take life, news stories, gossip about others, or propaganda from governments, businesses, or educational systems at face value. Unfortunately, there are many deceivers and snake oil salesmen out there. There is always more to the story than what is told to us, and what we are told is usually an attempt to sway our opinion for someone else's agenda. However, we serve our God, who is neither deceived nor does He deceive people. Psalm 119:160 says, *"All your words are true; all your righteous laws are eternal."* (NIV) He is trustworthy and faithful, and His words *"make wise the simple."* (Ps. 19:7, NIV)

Kyle Bauer

HUMILITY HAS ITS REWARDS

Proverbs 22:4

"Humility is the fear of the Lord;
its wages are riches and honor and life." (KJV)

Proverbs 16:18 says that pride goes before destruction and a haughty spirit before a fall. Solomon speaks directly to the end result of pride and being self-absorbed. Here in Proverbs 22:4, he makes the antithetical statement: The opposite of pride is humility. Pride leads to destruction. Humility leads to reverence and worship of the Lord. Reverence for and worship of the Lord yields riches, honor, and life.

Simply put, riches are things that are of great value to you. Honor is God's promise of others having regard for you. Additionally, life also has several meanings. Certainly, the life mentioned here infers long life. It also infers joy in living, living life to the fullest, and experiencing fulfillment. What a wonderful promise.

Wages are generally associated with cost, the outlay or reduction of something of worth. However, Solomon highlights the exact opposite. He uses a wage in the context of something having been earned, wherein value or worth is increased, not as something which has a cost, an expense that reduces overall value.

The takeaway is to understand how much God values humility, which is willing service intertwined with confidence in Him. As one practices the submission inherent in humility, they become more and more in awe of God, more respectful and reverent of God. The outcome, the wages earned (rather than the cost), are riches, honor, and life. Again, what a wonderful promise.

Father, I thank you for giving me the opportunity to grow in humility before you. Thank you for being such a loving God as to offer such great reward for my service to you. Help me, Lord, to grow in humility. Help me to decrease so that you may increase. I give thanks to you, Lord, in Jesus' name. Amen.

Lloyd Speese

CARELESS ANGER

Proverbs 27:3

"Stone is heavy and sand a burden,
but a fool's provocation is heavier than both." (NIV)

While we live in these earthen vessels, there will always be some personalities that will rub us the wrong way. This verse paints a vivid picture of this truth: Heavier than a large stone and more cumbersome than a bag of sand is the unreasonable and excessive anger of fools. Such people either do not know how to control their rage or could care less about the consequences of their stupidity by throwing a tantrum. This, of course, is a heavy burden to bear for those around them.

It is at times like these that we must keep our own spirit in check and not fall into the same trap of overreacting. A fool may not care what he says or does when he is provoked, but we must remain patient and self-controlled. *"Better a patient person than a warrior, one with self-control than one who takes a city."* (Prov. 16:32, NIV)

How many times have we been guilty of acting stupidly! Whether provoked, annoyed, grieved, or peeved, we were offended. Sadly, the pettier the offense, the more burdensome we become—not only to those around us, but to ourselves.

Lord, grant us wisdom, grace, patience, and humility to avoid becoming fools. Protect us from the vengeful wrath of rebels. Help us to steer clear of provoking them. However, if we do, help us to get out of their way!

Karen Heimbuch

GOOD LEADERSHIP

Proverbs 20:8

"When a king sits in judgment, he weighs all the evidence, distinguishing the bad from the good." (NLT)

Good and righteous leadership will weigh all the possible evidence when determining a case and passing judgment. A righteous judge will distinguish between the good and the bad. Whether it be a judge in court or among our own lives within our very own situations, good leaders must always judge righteously.

Proverbs 20:8 describes a king sitting in judgment. My first thought, probably like many of you, is of our God-King, who sits on His righteous throne. I am confronted with the reality that one day our lives will be judged by the Lord, and when I reflect on my life, I tend to think of my inadequacies, faults, and shortcomings. If we are honest, we all know we deserve a guilty verdict because we all have sinned. However, because of the precious sacrifice of Jesus, the Lord can legally dismiss our court case and grant us righteousness, all because of Jesus! The Lord is a righteous judge, and by His example, He expects us to use sound judgment in every situation.

Has anyone ever brought up a case against you? Perhaps someone in grade school, at work, within your family, or even within the church? Just as you would want a fair trial and a righteous judge with no bias who weighs all the evidence and distinguishes between the bad and the good, we must become leaders who similarly exercise wisdom. Our King set an example for us to follow. When we find ourselves in any situation involving discernment and judgment, we also must weigh all the evidence and distinguish between the bad and the good.

At the end of the age, our King will sit in judgment. He will weigh all of the evidence and truly distinguish between the bad and the good. So, until then, let us be sure to live in righteousness and judge situations fairly in our own lives.

Victor Miguel Rivera

THE WICKED ARE CRUEL

Proverbs 12:10

*"The righteous care for the needs of their animals,
but the kindest acts of the wicked are cruel." (NIV)*

Righteous people are honorable, upright, virtuous, honest, and put others before themselves. They regard the lives of animals, know their worth and value (Gen. 1:21) and choose to care for the animal. Concerned with the well-being of the animal in their care, they provide sufficient food, do not overwork it, and allow it proper rest from labor. If the animal has any health disorders, they will help bring healing. A righteous man will also have concern and care for wild animals if necessary.

God has given us stewardship of the animals, and it is His will that men show mercy to them.

Wicked people are unethical, manipulative, self-centered, shameless, dishonest, and cannot be trusted to be good-willed toward a person or animal. The very kindnesses of wicked people can be intended merely as a cover for mischief. Often cruelty is mixed in with what seems like merciful actions. Wicked people will sometimes pretend to show mercy for selfish gains.

This verse shares truths about righteous people and their actions as well as wicked people and their intentions. By observation, look at the people you allow to walk with you and speak into your life. Do they walk in righteousness, or do they behave cruelly to others?

God calls us to a higher standard in 2 Corinthians 6:11-18. Ask yourself, who do you spend your time with? Whom are you allowing in your life that may have wicked intentions?

Ask God for direction on how to handle any wickedness that may be rising up in your life because of the people you are around.

1 Corinthians 15:33 says, *"Do not be deceived: 'Bad company corrupts good morals.'"* (NASB)

Jill Alvarado

FINANCIAL FOOLISHNESS...

Proverbs 17:18

*"It's poor judgment to guarantee another person's debt
or put up security for a friend." (NLT)*

Poor judgment seems good at the time, but it is too late to undo a bad mistake when the consequences are revealed. This proverb deals with financial agreements where one party agrees to be a guarantor on a loan or other type of debt, and it is with a friend or neighbor. The most common purchases or loans I hear of people co-signing are real estate and vehicle loans. It is one thing to co-sign for a family member where you hopefully know the person well enough to know if they are able, of good character, and will repay the loan. It is altogether a whole different matter to do that for a friend or neighbor. That is all kinds of foolish. If the other party fails to pay the debt, you will be required to pay it in full. Additionally, while the debt is still active, it affects your credit rating, whether they make the payments on time or not, and affects how much money you can borrow for any other need. It will also affect the interest rate that you pay.

Poor judgment is the opposite of wisdom. The unspoken wisdom of Solomon here is to avoid financial entanglements that only have potentially negative consequences. Wisdom requires us to think first (of all the possible negatives that can come out of an agreement) before we act and to get wise counsel from those we respect (then follow the advice). Wisdom can help us avoid a great deal of sorrow and financial loss.

Martin and Bea Laufer

USE IT WISELY

Proverbs 30:32

"If you play the fool and exalt yourself,
or if you plan evil, clap your hand over your mouth." (NIV)

I'm going to go out on a limb and guess that everyone reading this devotional is not going to plan to do evil things. However…

It would probably be safe to say that we have all talked about our accomplishments, but have we ever felt that we stepped over the line and fell into boasting? We are all prone to boasting (exalting ourselves) and foolishness. So, be wise, and before the thought passes from your brain to your lips, clap your hand over your mouth! Before you open your mouth and stick your foot in it, take a moment to pray.

How many times have words flown out of your mouth that you wish you could take back the second they left the hangar? How many times have you wanted to tell people how you were the one to solve the problem? How many times has someone told you their particular experience, and you have to tell them your story that is bigger and better? How many times have you wanted to be so right that you crushed another person's spirit? How many times did someone else tell you to just shut up?

I can raise my hand to all those questions, and I have asked the Lord to forgive me for every misstep and help me to do it His way. Knowing God's Word and learning how to downshift to prayer (instead of flapping my lips) has helped me. It will help you too.

There is power in your words. The Bible says that the power of life and death is in the tongue. Use it wisely. Bless someone with it.

Pat Nannarello

DON'T TOUCH THE RIGHTEOUS

Proverbs 24:15-16

"Don't wait in ambush at the home of the godly,
and don't raid the house where the godly live.
The godly may trip seven times, but they will get up again.
But one disaster is enough to overthrow the wicked." (NLT)

It could not have been easy for young David, after being anointed as the future king of Israel and knowing his inheritance and future lay directly in front of him, to remain humble in the face of so many wicked attacks by Saul, the reigning King. The Scriptures indicate that Saul had long lost his spiritual favor with God through his disobedience yet dealt treacherously with David, who had done nothing but be loyal to God and King. Later in David's life, like Saul, David's rebellious son, Absalom, also dealt treacherously with him. It would not be hard to imagine that depression and doubt were no strangers to the heart of David. There is little doubt that these issues caused David to cry out to the Lord.

Yet this proverb is a powerful warning to the wicked who would dare to rise against the righteous and a chilling declaration by the Lord that, ultimately, He will rise up on their behalf. The righteous man may fall seven times, but the Lord will raise him again. But for the wicked, calamity surely waits for them.

In the case of David's enemies, both met an untimely death in judgment for having risen up against the righteous. God will vindicate His people in the end, and those who rise up against them will have to face the consequences of their actions. God will not let them get away with it.

Take heart, my soul, and know that the same God who stood up on David's behalf and brought his enemies down is the same God who will stand up for you.

Jose Nolasco

NOT ON THE LIST OF THE FRUIT OF THE SPIRIT

Proverbs 30:13

"There is a generation rising that is so filled with pride,
they think they are superior and look down on others." (TPT)

This proverb, written nearly 3000 years ago, speaks directly to what we see today in 2023. We see the spirit of pride acting out in many forms in our workplace, on television, on social media, and in our neighbors and families like never before.

God wrote this warning to let us know that when we see it happen, to not fall into the temptation of pride or behave in this spiritually destructive manner. Proverbs 16:5 says, *"The Lord detests the proud; they will surely be punished."* (NLT) 1 Peter 5:5 tells us, *"God opposes the proud but gives grace to the humble."* (NLT)

We want to lead a lifestyle that brings us closer to God and forms us more into His character and nature. God is love, and he looks at us through eyes of love and acceptance and welcomes us to be part of His family. It was His love that drew us to Him, and it is that same love that saved us from a life of sin and death.

Pride is not listed among the fruit of the spirit! We have already mentioned how God feels about it. Are you hiding pride in your heart? It may be time to do a spiritual heart checkup! Ask the Holy Spirit to reveal anything you are holding on to or hiding in your heart. Then confess the sin and ask God for forgiveness and cleansing from it. When you allow the Holy Spirit to do the work in your heart and mind, you can count on Him to do a perfect job and bring healing and restoration.

Debbie Speese

EVERY IDLE WORD

Proverbs 18:2

"Fools have no interest in understanding;
they only want to air their own opinions." (NLT)

It is as if this proverb were written especially for our day and age. Today's social media world has given unprecedented voice to the opinions of fools. All you have to do is read any comment on the post of any current event, and the fury of every opponent of the original comment is quickly revealed. "Conversations" degenerate rapidly into petty fights and degrading insults. Their opinions are not for objective truth but for their personal agenda.

The fact is that foolish people are fools regardless of who they are, where they are from, or when they lived. We were all born into the foolishness of sin.

> "The times in which we live are decadent. It is evident we are now approaching the end of the age. Everyone has disregarded the law. Children no longer obey their parents. Everyone is eager to write a book."
> —Ancient Chaldean tablet, 2800 BC[3]

For as much as things change, they stay the same.

There is a difference between airing opinions and having a conversation. Conversation requires two participants with open minds willing to respectfully listen to each other. Merely spouting opinions is the antithesis of conversation and can almost be labeled as the definition of social media. Someone lacking understanding, knowledge, or wisdom will quickly jump to unfounded conclusions and have knee-jerk reactions. I am not aware of anyone whose mind, much less their heart, was changed by someone foolishly "airing" their opinions.

This is not Wisdom. Wisdom remembers Jesus' warning that we will give an account for every idle word we speak—or type. Wisdom is slow to speak, quick to listen, and ready to fully understand a situation before rendering judgment.

Kyle Bauer

---

3   The claim of the age of this saying is disputed. Nevertheless, it is a very old saying, at the very least it was not written in our era, and it makes the point!

KINDNESS

Proverbs 16: 24

*"Kind words are like honey—sweet to the soul
and healthy for the body." (NLT)*

I have a wonderful friend who prays for me daily. She sends me a text every morning with a prayer and a blessing. Someone in the world thinks about me and loves me enough to stop and pray a blessing over me. Some days this simple act of kindness will bring me to tears. The Bible verses she sends me surround my day, encourage me, and give me strength. Her loving thoughtfulness has changed my life.

The storyline of a favorite movie of mine, Evan Almighty, tells the tale of the main character, Evan, who God calls to build an ARK. He fought it tooth and nail but eventually gave in and was obedient to follow God's direction. He was mocked, jeered at, and stripped of his duties at work, but he was faithful to complete his mission, and in the end, saved the people and animals in his neighborhood from being destroyed in a flood…in typical Hollywood fashion. But the last few moments of the movie tell the whole story. We see Evan and God standing underneath a tree, and God reveals how Evan has changed the world. It was by kindness. He learned along the way to be more loving with his family, to take in a stray dog, and to show Acts of Random Kindness to those around him. ARK…Act of Random Kindness.

Sometimes your kind words will carry a hurting soul through difficult or fearful times. They can lift spirits and change the course of someone's day. They will help someone remember that they are not alone or give them the strength to do the right thing.

Who are you blessing with a kind word? Does the Lord bring someone to mind? Next time He does, pray for them and reach out with a word of kindness to bless them. You may never know how much it means, until you come into eternity, what one small word or deed can do.

How do we change the world? Let's remember the ARK…One Act of Random Kindness at a time.

Michelle Glush

ANGER OR JESUS

Proverbs 22:24-25

*"Don't befriend angry people or associate with hot-tempered people,
or you will learn to be like them and endanger your soul." (NLT)*

Did you ever have a friend who was mad at another friend and wanted you to be mad at them too? I experienced this in grade school, and somehow in 2020, this juvenile behavior seemed to rear its ugly head again all around me.

This proverb says not to make friends with an angry person, or you will become like them.

As I was reading my bible during the year-of-our-Covid-2020, I came upon this verse and marked it with giant exclamation points!!! Everyone was angry. The Right was angry. The Left was angry. I was getting bombarded from both sides with vitriolic hate speech. And the news was making me angry! People wanted to be angry, and they wanted you to be angry with them!

I do not know about you, but I do not like to be angry or upset. It is just not healthy. So, I had to turn everything and everyone off. The only calm and peace I found was with Jesus. I also had to fight to stay aligned with Him because the din of opinions was everywhere. Have you seen a dog cover his ears because of a piercing or dissonant sound? That is how I felt with everyone railing at me. It made my teeth hurt. I kept praying, "Jesus, you know what is going on. I do not know and do not need to know because I cannot fix it. But Lord, Your will be done."

Being angry also makes you ugly. Ugly outside (ever notice someone's contorted face when they are screaming at you?) and ugly inside (ever notice the darkness that reveals itself?). The enemy steps into that ugly mess and sets the hook deep inside you. This is the endangering of your soul that proverbs is talking about. Keep your focus on Jesus at all times. Jesus brings calm. Jesus brings light. Jesus brings peace—the peace that passes all understanding (Phil. 4:6). Choose Jesus.

Pat Nannarello

NOVEMBER

My son,

obey your father's commands,

and don't neglect your mother's instruction.

Keep their words always in your heart.

Tie them around your neck.

When you walk, their counsel will lead you.

When you sleep, they will protect you.

When you wake up, they will advise you.

For their command is a lamp

and their instruction a light;

their corrective discipline

is the way to life.

—Proverbs 6:20-23

DRENCHED IN GOD'S BLESSINGS

Proverbs 28:20

"Life's blessings drench the honest and faithful person,
but punishment rains down upon the greedy and the dishonest." (TPT)

We live in a world filled with greedy and dishonest people, those who are dead set on gaining more and will stop at nothing to obtain it. They will lie, cheat, and steal in order to achieve power. They are guided by their evil intentions, and honestly, it can be frustrating to see their success, especially when you may be doing all you can to lead a righteous lifestyle but are barely making enough to cover the monthly bills. But this begs the question: Are they really successful? If sin produces the rain of punishment, are money, cars, and extravagant homes obtained by greed and dishonesty really worth it?

As believers, we can choose to either sulk in the frustration of the greedy person's success, or we can choose to change our focus and concentrate on the promise set forth in Proverbs 28:20 – the honest and faithful person will receive life's blessings. We must see the gifts that will inevitably come when we pursue righteousness – joy, peace, patience, gentleness, self-control, unconditional love, godly character, supernatural power, a sound mind, grace, mercy, and the list goes on! The honest and faithful will receive an abundance of God's blessings, so much in fact that we will be drenched in them! These blessings are far better than the fleeting material possessions that people strive after.

Have you ever been drenched in something? It's like being soaked in the splash zone at Sea World or having a bucket of Gatorade dumped on you at the end of a sporting event victory. Think about the glory of being drenched by God's favor in exchange for honesty and faithfulness. To be thoroughly saturated in the blessings of God sounds far better than feeling the rain of punishment. It is one choice that seems to have an obvious response. I hope you decide to allow yourself to be drenched by the Lord. I guarantee you won't regret it.

Jennifer Shank

"I KNOW WHAT YOU DID LAST SUMMER"

Proverbs 22:12

"The Lord preserves those with knowledge,
but He ruins the plans of the treacherous." (NLT)

Have you ever been lied to? Have you ever lied? Have you ever been caught in a lie? Can you lie to yourself? Do you know the truth? Will you tell the truth? I know, a lot to think about.

The word preserve means to keep something as it is, especially to prevent it from decaying or being damaged or destroyed. Knowledge is truth. The word treacherous is described as guilty of or involving betrayal and deception.

I will ask you to ponder another question. Have you ever told the truth knowing it would cost you something? Have you ever lied so it would not cost you?

2 Samuel 11-12 tells the story of David and Bathsheba. If you want to understand treachery, betrayal, and deception, read that passage. It would make for a good soap opera. King David slept with another man's wife, got her pregnant, and tried to get her husband to sleep with her to cover it up. When that did not work, he arranged to have him killed. Crisis averted, or so he thought. Then, in comes the prophet Nathan basically saying, "I know what you did last summer!"

Because of the treachery he had committed, family life around the palace went downhill. Please read the story when you have time. In David's attempt to preserve his image, he ruined his family. Telling the truth is not an easy task, especially when you have sinned against someone. But God always provides a way for restoration. He wants to preserve you. David tried to preserve himself by lying. Proverbs 12:19 says, *"Truthful lips endure forever, but a lying tongue is only for a moment."* (NASB)

So, before you try to save your skin by withholding knowledge or lying, ask yourself, do I want my plans ruined, or do I want to be preserved by Him? I will say this much; I never want to have Nathan come up to me and say, "I know what you did last summer!"

Fred Alvarado

CROWN OR CANCER

Proverbs 12:4

*"A worthy wife is a crown for her husband,
but a disgraceful woman is like cancer in his bones." (NLT)*

In Genesis 2:18, God said it was not good for man to be alone, so he made the woman. It was important to God for a man to have a wife as his helper and companion for life. However, not just any woman is apt for this task, but she who is "worthy." A worthy wife values herself as a child of God and values her husband as the man God gave her to respect and honor as the head of the household. She brings worth, honor, and respect to the marriage relationship and crowns her husband with beauty, value, and glory. Perhaps someone reading this would say, "but my husband should be a crown for me, too!" But this is not what this verse says. God gave the title of being a crown to the wife and not the husband. As wives, we could crown him with beauty or destroy him with rottenness—cancer—through honoring or dishonoring our husbands.

The saying goes, "Happy wife, happy life." This is true to a certain extent, but it is incomplete—as if the wife's happiness is the only one that matters! It has been my experience that a happy husband contributes greatly to a happy family, and we wives have a lot to do with that. A happy husband reflects a happy home.

Every day, we have the choice to be a crown or cancer. The words we say, the tone of voice we use, the encouragement or discouragement we show through the respect we give to our husbands. We can encourage them with our loving and positive words, or with negative words we can make them feel like the scum of the earth. When he is getting ready for work, is he encouraged by you, or is he criticized for his shortcomings? One of these makes us a crown and the other a cancer. What about other areas of your life and relationship? I know husbands have responsibilities to us as wives, but this proverb deals specifically with us as wives and our influence. So, what will we be? Crown or cancer?

Teresa Bauer

HERMENEUTICS

Proverbs 21:16

*"The person who strays from common sense
will end up in the company of the dead." (NLT)*

Common sense is wisdom, born from simple observation and critical thinking, that engages the use of the brain God gave us. From these critical observations, we can make fairly sound judgments on many issues of daily living, ranging from relationships to household chores to organizing our lives.

As a pastor, much of my time is spent reading, praying, listening to the Lord, and studying the Bible in preparation for preaching and teaching in the church. To do this effectively, I engage in spiritual, thoughtful, and academic exercises. The spiritual has already been mentioned, and being thoughtful is thinking critically and practically about the Bible. But the academic discipline is called Hermeneutics, which is the interpretation of the Bible. In Hermeneutics, there are several rules that must be followed in order to arrive at an accurate analysis of the text. Three of the most basic rules are:

- A *text* without a *context* is nothing more than a *pretext—which is little more than an excuse to read whatever you want into the scriptures.*
- A text can never mean what the author never intended it to mean.
- The simplest reading of the text is often the most correct reading of the text.

We apply hermeneutics to our lives every day in the interpretation of daily living. We observe our lives, work, and relationships within a context that allows us to rightly analyze what needs to be done. We cannot make wise decisions in day-to-day living if we cannot "read" the context of people or situations. Also, applying common sense assessments of our surroundings is often the correct decision to make, and doing otherwise rarely leads to anything healthy or productive.

This proverb says that straying from common sense—using our brains—leads to bad decisions that will lead to death. Should I light fireworks in my house? Should I get drunk and then get behind the wheel of a car? Should I road rage the guy next to me? Should I cheat on my spouse? Should I steal from my job? Should I gamble away my life's savings? Bad hermeneutics—both in the Bible and in life—lead to bad conclusions. Use your brain and save your life!

Kyle Bauer

STAYING CALM

Proverbs 12:16

"A fool is quick-tempered,
but a wise person stays calm when insulted." (NLT)

Growing up as an at-risk youth among street life and violence, I witnessed several quick-tempered individuals jeopardize their lives. I saw countless fights, acts of verbal aggression, and vicious threats, all starting because of a quick temper. Several of these instances resulted in severe injury and imprisonment. Truly foolish.

Proverbs 12:16 states that there is wisdom in staying calm when insulted. It also tells us that it is foolish to be quick-tempered. Real-life situations teach us the dangers of letting anger and violence dictate our behavior. In school, physical fights led to expulsion, punishment, and injury. In everyday situations, being quick-tempered can lead to termination of employment, broken relationships, closed doors, burned bridges, and even jail time. Quick-tempered people cause all sorts of harm, both to others and themselves. But the Lord gives us a spirit of self-control, because He cares for our well-being.

Have you ever witnessed an incident where an individual is insulted or verbally attacked, yet they choose not to respond? I worked in the security field for about five years and had to become an expert at de-escalation. I encountered countless quick-tempered individuals ready to cause trouble and do harm in more ways than one. However, I successfully prevented situations from becoming bigger than they already were through calm and even-tempered de-escalation techniques. By keeping calm, we avoided any harm from coming to the public, the aggressor, or myself. Imagine how many fights, how much pain, and how many relationships could be saved if we chose to stay calm rather than foolishly act out. Proverbs 15:1 says that a soft answer turns away wrath.

Let us follow Jesus' powerful example the next time we are insulted. He showed us how to stay quiet, develop an even temper, seek calmness, and choose peace over violence. Jesus suffered frequent insults and attacks, yet He taught us how to respond by His actions. So, let's respond to people with the same spirit that Jesus gives us.

Victor Miguel Rivera

CONTROL YOUR EMOTIONS

Proverbs 24:28-29

*"Do not testify against your neighbor without cause
—would you use your lips to mislead?"
"Do not say, I'll do to them as they have done to me;
I'll pay them back for what they did." (NIV)*

God made us emotional people, but He also made us rational. He gave us both a heart and a brain. There are many circumstances in life that provoke powerful emotions in us, both good and bad. When we act purely from emotion, we can take a step too far and find ourselves falling off the cliff of reason into the abyss of negative emotions, like anger, which can lead to revenge.

In the 1880s, a legendary and deadly feud began between the Hatfields and McCoys that culminated in an appeal to the U.S. Supreme Court in 1888. The origin of the feud is obscure; some say it was politics, while others claimed it involved stolen livestock. Whatever the cause, it started with strong feelings and acting out of emotion.

Today, we continue to see gossip and slander against neighbors, families, and friends that result in hurt feelings, rejection, and misunderstandings. We allow our feelings and emotions to take control of our tongues and actions. Our resolve to "get back" becomes so strong that our ego and pride rise up in us, opening the door to evil actions.

Many times, we are told in Scripture not to take revenge but to seek after the good. It can be difficult, especially when our feelings are involved. But we must rise above momentary feelings and show restraint and wisdom with our words and actions; yielding to God is where you will find His peace.

Romans 12:19 says, *"Never take your own revenge, beloved, but leave room for the wrath of God, for it is written, 'Vengeance is Mine, I will repay,' says the Lord." (NASB)*

Do you have a place in your life, in your heart, where unforgiveness lives? Have you found yourself participating in gossip or slander? Ask God to reveal it and remove whatever hinders you from a closer relationship with Him.

The theologian Isaac Burrow said, "It is commonly said that revenge is sweet, but to a calm and considerate mind, patience and forgiveness are sweeter."

Jill Alvarado

THA...THA...THAT'S ALL, FOLKS!

Proverbs 26:27

*"Whoever digs a pit will fall into it,
and he who rolls a stone will have it roll back on him." (NKJV)*

In the classic cartoon series, Bugs Bunny was never caught by his rival, Elmer Fudd. Time after time, Elmer would go to great lengths to lay traps to capture this "wascally wabbit." But try as he may, every trap ended up only catching or hurting the one who laid the traps.

In the case of this proverb, God is not trying to show us how to catch a rabbit but instead is giving a warning to those with no good intentions and lays traps for the innocent. In biblical times, those who dug pits would do so to cause harm to people and animals. They would often cover the hole so that it would not be seen, and someone would innocently fall into it and be trapped. A perfect example is the story of Joseph and his brothers. They hated their brother Joseph so much that they formed a plan to capture and rid themselves of him by his slow death in the pit they had dug for him.

In the case of someone rolling a stone, it was a common practice that thieves and robbers would do to catch innocent travelers on their way through a valley. The robbers would release a rock to roll into the unsuspecting travelers and then would rob them of their goods and their lives.

This proverb is a warning to those who choose to lay traps and harm the innocent that He will make their actions return to them.

Jose Nolasco

SEARCH YOUR HEART AND WATCH YOUR MOUTH

Proverbs 10:19

"When there are many words, transgression and offense are unavoidable, but he who controls his lips and keeps thoughtful silence is wise." (AMP)

I know from experience—and I am sure you do too—that too much talking, especially when talking about other people, usually ends up very bad. I remember when I created a big problem and hurt someone I loved by gossiping. I was letting my mouth run with what my uncle calls "verbal diarrhea" and was bad-mouthing a relative to a mutual friend, who also happened to be my cousin's best friend. That's just stupid on stupid! That person ended up repeating what I had said to my cousin. My foolish mouth caused pain and nearly broke a relationship with someone I love.

No one ever means for their words to reach the ears of the person they gossiped about, but I realized a couple of things. First of all, my gossip-filled talk was sinful. Secondly, my problem with my cousin was not as much about her as it was with my own judgmental heart.

Jesus said it Himself in Matthew 12:34, *"For the mouth speaks what the heart is full of."* (NIV)

Just as my talk was judgment-filled, so was my heart. In searching the contents of my heart, I find that I have become wiser.

Just as wisdom is found in silencing and restraining the mouth, it is also found in searching and dealing with the heart. If what comes out of our mouths is rotten, then maybe we should look inward to see what is going on in our hearts.

Joshua Bauer

BEYOND MURDER

Proverbs 16:29

*"Violent people mislead their companions,
leading them down a harmful path." (NLT)*

Proverbs 1:10-18 says, *"My son, if sinful men entice you, do not give in to them. If they say, 'Come along with us; let's lie in wait for innocent blood, let's ambush some harmless soul; let's swallow them alive, like the grave, and whole, like those who go down to the pit; we will get all sorts of valuable things and fill our houses with plunder; cast lots with us; we will all share the loot'— my son, do not go along with them, do not set foot on their paths; for their feet rush into evil, they are swift to shed blood. How useless to spread a net where every bird can see it! These men lie in wait for their own blood; they ambush only themselves!" (NIV)*

The violent set traps for others, but they will fall into them. I am confident that those reading this book are probably not hanging around with murderers. So, spending time with or following those who are violent, according to the Bible, can be applied to more than just murderous intentions. The word for violence in Hebrew is also interpreted as injustice, cruelty, oppression, and wrongdoing. The book of Malachi, for example, designates divorce as an act of violence. But here, their violent intentions are more than "shedding innocent blood." They intend to take advantage of someone else for their own personal gain.

Proverbs is clear: This type of behavior will only lead to destruction. God is just, and He is reciprocal. He will turn evil plans back on the evil people who make them. Psalm 1 tells us we should not walk, stand, or sit with evil people. They think they are tough and invincible but have no weight or substance and will be blown away like chaff and destroyed.

Heavenly Father, I want my life to have substance and leave a lasting legacy for generations to come. I want to make disciples who will disciple others to disciple others (2 Tim. 2:2). Let me not fall prey to deceitful people who come to steal, kill, and destroy, but rather let me impart life and love to others in Jesus' name.

Stephen Larkin

HIGH VOLTAGE—BEWARE!

Proverbs 15:10

*"Severe punishment awaits the one who turns away from the truth,
and those who rebel against correction will die." (TPT)*

Most people are not exposed to deadly situations as a soldier would be. While researching for a writing project, I came across this account of a soldier: "I was ordered by my commanding officer not to touch alcohol, at least for an entire day before I was to stand guard and patrol. I disobeyed, and when I went on duty, I actually fell asleep! My partner saved my butt by waking me up before I was found out. Lesson learned. I never touched alcohol again anywhere close to my patrol hours. I could have easily faced a dishonorable exit from the military and an early end to what became a distinguished period of service to the country, myself, and those with whom I served."

Similar to this soldier's story that serves as a lesson to us, this proverb is a warning like a placard that reads, "High voltage—Beware!" Those who touch something so highly charged with moral, spiritual, or, yes, physical energy will feel the consequences. Then why do we touch? The truth is that we all want to know what lies on the other side of the warning. There are so many opportunities to test God's warnings along with the more observable ones found on earth. The larger question remains: What causes us to want to know what lies beyond God's warnings? What is the lust that drives us? Then this proverb quickly becomes another placard advising the reader to "stay in your lane." The harm is in not complying with God's correction. If people really believe that God's warnings are sure and accurate, many would be spared so much. Something to think about.

Juline Bruck

WISE PURSUITS

Proverbs 21:21

"The one who pursues righteousness and love
finds life, bounty, and honor." (NET)

Worldly pursuits typically fall under the major categories of fame, fortune, and power. Such pursuits are foolish and dangerous. They have purposely left God out of the picture, turning to Satan instead via occult practices and secret societies. These pursuits distract and hinder lost souls from experiencing the eternally abundant life in Christ.

Rather than pursuing the temporary and vanishing vapor of this world, this verse encourages us to fix our gaze on the One who is righteous, the God who is love.

"The one who pursues…" is eager, diligent, and fervent to "follow after" (MEV), "earnestly seek" (AMP), and "go hunting for" (MSG). According to Benson, this is the one who constantly endeavors to attain and exercise righteousness and love. How does one pursue these virtues? With great focus and care, always pressing forward.

These two attributes, *"righteousness"* and *"loyal love,"* depict the lifestyle of the believer who is pleasing to God and a blessing to others. The first term means that he will do what is right, and the second means that he will be faithful to the community of believers.

Pursuing righteousness and love lead to the unexpected bonuses of *"life, bounty, and honor."* Remember King Solomon? All he asked for was wisdom. God was so pleased with his request that He also promised to give him what he did not ask for—riches, fame, and long life (1 Kings 3:10-14).

"But first and most importantly seek (aim at, strive after) His kingdom and His righteousness [His way of doing and being right—the attitude and character of God], and all these things will be given to you also." (Matt. 6:33, AMP)

Karen Heimbuch

FEAR OF THE LORD

Proverbs 28:14

"Blessed is the one who always trembles before God,
but whoever hardens their heart falls into trouble." (NIV)

Proverbs 1:7

"The fear of the Lord is the beginning of knowledge,
but fools despise wisdom and instruction." (NKJV)

Before Christ (BC), I was a control freak. Even After Christ (AC), I continued trying to control everything. I wanted to know all the facts of a situation to make an informed decision. But, becoming more and more a follower of Jesus, I learned that even with all the facts, I could not know everything in order to make the best-informed decision. Only God can know it all. And, yes, I stepped in it more times than I care to say.

As my walk with the Lord progressed, I was called upon to mentor a young single woman with two children living in the middle of an untenable situation. Heavy! I realized that God had put somebody in my path who I could help. I knew it was a huge responsibility, and I could not do it without Him guiding my every thought, every step, and every decision. I did not want to be responsible for giving her guidance outside of God's parameters. I have to admit that during the course of the mentoring, my flesh did rise up from time to time, but God (I always love that "but God"), in His infinite wisdom, had also given me a smart young woman who could handle my tough, no-nonsense personality.

When you are confronted with a situation that you know you are not equipped to handle (which translates to "every situation"), do not be stubborn or hard-hearted. Instead, respect your Maker and lean on Him. Read your Bible and follow His commandments, for blessed is the one who trembles before the Lord.

PS: Twenty years later, she is an amazing woman of God. Thank You, Jesus!

Pat Nannarello

LONELY AT THE TOP

Proverbs 10:2

*"Gaining wealth through dishonesty is no gain at all.
But honesty brings you a lasting happiness." (TPT)*

How does the bible define wealth? The Hebrew word here actually refers to "treasure" as in something valuable that is gathered and stored, piled up, for gain. Solomon presents wealth as being defined within method and intent. Specifically, how did one gather, store, or pile up what they value? Was it done honestly, with pure intent? Simply put, lying is defined as actions or words used with the intent to deceive. Did a person acquire wealth by lying or deceiving others? If so, Solomon infers a person to be mistaken in assuming they have gained at all from this existence. Why? They have what they want, don't they?

Does the deceitfully wealthy person want recognition, power, or autonomy? What do they truly consider to be "gain"? Are they truly happy? These outcomes are hard to define apart from the association with others. What good is it to have something valuable, stored, or piled up with no one to recognize you for it or share it with you? The underlying premise is to recognize that deceitfulness cannot create the true outcome of gain, especially if ultimate gain or happiness involves other people. I am reminded of the statement "it is lonely at the top." I suggest this is because you now cannot trust the persons you have stepped on and stepped over to get to the top (wealth/gain), and they certainly do not want to associate with you. What a conundrum.

In the end, clearly Solomon presents true wealth, treasure, and lasting happiness is achieved by honestly gathering, storing, and piling up things that are valuable, to you and others, by including them. Achieve with others, not at the expense of others. In so doing, happiness (with others) will be the lasting outcome. Wealth and treasure are people, not solely possessions.

Lloyd Speese

DECLARED RIGHTEOUS

Proverbs 10:16

"The wages of the righteous is life,
but the earnings of the wicked are sin and death." (NIV)

We, as believers, are declared righteous in God's eyes when we accept Christ as our Lord and Savior. We exchange our unrighteousness and sin for the righteousness of Jesus. Salvation is a gift we did not have to work for, but it is attributed to us as wages! We are given a new life to live here on earth, and eternal life with Him, all because of the precious blood of Jesus.

But in contrast to the wages of the righteous are the wages of sin. The earnings of the wicked lead to death. Their sinful deeds, self-seeking way of life, and indifference to God are being added to their account, and in the end, they will pay the ultimate price—their life. But God does not rejoice when a soul turns away from Him and chooses death; the Bible says in Romans 6:23, *"for the wages of sin is death but the Gift of God is eternal life in Christ Jesus our Lord."* (NKJV)

Everyone loves to quote John 3:16 (and rightly so), but listen to what 3:17-18 says, *"For God did not send his Son into the world to condemn the world, but to save the world through him. Whoever believes in him is not condemned, but whoever does not believe stands condemned already because they have not believed in the name of God's one and only Son."* (NLT)

God is not condemning the world!

Whosoever believes in the Son will not be condemned and will have both forgiveness of debt (sin) and eternal life, but whoever does not believe is condemned already. People do not go to hell FOR the wages of sin because Jesus paid their debt. Did I get your attention? They receive the wages of their sin by not believing in Jesus and appropriating the payment He made on their account, and because of that, their sins are not forgiven, and they carry that weight along with them to hell.

Jesus paid the price for our sin (debt) and transferred His wages—His life—into our account. Have you ever asked Jesus to be the Lord of your life? If not, see the prayer at the end of the book, and do it now.

Debbie Speese

JUSTICE AND LIFE

Proverbs 12:28

"In the way of righteousness is life, and in its pathway,
there is no death." (NKJV)

Human nature tends to challenge anything that God proposes for our benefit. From the beginning, God told Adam and his wife that they would surely die if they disobeyed His word by eating from the Tree of the Knowledge of Good and Evil. Conversely, if they obeyed, they would experience nothing but God's life and goodness. However, they chose death along with all its consequences, and it is startling how many times we choose ways of living that go against the life God desires to give us.

Proverbs 12:28 states that walking in God's righteousness will bring us many benefits, one of which is abundant life. In applying this to the New Testament, righteousness—which is the opposite of sin—is received by accepting Jesus Christ and thus receiving eternal life instead of eternal death. Jesus said in John 14:6, *"I am the way, the truth, and the life."* Our future is guaranteed, knowing that there is life after the death of our physical bodies. If we stay in His righteousness, we will have eternal life with Christ.

There is no denying that we live in difficult times. Amid constant temptations and worldwide fear, we always have a choice to make: Will we choose God's way of righteous living or our human nature, which tends to go against God? However, God has given us His powerful, heavenly resources to stay in the way of righteousness in these dangerous and difficult times. *"For He, Himself has said, 'I will never leave you nor forsake you.'"* (Heb. 13:5) So let us choose God's life and righteousness!

Ricardo Chaidez

THE MEASURING STICK

Proverbs 10:29

"The way of the Lord is a stronghold to those with integrity,
but it destroys the wicked." (NLT)

My mother has a six-and-a-half-foot ruler she made from a board. Every year she measures the growth of all 13 of her grandchildren. Outside the official measurement, all the kids size each other up—straining—to see if they are taller than their cousins. Sometimes they try to slip on a shoe to gain height artificially, or they do the hand-to-forehead measurement in which one can always give himself or herself an advantage. But the only one that counts is being shoeless with the back to the giant ruler and grandma taking the official measurement.

God's Word is the measuring stick by which all of us will ultimately be assessed. When we measure ourselves against other people, we look pretty good, like the Pharisee in Jesus' parable, "thank you, God, that I am not like other people…."[1] Yet our judgments about ourselves may not be correct. An attitude of humility, a life of integrity, and increasing knowledge of and obedience to God's Word will keep us safe when our lives are finally measured by God. Adherence to His Word, not our ideas, will keep us safe in the end. His Word is light and life. [2]

God's Word is a stronghold (I think of a stone fortress) to those who walk in it, but this same Word applies to all, even to those who reject it. Jesus speaks of Himself as a stone. There is safety in the Rock that never moves, but "anyone who stumbles over that stone will be broken to pieces, and it will crush anyone it falls on."[3] In other words, God's Word is either safety or judgment, for by it, all lives will be measured. There is no middle ground.

As the Psalmist wrote:
> *"Oh, that my actions would consistently*
> *reflect your decrees!*
> *Then I will not be ashamed*
> *when I compare my life with your commands."*[4]

Kyle Bauer

---

1   Luke 18:9-14 (NLT)
2   Psalm 119:104; Proverbs 3:1-8
3   Matthew 21:44 (NLT)
4   Psalm 119:5-6 (NLT)

GOD KNOWS YOUR NAME!

Proverbs 22:29

*"Do you see a man who excels in his work?
He will stand before kings; He will not stand before unknown men." (NKJV)*

God knows your name! He formed you and gave you the gifts and talents to be who He created you to be and to do what he created you to do!

When Moses was leading the children of Israel in the wilderness, God gave him the plans to build the Tabernacle where He could meet and commune with His people. Not only did God give Moses the exact measurement, foot by foot, but He also told Moses the specific men who were to do the work!

Exodus 35:30, 34-35 says, *"…Moses said to the children of Israel, 'See, the Lord has called by name Bezalel the son of Uri, the son of Hur, of the tribe of Judah; and He has filled him with the Spirit of God, in wisdom and understanding, in knowledge and all manner of workmanship…and He has put in his heart the ability to teach, in him and Aholiab the son of Ahisamach, of the tribe of Dan. He has filled them with skill…'" (NKJV)*

God gave Bezalel and Aholiab the wisdom, knowledge, understanding, and skill to do their job. Since we know God is no respecter of persons, He will do the same for you and me. Ask God to fill you with His Spirit, wisdom, understanding, and knowledge. God says in His Word, if anyone lacks wisdom, let him ask! He would not tell you to ask if He did not intend to provide it.

I have heard it said that it takes about 10,000 hours of practice for someone to become a master at their craft. If you want to "stand before kings" and be good at what you are called to do, you need to be diligent and put the time in. The place to start is to ask God to give you wisdom, understanding, knowledge, and skill. Just as you ask for your daily bread, ask for daily wisdom.

God will give you what you need to fulfill the call He has for your life. Work hard, walk humbly before Him, and ask for His wisdom. God knows your name!

Michelle Glush

LOVE YOUR ENEMIES

Proverbs 25:21

*"If your enemies are hungry, give them food to eat.
If they are thirsty, give them water to drink." (NLT)*

I genuinely believe that (after accepting Jesus) being kind to your enemies is the greatest thing on earth you can do. I am willing to hear otherwise, but this is the crux of where God meets us in our transgressions; we are literally called enemies of God until He saves us. Enemies can be nothing else but enemies until Christ takes hold of their hearts.

To love an enemy and not give back what they are dishing out to you is essentially being Christ-like to them. (It is also a picture of God's patience with us when we did the same to Him.) If you have an opportunity to one-up someone who has hated on you, don't. Leave it alone, and let God do the work in their hearts. Our job is to love.

Before the Apostle Paul came to know Jesus, his name was Saul, a persecutor of Christians. Later, he became known as Paul—it is as if his name change reflected the inner change! Saul had an encounter with the risen Jesus Christ and later experienced the love and hospitality of Ananias, a follower of Jesus. This set Saul on his way to following Jesus and being transformed from a persecutor of Christians to a propagator of the Gospel.

In western culture, where walking away from a relationship at the slightest inconvenience is the norm, it is hard to wrap our minds around the concept of being kind to our enemies. Jesus asks us to put aside our need to be right. We are to love our enemies and do good to those who spitefully use us. This is the command that, just as the disciples asked Jesus, causes us to ask Him as well, "Lord, increase our faith." But as we do, we will see the "Sauls" in our lives turn into "Pauls," and enemies of Christ become disciples who will go out and change the world.

Rachael Hopkins

OBEYING GOD'S VOICE

Proverbs 28:9

*"One who turns away his ear from hearing the law,
even his prayer is an abomination." (NKJV)*

Ever wonder what God thinks about prayers from one who is actively disobeying His Word? This proverb addresses this very issue. By this proverb, we can understand how God views obedience: We are either actively obeying, or we are not, and merely hearing God's Word is not the same as obeying it.

Disobedience can just as easily be found in believers as in nonbelievers. It is easy to simply hear God's Word by reading it or hearing a sermon, then let it pass from one ear and out the other, never allowing it to penetrate the heart and transform us to be more like Jesus. In this proverb, to "turn away" is significant to understanding the issue. If we turn away from God's Word, we obstruct the work of God's Word within our hearts, affecting the power of our prayers.

Interestingly, the people who got the brunt of Jesus' criticism were the least likely candidates we would have thought of—the most religious and even some of the teachers of God's Law. For they, supposedly knowing what God wants from them, resisted it by replacing God's laws with their own rules and regulations—teaching their own rules as if they were the laws of God! Jesus used their long, loquacious prayers as an example of how not to pray! Jesus referred to them as hypocrites and whitewashed tombs. They appeared to be clean and holy all the while their hearts were full of the death and decay of human rules that ran contrary to God's laws.

The wisdom to be found here is that to hear His Word and not obey it creates a barrier to one's prayers being heard by God. It is not that we have to "pay to play" or that we are accepted by our works, but in Jesus' words, we are His friends when we obey His commandments (John 15:14). Let us, therefore, seek to be doers of God's Word so that all our prayers will humbly and gracefully make their way unimpeded to the throne of the living God.

Jose Nolasco

BY WISDOM, THE HOUSE IS BUILT

Proverbs 24:3-4

"By wisdom, a house is built, and through understanding, it is established; through knowledge its rooms are filled with rare and beautiful treasures." (NIV)

Have you noticed that whenever you buy furniture online, it always comes with instructions? Many people have said, "if only life had an instruction manual that we could follow!" Well, life comes with a manual. It is God's Word—the Bible. In the pages of God's Word, we find wisdom, knowledge, understanding, and good judgment. The beginning of wisdom is the fear of God (Prov. 1:7, 9:10)

I like to fix things and put things together. When I read the manual for furniture I have bought, I always check to make sure all the pieces are there and that I have all the necessary tools. If any of the hardware is missing (e.g., missing screws), I still make it happen. But if the furniture is missing a key piece, I have to return it. Some of us come to serve God with some missing screws, damages, and stains. The Lord is gracious and accepts us as we are, but that does not mean He will allow us to stay that way.

Wisdom is found in God, and He has the perfect building plan. To build a strong house in the Lord, we need stable foundations and pillars that can bear the weight of daily life. Problems and struggles can come suddenly, but If you walk in the fear of the Lord, your house will stand because of the solid foundations you have built upon the rock—Jesus Christ (Mark 3:25). Read your manual; read the Bible.

Alicia Suarez

EARS TO HEAR AND EYES TO SEE

Proverbs 20:12

"The hearing ear and the seeing eye,
the Lord has made them both." (NIV)

The simplicity of this proverb is self-evident. As The Message version of the Bible translates it, *"Ears that hear and eyes that see—we get our basic equipment from God!"* However, it is much more than the simple physical body parts that this proverb is speaking to.

Psalm 25:14 tells us, *"The secret counsel of the Lord is for those who fear Him, and He reveals His covenant to them."*[5] The New Living Translation says, "The friendship of the Lord"[6] instead of the secret. A valid way to translate this concept is to say that God has "secrets close friends share with each other." Another translation says:

> *"The secret [of the wise counsel] of the Lord is for those who fear Him, And He will let them know His covenant and reveal to them [through His word] its [deep, inner] meaning."*[7] (AMP)

There is a deeper meaning to these verses in Psalms and Proverbs that complement each other. God gave us more than physical equipment to see and hear. We are primarily spiritual beings that occupy the vehicle of our physical bodies until we receive our heavenly bodies.[8] We have our spiritual person with the same equipment as our physical person—eyes that see and ears that hear. We have the capacity to live in two realms at the same time; God has given us the ability to hear and see both in the physical and the spiritual realms. As we cultivate our relationship (friendship) with God, He will give further revelation of Himself and open our eyes and ears to know His "secrets-shared-between-friends." Fear Him and become His close friend. Listen to His voice, know His heart, and see new things about Him!

Kyle Bauer

---

5   Holman Christian Standard Bible. Copyright © 1999, 2000, 2002, 2003, 2009 by Holman Bible Publishers, Nashville Tennessee. All rights reserved.

6   New Living Translation, copyright © 1996, 2004, 2015 by Tyndale House Foundation. Used by permission of Tyndale House Publishers, Inc., Carol Stream, Illinois 60188. All rights reserved.

7   Amplified Bible. Copyright © 2015 by The Lockman Foundation, La Habra, CA 90631. All rights reserved.

8   See 2 Corinthians 5:1-10

A SAFE TOWER

Proverbs 10:15

"A rich man's wealth becomes like a citadel of strength,
but the poverty of the poor leaves their security in shambles." (TPT)

In reviewing this verse in eight different translations and then pondering it together, we realized there is an underlying truth that is the foundation of this verse: Life is not fair, it is not predictable, and it is not secure. So how do we want to deal with it?

We experienced a teaching moment many years ago when paying the monthly bills. I added up the interest from all the credit card debt and the car loans. I discovered we were paying over a thousand dollars a month just for the interest on our debt (not including the mortgage). Reality hit me: It was money we were paying for nothing! I resolved at that moment to create a plan to end any debt that did not even have tax benefits like the mortgage.

When we look at verse 15, we see two results based on choices made and actions taken. The results are "Citadel of Strength" or "Security in Shambles." These apply equally well to finances as they do to faith. Where will we be in a crisis? Are we students or drop-outs? In a financial crisis, we need a secure plan, strength of character, financial reserves, and wise counsel. The alternative is to live without thought of tomorrow and no reserves for a time of need.

Solomon would say it is better to be safe in a strong fortress than in a tent on a Balboa Boulevard sidewalk.

We are called to make a choice about which way we will live. Poverty requires no effort. Success requires diligent pursuit.

We have learned that sometimes life is not fair, it is not predictable, and it is not secure. It is in those times of despair that the discipline of our daily abiding in the Lord and His Word and ways becomes our safe tower and stronghold. We have testimonies to prove it.

Martin and Bea Laufer

TEMPERED

Proverbs 14:29

"He who is slow to anger has great understanding
[and profits from his self-control],
but he who is quick-tempered exposes
and exalts his foolishness [for all to see]." (AMP)

According to Mead Metals, *tempering* is the process of heating steel to a high temperature, though below the melting point, then allowing it to cool in still air. This process improves the machinability of the hardened steel while reducing the risk of cracks due to internal stresses.

In the same way, we see this verse contrasting the tempered person (who is "*slow to anger*") with the non-tempered person (who is "*quick-tempered*"). God is looking for cool-headed people; folks who have learned that Christ is our wisdom. Though God increases the fire in our lives, yet He will not allow us to melt. It is only after we have cooled in His presence do we begin to understand the need for patience and self-control. We are being tempered. We are slower to anger, slower to take offense. We understand ourselves better, as well as human nature.

On the other hand, a quick-tempered person will crack under stresses, whether internal or external. His impatience will cause him to lose control of his temper. He is easily provoked. Although he thinks he is acting like a big man, he is really acting like a big fool.

Therefore, let us not be "hasty of spirit" (KJV) or "angrily impulsive" (OJB), for "a quick-tempered person stockpiles stupidity." (MSG) Instead, let us submit ourselves to God our Father, who tempers us "to be conformed to the image of His Son." (Rom. 8:29 NIV)

Karen Heimbuch

YOU ARE YOUR HEART

Proverbs 27:19

*"As in water face reflects face,
so a man's heart reveals the man." (NKJV)*

"For as he thinks in his heart, so is he." Proverbs 23:7 (NKJV)

If you want to know what someone is really like, just let them talk. You will find out a myriad of things about them. You will learn their favorite color or song, their pet peeves, what they think about politics, and where they are or are not in their spiritual walk with the Lord.

One of my favorite Scriptures is Luke 6:45, *"A good man out of the good treasure of his heart brings forth good; and an evil man out of the evil treasure of his heart brings forth evil. For out of the abundance of the heart his mouth speaks."* (NKJV) What you have in your heart will be what you dwell on, what consumes you, and what comes out of your mouth. So, to put it in context with Proverbs 27:19, just as you see a reflection of yourself in water, what you see in your heart is a reflection of you.

Unlike what fitness gurus tell you, you are not what you eat. In Matthew 15:11, Jesus tells the crowd, *"It's not what goes into your mouth that defiles you; you are defiled by the words that come out of your mouth."* (NLT) I am not saying that you can make a daily diet of chips and soda and live a long and healthy life! But I am saying that it is what you put into your heart that matters most of all. It can either draw you closer to the Lord or serve as a catalyst to harden your heart and draw you away from Him.

Putting good things into your soul and spirit is just as important as the good healthy, nutritious food you put into your physical body. You would not drink poison and expect to live, then why would you listen to the negativity of the world or the lies spewed by the enemy and expect your spirit to thrive?

What we talk about matters. I believe the Father is leaning over the windowsill of Heaven, listening for those whose hearts are toward Him and smiling when He hears us praising His name. What's in your heart?

Michelle Glush

LAZINESS

Proverbs 10:26

*"As vinegar to the teeth and smoke to the eyes,
so are sluggards to those who send them." (NKJV)*

Have you ever worked with the wrong person? A person who just doesn't give a rip? Lazy people do not just irritate their employers, they irritate their co-workers, as well. So why are they there in the first place?

Some definitions of sluggard are lazy, shiftless, apathetic, and good-for-nothing. I love how the Passion translation renders this verse: *"To trust a lazy person to get a job done will be as irritating as smoke in your eyes—as enjoyable as a toothache!"*

I once hired a person for an important position. I neglected to check in with the Lord first. This person was so incompatible with our workplace that they made the people around them sick. I mean literally physically ill. In this case, it was not that they were "lazy" per se; they did not want to do the job as prescribed. Apathetic, for sure. If the boss asked this person to do job X in a particular manner, they would do job Y. They performed every task in a contrary way, which meant other people would have to redo it. There was definitely a rebellious spirit in this person, which cast a pall over the office that made us sick. More than a toothache! It was so bad we sought medical attention, and the doctors told us to leave our jobs. Instead, we decided to get rid of the negative person. We never recognized the extent of the negativity until the person was gone. New person hired. Darkness gone. Lights went on. People smiling. People healthy. The change in the office was that obvious.

We are called to do everything "as unto the Lord." We are always to bring our best to God. He gave us His best in giving us His Son, Jesus Christ, so why would we bring Him any less? Being lazy, shiftless, apathetic, and good-for-nothing is not how we honor God.

Pat Nannarello

THE SECRET LIFE

Proverbs 11:18-20

"The Lord detests those whose hearts are perverse,
but he delights in those whose ways are blameless." (NIV)

Every one of us has decisions to make that no one will ever know about. It could be a morally righteous decision or one that is unrighteous; either way, no one else would ever know what action was taken behind closed doors.

Proverbs 11:18-20 makes a clear distinction between the person who acts with a perverse heart and one who acts righteously. God sees both, is aware of both, and conveys that there are significant outcomes for either. For the person who pursues righteousness, they gain life. On the contrary, one who approaches life with a perverse heart paves the way to their own death. Ultimately, one is either gaining life or walking towards destruction; there is no middle ground

I have often found myself frustrated and questioning God about whether following Him is worth it when I do not have everything I want in this life. Then I see others who are sowing unrighteousness and have the very things my heart desires. The Holy Spirit, in His gentleness, reminds me to shift my focus on God and release my frustrations to Him before they take me over and impact my actions behind closed doors. I have seen that when I compare my life to others, I act as though I know what is in their hearts when I really need to pursue my relationship with God to gain life from Him and not compare my life to others.

Only God knows our hearts and truest intentions. He is the rewarder and the sovereign Father. If we keep pursuing His ways, we will gain delight in Him, and He will continue to show us His goodness beyond what we can comprehend. This can only be accomplished through how we spend our time behind closed doors. Where is your time going? Retreat to Him. Linger to hear from Him. Do not rush through your day depending on your own strength and understanding. What you do in secret matters, and as you spend time with God, you will gain unfathomable rewards. (Matt. 6:6-7)

Cynthia Medrano

DEEP ROOTS

Proverbs 12:3

"Wickedness never brings stability,
but the godly have deep roots." (NLT)

We see it all the time: Governments around the world that are based on lies, violence, corruption, greed, ambition, theft, and bribes never bring stability to any country. Yet, at the time of this writing (Summer 2022), we see the same corruption happening in our country at unprecedented levels. As a result, we see racial, financial, economic, social, moral, political, and geopolitical instability not previously seen before. Psalm 89:14 says that the foundations and stability of God's Throne are righteousness, justice, truth, and mercy (love). When these are not present, the governmental foundation cannot last.

Corruption and politics, however, are certainly nothing new; they are more synonymous than anything else. Amid a chaotic world filled with so much wickedness, there is something that brings stability to our lives: godliness. The metaphor employed in this proverb for godliness (and elsewhere in the Bible) is a tree with deep roots.

Psalm 1 speaks about the wicked and the godly by directly contrasting a deeply rooted tree with chaff. The blessed people do not do as the wicked; rather, they delight in the Word of God and diligently keep their minds on it all the time. This will make them like fruitful trees planted by streams of water. The wicked, however, are like the chaff that surrounds the kernel of wheat. It is easily separated and easily discarded.

The imagery is clear: trees are strong, weighty, and the deep roots in God's Word keep them from blowing over in the fiercest of storms. They are filled with fresh, green leaves and nutritious fruit. God's Word gives us a firm foundation into which we can sink deep, unshakeable roots, regardless of what is happening in the world around us. Yet those who insist on selfish ambition, immorality, and the total rejection of God's Word are little more than the thin, papery chaff blown away by the slightest breeze. Proverbs 12:3 and Psalm 1 are unequivocal: wickedness will not last long term, but the righteousness of those who hold fast to God's Word will stand forever.

Kyle Bauer

A FLOWING FOUNTAIN

Proverbs 15:2

"Knowledge flows like spring water from the wise;
fools are leaky faucets, dripping nonsense." (MSG)

Imagine you are in the middle of the desert, and the sun is beating down on you. You are sweating and in need of water to soothe your dry throat. As a source of water, would you choose a leaky faucet dripping one water droplet at a time or a fountain flowing with fresh, abundant, and never-ending water? The answer may seem obvious. However, when put into the context of Proverbs 15:2, every time we hear advice, guidance, or even suggestions from someone, we have to discern whether we are about to drink from a leaky faucet or a fountain of spring water.

When we have a dry throat and are in desperate need of water, we would go to any source to quench our thirst. In the same way, when we feel like we are stuck and need guidance from someone, we tend to absorb any piece of advice given to us. However, Proverbs 15:2 warns us about who we should listen to when seeking guidance. A fool giving advice will leave us empty and unquenched, because their words are nonsense and have no substance. But the words of the wise bring abundant knowledge, because their guidance flows from the Holy Spirit: "For He has satisfied the thirsty soul." (Ps. 107:9)

The next time you receive advice from someone, before you take it in and follow through, pause and seek God first: "Let no one deceive you with empty words." (Eph. 5:6) God does not want us to spend our time drinking from leaky faucets when we are craving flowing water. Instead, He wants us to receive knowledge from those who are wise and who offer an abundance of water when we feel like we are in the middle of a desert.

Amelia Montantes

ARE YOU LISTENING?

Proverbs 16:21

*"The wise are known for their understanding,
and pleasant words are persuasive." (NLT)*

"Is he listening to what I just said?"

Most people understand what it's like to buy a car. The whole dealership experience. The negotiating process. It can be overwhelming for the customer and the salesman. Meeting someone for the first time. Trying to figure out the needs and wants while trying to "make the sale." Overcoming obstacles. Back and forth with the questions, answers, offers, counteroffers, and legitimate expectations vs. unrealistic expectations.

As of the writing of this book, I have been in car sales for 20 years. At my store, we have one particular salesman, Vig, who has consistently sold 25 to 30 cars per month for 24 years. No one comes close to Vig, though they try. What's his secret? Vig seeks to understand his customer first—their wants and their needs. In this proverb, the wise seek understanding. Vig's understanding is not based on how he feels or his emotions. He addresses the concerns of his customer first and not his own. So, when he begins to speak, he responds to what they have told him. Vig's response is pleasant and persuasive to his customer.

It is a lesson in listening. Imagine if we had the same discipline of understanding what someone is trying to tell us. When we have understanding, we acknowledge that we are listening. The words we then speak are directly to what they have said. Verse 23 says, *"the heart of the wise teaches his mouth and adds learning to his lips."* Do we listen with our ears or heart?

I would love to say I am a master of this concept. I fall short. In my conversations with my wife of 36 years, I have seen the difference between understanding and just hearing. When she sees that I understand her wants and needs, my words are more pleasant and persuasive. I do not just listen with my ears, I listen with my heart. When I listen with my heart, I speak from the heart. I speak to my wife's heart. I cannot imagine being more pleasant and persuasive than that.

So today, try to gain understanding of someone. Doing so will make you wise, and you will speak with pleasant and persuasive words.

Fred Alvarado

375

A DIFFICULT TEST

Proverbs 27:21

*"The purity of silver and gold is tested by putting them in the fire;
the purity of human hearts is tested by giving them a little fame." (MSG)*

Just as fire purifies precious metals, God allows us to experience the fire of recognition, fame, praise, honor, and admiration from other people, and He is watching and measuring our internal heart responses.

We have all seen fame and praise from the masses turn young celebrities into self-absorbed monsters, and we are rightly repulsed by their actions. Pride, disdain for others, and condescension are ugly, and nothing brings it out of the heart more quickly than being lifted up by other people. But what makes us think our response to the same idolization would be any different?

I was 25 years old and in my first pastoral assignment. I was never given a chance to preach at this church, but my friend was—all the time. It irritated me. I knew I could preach and had great things to say. Then, one Sunday, I saw my friend was preaching again, and I became angry. Then, it was as if God suddenly put His finger on my chest and fiercely said, "Why do you want to preach? For My glory or yours?"

Before God allowed me to preach, He had to settle with me about what kind of man I was going to be. He had to first deal with my heart, which could have easily become ugly and prideful the moment the first person said, "Pastor, that was really good."

What about you? Do you react to praise with visceral joy and butterflies in the stomach that suddenly go to your head, thinking, "I must really be something!"

God is watching our responses in every situation. *He is measuring what we really want and who or what we really love.* These attitudes will be revealed in this test. The irony is that those who seek honor for themselves will never get it from God, but God gives great honor to those who choose humility and will deflect the glory given to them back to Him.[9]

Kyle Bauer

•

---

9   Psalm 138:6; Isaiah 2:12, 23:9; James 4:6, 10

DECEMBER

Follow my advice, my son;

always treasure my commands.

Obey my commands and live!

Guard my instructions

as you guard your own eyes.

Tie them on your fingers as a reminder.

Write them deep within your heart.

—Proverbs 7:1-3

THE DOORS OF HUMILITY

Proverbs 15:33

"Fear of the Lord teaches wisdom;
humility precedes honor." (NLT)

The whole premise of the book of Proverbs is to 1) get wisdom and 2) understand that the beginning of wisdom is in fearing the Lord. If the fear of the Lord teaches wisdom, then Proverbs 15:33 gives a key insight into gaining His wisdom and receiving the honors He desires to give—be humble and humility will bring honor. Many times, in both the Old and New Testaments, the Bible says that God lifts up the humble and brings down the proud. God has a very special place in His heart for humility, but pride is hateful to Him.

Some time ago, while I was in prayer, the Lord gave me a vision of Heaven's courts. I saw a grand entryway with enormous golden doors and many angels flanking a magnificent red carpet—a truly worthy entrance for the King of kings. In the vision, however, I did not see the Lord going in or out by this way. I walked around the building where I saw plain wooden doors. They were beautiful and very tall, but they were not anything special. I asked the Holy Spirit what He was showing me, and He replied, "These are the doors of humility. These are the doors by which I usually come and go."

God made His grand entrance into our world by way of a baby born in a stable. Jesus came not to be served but to serve. Jesus took the form of a servant, and He washed His disciples' feet with a towel. Jesus was obedient even to the point of death on the cross. Jesus came to save our lives by giving His life up. Though He continues to be God, Jesus has forever relegated Himself to a human body, thereby giving up more than we will ever know. Humble is who God is, and humility always seeks to love and serve other people. Psalm 18:35 says, *"…Your [humility] gentleness has made me great."* (NKJV)[1] In Jesus' humility, He has also received God's highest honor (Phil. 2:5-11). As we humble ourselves at all times and in all things, never seeking our own position or glory, as we serve others, we will find God honoring us as those who act as He does.

Kyle Bauer

_____

1   The HCSB translates it humility whereas most other translations use gentleness.

WHAT IN THE WORLD IS HE *"DOINGS?"*

Proverbs 20:11

"Even a child is known by his doings,
whether his work be pure, and whether it be right." (KJV)

I can tell you some of my "doings." When I was 10, I snuck out of my bedroom window and rode my bike to the store to buy three chocolate doughnuts, only to be caught by my mom on the way home. When I was 6, I rode my bike down a hill into cross traffic. When I was 14, my friend and I rode our roller skates down a hill, traveling up to 35 MPH (read about it in "Another one bites the dust"). Finally, the pièce de résistance, when I was about 12, I thought it would be a great idea to take a can of gas into our backyard and pour it out in an artistic fashion, with twists and turns, light it on fire, and watch it burn only to watch it run its course back to the can of gas. God only knows why it did not blow up in my face. I believe this will be the first time my parents have heard that story. Sorry about the grass, mom and dad.

There are countless other "doings." I eventually grew out of these foolish acts, sooner than later. Proverbs 22:6 says, *"Train up a child in the way he should go, and when he is old he will not depart from it."* (NKJV) My mom especially adhered to 22:6, and because she did, there were many other "doings" that were not dangerous and reckless.

I am still my mom and dad's child. I am also a child of God. Now that I am older and growing closer to my heavenly Father, I must be careful of my "doings," because they will become what I am known for. In John 13:35, Jesus said, *"By this* all will know *that you are My disciples, if you have love for one another."* (NKJV) Our "doings" should be a reflection of Jesus and His love. Ask yourself, "Am I known for my good doings or bad doings? Will others know I am a disciple of Jesus?"

So, as you go about your daily "doings," just remember someone is watching and saying, "What in the world is he doings?!"

Fred Alvarado

PAY ATTENTION

Proverbs 10:5

*"A wise youth harvests in the summer,
but one who sleeps during harvest is a disgrace." (NKJV)*

My husband used to say to me, "You have GOT to pay attention to what is around you." His father and his best friend were law enforcement, so he learned throughout his life to pay attention. He also spent 30+ years in the film industry in the grip and lighting departments. Those are the people who make things magically happen for films. There was a lot of creative problem-solving, and I watched, listened, and learned.

Proverbs 10:5 is not just about being wise and young or young and lazy. It is about paying attention in your life no matter your age. As you go through life, you inevitably will gather knowledge, and the harvesting of your experiences will give you tools to apply that knowledge to circumstances you face. Now you have a choice—you can use that information or let the circumstance dictate the outcome.

One extremely rainy day, about nine months after my husband died, my backyard was flooded. The water on my patio was at least 18 inches deep. I found myself at the local equipment rental company renting a sump pump and 100-foot hose (think fire hose)! Donning my husband's rain gear, I set up the pump on the patio and ran the hose to the street. I was not happy. It was pouring rain, and I am a 5 feet 4 inches, 50-something woman hauling a fire hose in the middle of a torrential downpour and screaming at God: "I don't get it! I can make sense of why my husband died, but WHY DO I HAVE TO DO THIS??!" I still don't know, but I do know that paying attention to what my husband did prepared me to save my home.

This also applies to harvesting the Word of God. You learn the Scriptures so they become part of your being. As you fill your mind and spirit with God's Word, you will have an overflow of living water to minister to others and practice what the Bible says to do. If you don't pay attention, you miss all that the Lord has for you. Don't be lazy! Read your Bible! Pay attention!

Pat Nannarello

A REFUGE EVEN IN DEATH

Proverbs 14:32

*"The wicked are thrown down by their own evil,
but the righteous find refuge even in death." (CEB)*

Two profound truths are contained in these two short phrases.

First, *"the wicked are thrown down"*—they are crushed (NLT), overthrown (AMP), driven away (KJV), banished (NKJV), and ruined (NCV) *"by their own evil."* When such a person dies in their sins, he has no defense or hope of recovery, for he has departed this life without repentance or forgiveness. He is without faith in Christ; unjustified and unsanctified. The sins to which he clung are now inseparable from him. He cannot blame God for his demise, for "wicked people are killed by their *own* evil deeds." (Ps. 34:21, CEV)

Second, *"the righteous find refuge even in death"*—they have hope of eternal life, love, and joy on the other side of death. A literal and glorious heaven awaits those who have put their faith in Jesus Christ. Regardless of earthly pain or trials, dangers or distress, the righteous have resolute hope in the promises of God, for it is impossible for God to lie (Heb. 6:18).

"I have fought the good fight, I have finished the race, I have kept the faith. Now there is in store for me a crown of righteousness, which the Lord, the righteous Judge, will award to me on that day—and not only to me, but also to all who have longed for His appearing." (2 Tim. 4:7-8, NIV)

Karen Heimbuch

MADE IN HIS IMAGE

Proverbs 17:5

"Those who mock the poor insult their Maker;
those who rejoice at the misfortune of others will be punished." (NLT)

When God formed Adam and Eve, He "created [them] in His own image… male and female He created them." (Gen. 1:27) Adam and Eve knew they were made in the image of God, and that was enough for them. When the serpent entered the Garden, he mocked them, telling them they were less fortunate because their eyes had not been opened. The serpent deceived them into believing that being made in the image of God was not enough, and they needed to become like God. They believed the lie, and as Adam and Eve were expelled from the Garden because of sin, the Lord did not rejoice when He had to send them away.

When the serpent tempted Adam and Eve into taking the fruit to be like God, he was mocking that God had already made them in His image. In the same way, when we mock people, it is the same as saying that being made in the way God made them is not enough—they have to be better, smarter, or wealthier. Mocking a reflection of something is the same as insulting the original image, which is why we need to caution ourselves with how we speak toward others and what we think about them in our hearts.

The act of rejoicing dates back to when God created humankind: *"God saw all that he had made, and it was very good."* (Gen. 1:31, NIV) He rejoiced in His creations, because what He had made was beautiful in His sight. However, God did not rejoice when He had to send His creation away. In the same way, God calls us not to delight in someone's adversity, because we are rejoicing in the misfortune of His creation. Instead, we can provide comfort and reassurance just as God would do for us.

Every human being is a work of art by God, a masterpiece, including those less fortunate or those who encounter adversity. Because of this truth, we can ask the Lord to help us see people as He sees them so we can grow in how we speak and act toward the people around us.

Amelia Montantes

PARTIALITY IS NOT GOOD

Proverbs 24:23

"These things also belong to the wise:
It is not good to show partiality in judgment." (NKJV)

To show partiality in judgment is not good. (Period. Mic drop.)

You will pardon the colloquialism used above, but it is hard to add anything to such an important truth directly from the heart of God. Partiality in judgment is not only an offense to God, but also to our fellow man. Few things can be as harmful to society as a justice system that is partial to any person, group, or affiliation.

Interestingly, the purpose behind the blindfold on the symbol of justice, the Lady of Justice statue you find in many courtrooms in America, is that justice is blind in order to render righteous judgments. However, justice has been placed under a microscope of late in our contemporary world, where issues of race, equity, and equal justice between political ideologies abound and are continually the topic of conversation in the news and around the water coolers of our society.

But you might say, I know this to be true in business, politics, or even the justice system, but isn't it great to know that it could never be the case in the church?

Not so, my dear brother and sister! We know that if this were not a problem for all men, including those within God's family, the writer of Proverbs would not have mentioned it. We must be vigilant to guard our hearts against unfairness, selfishness, or blindness to other people's needs or feelings. For proof, one needs only to go to the New Testament and see the dispute between the Jews and the Hellenistic believers. The Hellenists had noticed that their widows were not receiving equal treatment and monetary support. There was partiality, even though it was unintentional; fairness in the church was being overlooked. But it was rectified by the appointment of Holy Spirit-filled overseers to correct the injustice.

So let us be wise today and ask our heavenly Father to help guard our hearts against any possible influence or partiality. May we, by the power of the Holy Spirit, see all things through the lens of our Savior, Jesus Christ, and never fail to properly sow righteous judgment in every decision.

Jose Nolasco

WATCH YOUR MOUTH!!

Proverbs 10:21

"The words of the godly encourage many,
but fools are destroyed by their lack of common sense." (NLT)

What do your lips do? You are relieved of thirst by your lips. You breathe through your lips. Nourishment comes through your lips. Poison and death can come into you or out of you through your lips. Apparently, the lips are vital to life.

The godly, the righteous, and those who follow the Lord give life to many. Life and death are in the power of the tongue (Prov. 18:21) which is the inner working structure of the lips. Out of the abundance of the heart, the mouth speaks (Matt. 12:34). From the lips come life or death. Spiritually speaking, life comes from the function of the lips through the tongue to the hearers.

However, the foolish, the ungodly, and those who do not choose the Lord die for lack of understanding and a lack of knowledge. Clearly, godliness increases knowledge, common sense, and wisdom. In turn, what we feed ourselves through our mouth develops itself within us and produces an end result from within us. If you feed godliness into yourself, that godliness and its wisdom is exactly what will come out of you. This same godliness affects your heart, and from the abundance of a godly heart will come an abundance of godly productivity through you and then to others.

The question becomes how do you use your lips? How do you feed yourself? What goes into your heart through your spiritual lips, lifestyle, practice, and discipline? This, in turn, becomes what you feed to others, both literally and abstractly. Whatever is in you comes out and displays itself. Your true nature will be revealed.

Clearly, Solomon wants us to be aware that if we put foolishness into ourselves, it will come out. Furthermore, feeding on and then feeding others, either foolishness or godliness, is a choice. The foolish die for not having chosen common sense and greater understanding. In short, a lack of wisdom is life-threatening. Let this be food for thought, and let this be life for yourself and for others.

Lloyd Speese

RIGHT IN HIS EYES

Proverbs 21:2

"People may be right in their own eyes,
but the Lord examines their heart." (NLT)

Why do people, knowing the difference between right and wrong, do what is evil? They think and see themselves as doing right. The prideful do not want God to examine their heart, nor do they desire His correction. They choose to live their own way, and any way apart from God will end up being sinful. Even though they do not want Him to examine their heart, He will judge them according to their nature and actions. *"But I, the Lord, search all hearts and examine secret motives. I give all people their due rewards, according to what their actions deserve."* (Jer. 17:10, NLT)

The Lord has commanded His people to set themselves apart, to be holy because He is. (Lev. 20:7-8, NLT). We are to be holy, like Jesus, just as He is holy (Matt. 5:48). We do this so that we may walk blameless in His eyes and show God's goodness in living out His righteousness.

To be holy before Him, we must let Him examine our hearts and ask Him to renew us. *"Create in me a pure heart, O God, and renew a steadfast spirit within me."* (Ps. 51:10, NIV) He will renew our spirit; He will soften the hardened heart. (Ezek. 36:26, NIV). To stay holy, we are to continue reading the Bible and putting His commands into practice. *"How can a young person stay on the path of purity? By living according to your word."* (Ps. 119:9, NIV).

We need to keep our hearts ever before the Lord, so He can EXAMINE US SO WE CAN BE RIGHT IN HIS EYES INSTEAD OF IN OUR OWN EYES.

Joshua Bauer

STAND FAST IN GOD'S WORD

Proverbs 10:10

*"He who [maliciously] winks the eye [of evil intent] causes trouble;
and the babbling fool [who is arrogant and thinks himself wise]
will come to ruin." (AMP)*

This proverb references two types of people—the "winkers" and the fools.

A wink is a secret signal to those "in the know." In this case, the winkers are the ones who set forth plans of evil intent. The fools are the ones who continually speak arrogantly with empty words and promises.

In today's landscape, the most prominent winkers are the conspirators who believe they have the "secret truths" and perpetuate shaky and immoral ideologies in society. At the same time, the fools who follow these movements respond in harmful ways—as we saw the violence in the summer of 2020. The fools are those shouting ideologies, philosophies, ways of governance, etc., on public platforms to advance their own agendas. Unfortunately, there is an exhaustive number of "leaders" and movement pushers today who rise up as quickly as they disappear. They are motivated to create and feed their audiences' insecurities and fickle appetites to consume whatever is the next issue.

Are you winking in any direction that leads to a destructive end? Are you speaking too much on topics you don't genuinely know about? Are you creating narratives to fit assumptions that lead others into ungodly action? Are you jumping to conclusions?

Take comfort in God's faithfulness! It's scary to watch friends or family you love fall into these traps, willingly or unwillingly. I believe if we are misinformed but submitted to God, He will straighten our paths to His truth (the only truth), and we will walk (with His help) in His perfect ways. Evil will not endure forever. It is our job to stand fast in God's Word, love His truth, walk blamelessly, and, above all, love others.

Rachael Hopkins

GOD PROTECTS THE WIDOW

Proverbs 15:25

"The Lord tears down the house of the proud,
but he sets the widow's boundary stones in place." (NIV)

"God smashes the pretensions of the arrogant;
He stands with those who have no standing." (MSG)

These two different translations shed light on two similar groups needing God's protection. There are many references in the Bible to God's concern for widows. In the Old Testament, we read of a widow who listened to the prophet Elijah and received provision in her time of need. She had only enough oil left to make one loaf of bread for her son and herself before they were in danger of starving to death because of the famine in the land. As an act of faith, Elijah requested that she feed him first. Her faith resulted in provision for the duration of the famine. In another example, Jesus also took care of his widowed mother. While dying on the cross, He called out to his trusted disciple, John, to care for her.

The Bible also shares concern for the orphan and others who had no standing (family or status). Jesus told the disciples to *"let the little children come to Me…."* (Matt.19:14 NKJV) These are words for us to consider in today's culture when the lives of the little ones are not valued.

As with a coin, there are two sides to the story in this proverb—what the Lord speaks to the proud and arrogant and what He, in His love, speaks to those who have no one else to stand with and for them. It is difficult to understand in our culture when we see the proud prospering and the humble in want. We see the extremes in our world and cry out for answers. We do not always see the answer we were hoping for, but we know that God sees and, as Judge of all, will ultimately make things right. I like when Proverbs 15:3 states, *"The eyes of the Lord are in every place, beholding the evil and the good."* (KJV)

Those who only look out for themselves and their own interests do not reflect the heart of God. On the contrary, He is intensely interested in and loves to defend the defenseless, and when we stand up for others, we reflect God's heart.

Kathleen Stevenson

DON'T TAKE YOUR NEIGHBOR TO COURT

Proverbs 25:9-10

"When arguing with your neighbor,
don't betray another person's secret.
Others may accuse you of gossip,
and you will never regain your good reputation." (NLT)

Whether in your home, neighborhood, or wherever two people exist—wherever you find yourself and others—there is sure to be conflict. Two people can hardly agree on where to go to lunch after church! The New Testament sheds an understanding on the wisdom of this proverb in dealing with personal conflict. In Matthew 18:15-17, Jesus outlines three steps for healthy conflict resolution, and wisdom shows if we do these three steps, we'll never end up in court. However, there is a caveat: This wisdom is exclusive to the believer.

Step 1: Go to the person in a cool, calm, and collected spirit. This may take some preparation of heart and mind to avoid jumping into a confrontation when you are angry. With humility and grace, tell your perspective on the offense. If the person does not want to hear you out or come to an amicable agreement, take Step 2.

Step 2: Meet with the person a second time and bring one or two others along so they can hear the conversation and assess the situation and the responses. If the person does not want to reconcile, and one or both parties continue to be recalcitrant and refuse to forgive, continue to Step 3.

Step 3: If they still do not hear you or respond, then take it to the church, and if they refuse to listen [refuse to forgive and maintain the unity of the Body of Christ], treat them as you would a pagan or tax collector. If there is no remorse or desire for reconciliation, perhaps it is time to go see Judge Judy.

Chris Stanton

TALK IT OUT

Proverbs 18:13

*"He who answers a matter before he hears it,
it is folly and shame to him." (NKJV)*

More than once in my life, I have jumped to conclusions. Oh, it is so easy to do! We hear one thing and think we know the answer and the right thing to do. We are convinced of our own justice and righteousness. We are convinced there is no other option than what we know to do for the situation at hand. Things inevitably happen in life, the accusations fly, and equally inevitable is that we only heard one side of the story, and then we are put to shame with our knee-jerk reaction.

The child's teacher sends home a bad report and some sort of consequence. The child has a story that mom and dad readily believe. "My child's teacher hates him!" the parents exclaim. Then it comes out that the child was lying about everything. Oops! Now there is egg all over mom and dad's faces, and the situation needs redemption and forgiveness.

A while ago, I had to answer a matter, and fortunately, circumstances allowed me the opportunity to hear it first and come up with a solution before any meeting or corrective confrontation took place. I realized at that moment how much easier it was to come prepared, not with hearsay but with hard, first-hand evidence and context instead of moving on unsubstantiated rumors or hurt feelings. (By the way, hurt feelings are not evidence in a situation. Often, hurt feelings are misunderstandings that provoke harsh and unfounded responses that exacerbate the situation and bring further hurt instead of redemption and forgiveness.) The confrontation brought redemption between the parties involved.

Before we get our feelings hurt, let's go straight to the person and talk it out. Do not brood over it or react to only partial information, and be careful not to let your imagination attribute false scenarios or wrong motives unjustly to the other person. That never ends well.

It is good to come to a difficult conversation with an open mind, an open heart, and a willingness to listen to the other person. The goal is not to "exact a pound of flesh" but to bring truth and restore relationship. As they say in Spanish, "Hablando se entiende la gente." (Talking it out helps people understand.)

Kyle Bauer

LEADERSHIP DETERMINES FLOURISHING

Proverbs 29:2

"When the righteous are in authority, the people rejoice;
but when a wicked man rules, the people groan." (NKJV)

It's extremely important to understand that governments put into place by people will never be the "Utopian" rule that our hearts desire them to be. (Utopia—the shallow, sinful, human version of Heaven.)

For now, governmental bodies of power will always be stained by various forms of corruption. We can argue about what perfect policies look like and how helpful solutions can be implemented, but we will never fully escape sin's hold on this side of eternity. That being said, it is important to know that in any system, righteous leadership (those who seek after God's ways; operate in honesty, righteousness, and goodwill towards people) makes a massive difference in how these deeply imperfect systems function.

Have you ever noticed how life and creativity are sucked out of places where leadership does not honor God? God raises up a nation that exalts righteousness and will allow a nation set in its wicked ways to experience the consequences of its sin. This principle holds true for governments and any leadership, business, church, and family. When those in any role of leadership seek the Lord, everything under their influence falls into place. Solutions will be thought of that were never sought out before, resources will be given where there wasn't previous access, and the people under this wise, God-seeking leadership will flourish in ways they never knew they could. Leaders who love righteousness are, for those affected by their leadership, a cause to rejoice.

Rachael Hopkins

HOPE ENJOYED VS. HOPE DESTROYED

Proverbs 10:28

"The prospect of the righteous is joy,
but the hopes of the wicked come to nothing." (NIV)

I love the word *prospect*—it puts me in mind of prospecting for gold. When I was young, our family once toured a pyrite mine. Pyrite is also known as "fool's gold" for it bears a superficial resemblance to gold. Whereas gold is scarce and therefore precious, pyrite is the most abundant sulfide mineral found. Failure to recognize these differences causes one to look foolish.

The *prospect,* or hope, of the righteous "pans out" to be "true gold"; hope fulfilled brings joy. Righteous people are uncompromisingly upright, having honorable character and integrity. Wicked people oppose God and ignore His wisdom; sinners refusing the Savior. Their hopes, or expectations, will "pan out" as "fool's gold," ambitions perished, hope destroyed.

The surrounding verses list the blessings that come to the righteous: Their fear of the Lord prolongs their life (v. 27); their hope in the Lord brings them joy (v. 28); the way of the Lord is their stronghold (v. 29); godly wisdom and truth flow from their mouths (vv. 31-32).

In contrast: The years of the wicked are shortened (v. 27); the hopes of the wicked are frustrated (v. 28); the way of the Lord is the ruin of the wicked (v. 29); the tongue of the wicked is perverted and will be cut out (vv. 31-32).

The wicked look to what they have in hand while the righteous look to what they have in hope.

"...we eagerly await our adoption, the redemption of our bodies. For in hope we were saved. Now hope that is seen is not hope, because who hopes for what he sees? But if we hope for what we do not see, we eagerly wait for it with endurance." (Rom. 8:23b-25, NET)

Karen Heimbuch

WARNING SIGNS

Proverbs 11:29

"Those who bring trouble on their families inherit the wind.
The fool will be a servant to the wise." (NLT)

Danger!

When there is peril ahead, it is common for those in charge of public safety to place signs to warn of the danger. In public, such signs are normal and appropriate. However, it is not common to see these same signs on one's front door! In a sense, this proverb is placing a warning sign on the door of the heart of those who read it. The danger here is not from outside but from within. The peril itself is far more disastrous, so much so that if one fails to heed these warning signs, one will "inherit the wind," meaning complete destruction.

We hear the regrets of fathers or mothers who realize far too late in life that they spent all their time earning money or squandering time on personal interests rather than focusing on their children during the formative years. They tell a story of far too many hours spent on their own pursuits at the expense of their children who greatly needed their love and instruction.

Because of this, the children ended up raising themselves. As a result, by either hurt or neglect, they learned their moral and ethical behavior from the world, which ends up destroying them. Since the children did not grow up receiving godly counsel or loving reassurances as part of their upbringing, their love and respect for their parents grew cold, and they did not "honor" them. As a result, these children developed without understanding the command to honor their parents and did not reap the blessing but "reaped the wind."

The second part of this proverb is equally disturbing, because it is a warning that in the case of the folly created by the actions above, the foolish-hearted will serve the wise.

Take heart because the God of the universe put this warning sign here, as if on the door of your heart. Therefore, heed the warning and turn to the loving Savior. In so doing, you will not only save your life, but also change the lives of your family. So, what was once a disaster zone becomes a sanctuary for the humble and weary of heart. No matter where you and your children are in your story, God's kindness and redemption are always pursuing you.

Jose Nolasco

WISDOM, OR NOT…

Proverbs 17:24

"Wisdom is before him that hath understanding,
but the eyes of a fool are in the ends of the earth." (KJV)

I love the way Solomon thinks: Wisdom is worthless and not even visible to a person devoid of it. To have wisdom, you must have understanding. Without understanding, wisdom is worthless. Wisdom is all around us. Often, the wisdom we seek is right in front of us: In the Bible, as well as from pastors, teachers, family, and friends. Today, we can even Google it. We can literally be emersed in wisdom. The New International Version says, "A discerning person keeps wisdom in view, but a fool's eyes wander to the ends of the earth." Keeping wisdom at the forefront of our thoughts directs our actions. May God grant us the discernment to know wisdom and to apply it throughout our lives.

The fool on the other hand (Solomon does not mince words when he calls that person a fool) does not recognize wisdom and looks everywhere for it. Even to the ends of the earth it will be sought and not be perceived as wisdom when it is found. Therefore, the fool will not act wisely. Dear Lord, may we never be so blind as this.

A wise man by the name of Jim Rohn once said that we are given two examples in life: The example of what to do and the example of what not to do. It is equally important to know what not to do, what to avoid, as it is to know the right steps to take in life.

Which example are we? Are we the wise or the fool? Do we seek God for the insight that He often puts right in front of us. Or is He our last resort as our eyes wander to and fro looking for an answer. May God grant us the desire to seek and understand wisdom. May God show us how to apply it. May God also protect us from the inability to discern wisdom that we may harm no one.

Martin and Bea Laufer

A STENCH OR AN AROMA

Proverbs 13:5

"The righteous hate what is false, but the wicked make themselves a stench and bring shame on themselves." (NIV)

What is your initial reaction when you walk into a room with an apparent stench? Are you repelled? Do you cover your nose? Do you exclaim, "What is that smell?" These are all natural reactions to a lingering odor. Let's say someone has been living in that same room for months or years. They would most likely have gotten accustomed to the smell, because it would become familiar to them. But, to an outsider walking in, the stench is unpleasant and creates an uneasy feeling that is not inviting.

In the same way, when the wicked intentionally bring about destruction, chaos, and lies, they create an unpleasant atmosphere. This is an atmosphere—a stench—to which they grow accustomed to the extent that they no longer recognize there is an odor within their wicked ways.

I remember entering an environment that was unfamiliar to me. I knew most, if not all, of the people there were not followers of God, which was evident in how they spoke and interacted with each other. Their choice of language and the way they presented themselves were contrary to what I knew God's Word says.

According to Scripture, as disciples of Jesus, we are called to remain rooted in what is true and right (Phil. 4:8). The best way to do this is to know God's Word, the source of His holy truth, and apply it to our lives. The more firmly we are planted, the more we can enter environments with this uninviting stench, knowing well where we stand as children of God. So, before we begin our day, let us ask the Lord to help us not to be overwhelmed by the stench of any adversarial environments we may walk into but rather be overtaken by His truth, which is a pleasing aroma to us.

Amelia Montantes

PATHWAY THROUGH THE PROVERBS

HUMBLE IS HARD

Proverbs 18:12

"Before a downfall the heart is haughty,
but humility comes before honor." (NIV)

"Lord, I humble myself before you," I said in a time of prayer. Then I began to reflect—did I really? Did I just say it, or do I really mean it? How do I know if I am truly walking in humility before God?

As I talked to a very dear friend, I told him the title I had thought of for this specific devotional, and he laughed and shared the following quote by Benjamin Franklin:

> "There is perhaps no one of our natural passions so hard to subdue as pride. Beat it down, stifle it, mortify it as much as one pleases, it is still alive. Even if I could conceive that I had completely overcome it, I should probably be proud of my humility."

So how do we know we are truly walking humbly before God? The key is found in John 5:44:

> *"How can you believe since you accept glory from one another but do not seek the glory that comes from the only God?"* (NIV)

The key is whose glory are you seeking, God's or yours? If you are seeking honor from people, then you are looking for your own glory. But if you are seeking God's glory, walking in the fear of the Lord, and being willing to bow to (accept and do) His will, then you will receive honor from God.

So, how do you *seek* the glory that comes only from God? Micah 6:8, says,

> *"He has shown you, O man, what is good; and what does the Lord require of you but to do justly [to do what is right], to love mercy, and to walk humbly with your God?"* (NKJV)

Then, how do you *keep* on the path of humility? By acknowledging His Lordship, that He is God and you are not. Ask Him every morning to order your steps and yield to His plan and purposes, and keep an attitude of gratitude. Be willing to yield your life as a living sacrifice to the King who gave His life for you.

Do you want praise from men, or do you want honor from God? Only one of them is worth it.

Michelle Glush

THE INNER LIFE

Proverbs 20:27

"The Lord's light penetrates the human spirit,
exposing every hidden motive." (NLT)

God's light is more than illumination; it is a living light. In fact, the Lord is light itself. It is the first thing He created, and He "dwells in unapproachable light."[2] The Light of the Lord is His glory, wisdom, Word, holiness, and beauty. In God, there are no shadows, no darkness, death, sin, or ugliness.[3]

Light and darkness have nothing in common.[4] Therefore, no darkness should dwell in our hearts. We cannot live a dual existence by showing one life on the outside and living another on the inside. We cannot pretend to serve God yet conceal hidden motives of selfishness, greed, lust, or hatred. If we are hiding things in the deep recesses of our hearts, then we are harboring something other than the beauty of God's perfection in our hearts. Jesus said in John 3:19, *"And the judgment is based on this fact: God's light came into the world, but people loved the darkness more than the light, for their actions were evil."* (NLT) God created the light, and the first thing He did was to separate it from the darkness.

Such sins hidden in our hearts disallow for our spiritual health and set us up for future judgment. In Romans 2:16, the Apostle Paul says, *"And this is the message I proclaim—that the day is coming when God, through Christ Jesus, will judge everyone's secret life."* (NLT) Nothing hidden will remain hidden forever, but all will be revealed.[5]

A life pleasing to the Lord is a life lived in front of Him. We need to allow the perfect Light of God to fill us, expose our motives, and bring us to repentance and purity. This transparent life with God is expressed in Psalm 19:14, *"May the words of my mouth and the meditation of my heart be pleasing to you, O Lord, my rock and my redeemer."* (NLT)

Kyle Bauer

---

2   1 Timothy 6:16
3   See Genesis 1:4; James 1:17; Revelation 21:1-8, 22-25; 22:3-5
4   2 Corinthians 6:14
5   Luke 12:2-3

BE A FRIEND

Proverbs 16:28

"A perverse person stirs up conflict,
and a gossip separates close friends." (NIV)

It is funny when you look things up in the dictionary—you learn a lot! The word perverse is used a lot in our culture, but the definition is not what I expected. Perverse is defined as awkward, contrary, difficult, unreasonable, uncooperative, unhelpful, obstructive, or troublesome, among many others. Other Bible translations use the word troublemaker; in this case, it fits.

Troublemakers who gossip will end a close friendship. Whether the friendship is theirs or they stir up strife in someone else's, their selfish actions cause significant harm, and no one comes out unscathed. The troublemaker does not understand that they do not have the right to reveal other people's business. As my mother would say, "I told you, not the NBC news media. If I wanted them to know, I would have called them."

I worked with a person years ago who is the picture of that definition. She was never happy, never agreeable, and always speaking negative things about people, even those she did not know. She gossiped and stirred up strife among co-workers and was extremely destructive to the morale of our company. Because of her terrible behavior, she had no friends. People were either afraid of her because of her disagreeable nature or shunned her because she would talk about them or repeat everything they said.

Proverbs 17:17 states, *"A friend loves at all times…."* (NIV) To have a friend, you need to be a friend. That means being a person of love, integrity, trust, compassion, and respect. Ask God to show you where you need to improve on the "Friend-O-Meter," and cultivate a new friendship!

Debbie Speese

BEING BULLIED BY THE WICKED

Proverbs 10:11

"The words of the godly are a life-giving fountain;
the words of the wicked conceal violent intentions." (NLT)

When I read through the Bible, the Holy Spirit often connects words together for me. As I was reading Proverbs 10:11, I saw the interesting dichotomies between the godly vs. the wicked, giving vs. concealing, and life vs. violence.

There are definitely life-breathing and death-gasping tones in this proverb, which reminded me of my junior high and high school days. I used to be bullied by girls who didn't like me. They would whisper horrible names about me as I walked the hallways and, at times, would write hate-filled letters and stick them in my locker for me to find. I never quite understood why they hated me so much, but I had to press through the negativity and try not to believe a word they said. This was no easy task, and I recall crying about the harm-filled words many, many times throughout my adolescent years.

Although I may no longer have teenage girls calling me names every day, I do have an enemy named satan, and he tries to attack me with his wicked words. He conceals them in my thoughts and through the "critiques" of others. The thing is, he isn't just coming after me; satan is coming after the body of Christ, and he will continue his assaults as long as he can to destroy God's army one soldier at a time.

We must be diligent and recognize his tactics! When people speak into our lives, we need to pause and ask ourselves, "Who are the words coming from?" We should receive Christ-centered edification and bask in the life-giving fountain, but we must ask for discernment in identifying the bullying of the wicked so that we may hold captive their violent intentions and bring them under the submission of God's Word and what He says. Be on high alert, fellow soldiers, and only choose to receive the words of the godly!

Jennifer Shank

FINANCIAL FREEDOM

Proverbs 22:7

*"The rich rule over the poor, and
the borrower is a slave to the lender." (NIV)*

Newly married, my husband and I quickly learned that our jobs, our paychecks, and even what we did, did not fully belong to us because we became slaves to our debt.

In our youth, credit cards and "free" checks flowed into our mailbox daily; it was too tempting for us to ignore. Starting out on our life together, we quickly discovered the needs that arose, including insurance, groceries, rent, clothing, entertainment, etc. In our wisdom, we applied for new credit cards, and our debt grew. Not understanding revolving credit or finance charges, the bills started coming in. Unable to pay them off, we made the minimum payments with more credit offers coming in. Once we hit our limits, we just applied for a new card or wrote a credit card check to cover our expenses. As you can imagine, our debt was growing exponentially with no end in sight. We would try to ignore it, but the bills kept coming; we would rob "Peter to pay Paul" and justify every expense as a need.

Yet deep inside, we knew we were drowning in debt.

This verse explains where my husband and I found ourselves during the first years of our marriage. Every decision and every thought was influenced by our debt. We became slaves to the debt, and the lenders ruled over us. Nothing actually belonged to us except our debt.

But Christ is where we found our freedom. Once we submitted to God and His ways of handling money, we discovered how to manage it and find a way out of our debt. It was not an easy process, and it took us years, but God blessed our trust in Him and made what seemed impossible, possible. (See Mal. 3:8-12)

On reading this verse, where do you find yourself? Have you become a slave to something, knowing or unknowingly? What rules in your heart or mind or wallet? What controls your decisions—God or your desires? Do you faithfully tithe? Pray and ask the Lord where you need to surrender control and submit to His Word.

Jill Alvarado

THE LAW OF THE SECOND DONUT

Proverbs 25:16-17

"Do you like honey? Don't eat too much, or it will make you sick!
Don't visit your neighbors too often, or you will wear out your welcome." (NLT)

Let's look at this verse by today's standards: Do you like soda? Good! Have some! Just do not get diabetes from it. Do you love your neighbors? Good! Do not make yourself a pest, or they will not like you anymore!

I, and I am sure you too, have been at gatherings where food and desserts abounded. I purposely come hungry because I do not want to be inhibited by a suppressed appetite. I eat and enjoy. I get full. My eyes want more, but my stomach is telling me to stop—but I know this kind of food does not happen every day! So, I try a little more, and it is too much.

My brother came up with a "law" a while back. Not a legal law, but it could be akin to the laws of thermodynamics—maybe we can call this the *fifth* law of thermodynamics—it is the "law of the second donut." You walk into the office, and you see the classic pink box, and you know what is in it. You open the lid, see your favorite donut, and eat it. It is the best thing in the world. It is so good you want another one, and against your better judgment, you take it. Then the "law" kicks in. The second donut is *never* as good. It sits heavy, oily, and nasty in your stomach.

We all know the saying, "You can never have too much of a good thing." Well, according to this proverb, you can! This Scripture calls us to live in self-control and enjoy all things in moderation. Excess is a gluttonous spirit. Self-control and moderation are disciplines that keep our lives in reason and in godliness.

Kyle Bauer

BE INTENTIONAL TO INSTRUCT

Proverbs 22:6

*"Direct your children onto the right path,
and when they are older, they will not leave it." (NLT)*

The correct path to which Solomon refers is the path of following the way of the Lord. The New Testament says that Jesus is the way, the truth, and the life (John 4:16). Deuteronomy 6:7 says that we, parents, are to teach God's Word often to our children and to use every opportunity to talk about Him in daily, practical ways.

Here are some examples of things you can do: Sit at the dinner table and ask your children what they learned at church. When you are in the car, open a conversation about the goodness of God in your life and theirs. Take a walk around the neighborhood and ask about their school and what their friends talk about. Then take what they say and compare it to what the Bible says. When you correct your child, explain the reasons why it is important to obey by clarifying a biblical worldview. You will be surprised by how much of God's Word they absorb!

I have heard parents say, "My children were raised in church, but now they do not want anything to do with God." There can be many reasons why they do not want to go to church, but I wonder how much of Jesus was shown at home. Do our children witness a discrepancy between our faith and our home life? We need to model commitment to God in the way we want our children to follow. Do we love the Lord our God with all our heart, soul, and strength? Some say they raise their children in the ways of the Lord but do we consistently attend church? Are activities like sports or other events more important than gathering at the house of the Lord? Do we read the Bible? Do we pray, serve others, or serve at church? God is not impressed by our work, but all those areas are an expression of our love, commitment, and trust in Jesus.

Our children's knowledge of Jesus is not dependent on the church. The church is here to support what we teach them at home. You are their first example of Christlikeness. Let's be intentional to make sure they see it in us first.

Teresa Bauer

FOOT-IN-MOUTH

Proverbs 16:23

"The heart of the wise teaches his mouth,
and adds learning to his lips." (NKJV)

We all have moments where we have "put our foot in our mouth" and said something we wish we could take back. The apostle Peter did this as much as anyone. One moment being praised by Jesus and the next having the Lord tell him, *"Get behind me, satan."* (Matt.16:23)

This is an amazing concept. Our lips need to be taught. When we examine James 3, he tells us that *"no one can tame the tongue." "The tongue is set on fire by hell."* How can we *"praise God and curse our brother"*? So, this proverb teaches us to instruct our mouths. Proverbs 17:27 tells us that a wise person *"restrains his words."* We must learn to discern when to speak.

I find this so relevant for my life. I tend to say almost whatever comes to my mind, and especially when I am tired, I do not seem to have a filter. If I want to be wise, I will teach my mouth how to be quiet and give my mind time to filter through what I am going to say. I do not have to say everything that comes to mind (1 Cor. 6:12); that is foolish.

As we walk in the Spirit and not in the flesh, the fruit of the Spirit will manifest and grow in our lives. The Holy Spirit can empower us and help us with learning and applying self-control. When the challenge comes, pray in the Spirit before you give release to your tongue. Open your Spirit to the Holy Spirit before you open your mouth. By doing so, we will teach our mouths and grow in wisdom.

Heavenly Father, help me to have self-control over my tongue. I want fresh life-giving water to flow from my mouth, not bitter water. So, I choose to use my mouth to bless and not to curse.

Stephen Larkin

BEAUTY ISN'T ENOUGH

Proverbs 11:22

*"A beautiful woman who lacks discretion
is like a gold ring in a pig's snout." (NLT)*

By nature, we are drawn to beauty. God made us this way, because all He made reflects Himself, and our delight in beauty brings us into the awe of who He is. We were not created for decay with a body that fades away from its youth, nor to live in a world of physical and moral destruction. So, within the existence of both beauty and varied stages of deterioration, wickedness can play aesthetically pleasing tricks on us.

For example, I had a severe crush on a guy, and the more I talked with him, the more I had to wrestle with his beliefs that were in complete contrast to everything I stood for. He was a hot potato, but his heart was fragile and dark, and his mind was bound in deception.

This proverb, similarly, is saying here is a gorgeous woman, but her heart is filled with destruction and because she is choosing the path of death, walk away. She has nothing to offer. Likewise, people who propound their personal or political ideologies with grandiose words that sound nice, but have other intentions behind them, are also a path that leads to destruction.

So, where our natural inclination is toward beauty, this proverb is a warning for us not to be deceived by outward appearances. We must put on our discernment lenses and see beyond what appears beautiful to see the heart of the person or the issue.

Rachael Hopkins

LIFE-SAVING DISCIPLINE

Proverbs 13:24

"Whoever spares the rod hates their children,
but the one who loves their children is careful to discipline them." (NIV)

Over two decades of ministry, I have had to sit with many people whose adult children have walked away from the Lord. There are many reasons for this, and I would never cast blame, much less bring condemnation, upon any person for such a painful thing. Sometimes it is willful disobedience on the part of the child, or the child simply never had an encounter with Jesus. In other cases, pain was caused at the hands of church leaders that drove the child away. Reasons abound, but at the end of the day, adults make their own decisions. But rest assured, Jesus is working to reach them and bring them back! Keep praying for them!

I have also heard many parents' anguish over their children, saying, "But my son/daughter grew up with the Gospel! We were at church all the time!" Again, I realize that there are few cut-and-dry answers for this, but there are some important patterns that I have observed over the years that can be instructional for those with children still at home.

1. There is often a marked inconsistency between what the child observed in family life at church and family life at home. Everything was good, spiritual, kind, and keeping up appearances at church, but life at home was filled with anger and worldliness. Almost nothing turns a person off to God more than this inconsistency. So be the same person everywhere you are.
2. I have heard children complain that their parents were more attentive to the church and the people of the church than to them. There is no ministry more important than the family. Do not do church at the expense of your family, but do not do your family at the expense of being a disciple of Jesus, either!
3. I see many parents' lack of discipline in their child's life. It is easy to justify and let things in their life slide and let the child sass and throw tantrums with little or no confrontation. Yet discipline is an entry point of the Gospel into your child's life. Do not let sin take root. Instead, discipline with love and intentionality, and give them biblical understanding.

Kyle Bauer

SPILLING SECRETS

Proverbs 20:19

"He who goes about as a gossip reveals secrets;
therefore, do not associate with a gossip [who talks freely or flatters]." (AMP)

To be entrusted with a secret is to stroke the ego and tempt the soul—the honor of confidentiality versus the dishonor of gossip. Sadly, we have not only been victims of gossip ourselves, but we have also been perpetrators of the same, breaking trust and hurting feelings. Gossip is the unauthorized divulging of sensitive information to third parties, often without the full truth revealed or known. This verse warns us to steer clear of people who habitually cross this line.

The Bible forbids gossip, as it can lead to slander (Lev. 19:16a; Ps. 50:20) and incite bloodshed (Ezek. 22:9). Slander means speaking falsely about another, damaging their reputation. The seven things listed in Proverbs 6:16-19 that God hates concludes with "him who sows strife among brothers" (CJB). Gossip certainly spreads rumors and stirs up trouble that cause people, including family members, to fight.

A gossip is a talebearer (KJV), one who talks too freely (AMPC), a simple babbler (ESV), a flatterer (GNV), a blabbermouth (MSG), a slanderer (NASB), a chatterer (NLT), one who speaks foolishly (RSV), a busybody and deceiver (YLT). Avoid these kinds of people. Do not allow them to tell their tales and reveal secrets, for you can be sure that they will betray your secrets, too, and tell tales of you!

Instead, bring honor to God by honoring others as a trustworthy person who keeps a confidence (Prov. 11:13).

Karen Heimbuch

FOOLS DECEIVE THEMSELVES

Proverbs 14:8

*"The prudent understand where they are going,
but fools deceive themselves." (NLT)*

As a teenager, I heard of many singing and talent competition programs. Due to the popularity of the shows among my schoolmates, I decided to tune in one night. In these shows, thousands of people from all over the world come to audition before a panel of industry professionals. These shows produced some of the worst singing and talent auditions ever to be recorded and televised. To make matters even worse, several contestants with awful auditions would argue with the judges, stating that they were absolutely phenomenal and that the judges were mistaken.

Proverbs 14:8 teaches us that "…fools deceive themselves." It makes me wonder, just like the delusional auditioning contestants, if we have ever been led astray in areas of our lives. I am sure there are moments where we not only deceive ourselves, but also deceive others along with us. It is as if we are lost, denying direction from others, heading down a wrong path, and yet trying to convince ourselves that we are headed in the right direction. This can be applied to any area of our lives. We can easily be wrong, yet we try so hard to deceive ourselves into thinking we are right.

Proverbs 14:8, however, speaks about the "prudent" and how they understand where they are going. In contrast to the foolishness of self-deception, the wise understand their direction because their paths are lit, and their feet are led by the Word of God. They know where to go and where not to go because they are self-aware of what they are good at and what they are not.

The Lord desires that we become prudent, gain understanding, and fully know where He is leading us. Let us not become foolish and caught up in our own delusions, deceiving ourselves. Let us not fool ourselves to the point of public humiliation and self-destruction. Instead, let us seek His wisdom!

Victor Miguel Rivera

A PRUDENT MAN

Proverbs 14:18

*"The simple inherit folly,
but the prudent are crowned with knowledge." (NKJV)"*

It sounds simple enough, pun intended. So, let's break that down.

- Simple: Plain, basic, or uncomplicated
- Inherit: To take possession of
- Folly: Lack of good sense, foolishness
- Prudent: Marked by wisdom or judiciousness
- Crowned: A reward of victory or mark of honor
- Knowledge: Acts, information, and skills acquired by a person through experience or education

Have you ever heard of the acronym for KISS? "Keep It Simple Stupid." For the person who wants things the easy way, this proverb is for you. But it is more like a warning. What I have found in my life is that I grew the most when I was challenged the most. When I found things super easy is when I would get into trouble. There was nothing to challenge me, nothing to make me think hard about what I was doing, and nothing to refine me or enlighten me about the things of life. In my desire to keep everything easy, my brain was dulled. I lacked good sense, and I acted foolishly. I took possession of whatever folly was coming my way.

So how does one become prudent? There are multiple ways. For me, it was learning through the challenges that presented themselves throughout my life. Many of the difficulties were self-inflicted. Others are the ones that happen in life that I seem to have no control over, and I acquired some skills by having to figure them out. One thing is for sure, God was with me every time, whether I knew it or not. Romans 5:3-4 says, *"…we also glory in tribulations, knowing that tribulation produces perseverance; and perseverance, character; character, hope."* (NKJV)

I have come to know that although I may have faced adversity, God used those adversities to create the man I am now, a much more prudent individual than my younger self. In doing so, I have a mark of honor, a reward of victory that I must humbly say was God's love and grace over my life.

Fred Alvarado

THE GOD OF ETERNITY

Proverbs 30:4

"Who but God goes up to heaven and comes back down?
Who holds the wind in his fists? Who wraps up the oceans in his cloak?
Who has created the whole wide world? What is his name—and his son's name?
Tell me if you know!" (NLT)

His name, you ask? The Great I AM.

God IS. Not He was. Not He will be. He eternally IS.

He IS the Beginning—the Alpha. He IS the End—the Omega. He encompasses all and every moment in between. There is never a moment when He is not.

All things were created by Him, and all things exist in Him. His Word formed the Universe, and it is His Word that holds the Universe together.

The Word that He spoke thousands of years ago still carries the same power as the day He spoke it. His words do not lose their power, and His Word will not (no, not ever) return to Him void. The promise He spoke is continually active and being fueled by the power of His Word.

In Genesis 15:5, God promised Abraham that his descendants would number as the stars in the sky. Abraham did not even have a son yet, and he was well into his later years. Yet, God spoke it, and Abraham believed God, and it was counted unto him as righteousness (vs. 6). Twenty-five years Abraham waited. But the word of promise that God gave to Abraham (now 100) brought he and Sarah (now 90) a son. Abraham never saw the untold numbers of his descendants, but he saw the seed, and God's faithful promise—His Word—still came to pass.

Has the Holy Spirit whispered a Word of promise to you about your future? Are you still waiting for it to be fulfilled? Be encouraged! The word is still as alive and active today as the day it was spoken. There is no law of diminishing returns when it comes to God's Word.

"…he who comes to God must believe that He IS, and that He is a rewarder of those who diligently seek Him." (Heb. 11:6, NKJV)

Because He IS, we can be assured that His Word will never fail. Not one.

Michelle Glush

409

THE ULTIMATE WISDOM OF GOD

The Bible gives us wisdom for daily living, but this wisdom is for a purpose. The purpose is beyond gaining success in this life or avoiding problems with other people, it is wisdom that instructs our lives to live in a way that pleases God. God, who is the Author of all wisdom, instructs people to live as He does. God also gives us instructions far beyond this temporary life here on Earth; He gives us wisdom for eternity! 1 Corinthians 1:24 says that Jesus Christ is the wisdom of God. God's wisdom was that Jesus pay the price for our foolishness. Foolishness is epitomized in sin. It is our sins that separate us from a relationship with God. No matter how much we apply these Proverbs to our daily living, only the ultimate wisdom of God in Jesus Christ can save us from sin through total forgiveness.

What we have done in the past is passed, and there is nothing we can do to change it. But we can ask for forgiveness—and God freely offers it through the death of Jesus Christ on the cross and His resurrection from the dead. He lived the life we should have lived, and He died the death we should have died. He freely offers to exchange the foolishness we have committed in order to receive the life of His wisdom through Jesus. Inviting Jesus into your life and receiving His forgiveness is the wisest thing anyone could ever do! Once we receive God's ultimate wisdom in Jesus Christ, we live according to the daily wisdom found in the rest of the Bible.

If you have never received Jesus Christ, you can do it right now. Put your faith in Him. Apply His death and resurrection to your life by saying this simple prayer in faith, and then living in the wisdom that pleases Him. Pray:

Jesus, I know I have sinned, and I ask for your forgiveness. I believe you died on the cross for me and that you rose again to life so I could have your life. I receive it now. Fill me with your Spirit so I can live in the fullness of your wisdom all the days of my life. Amen.

www.ingramcontent.com/pod-product-compliance
Lightning Source LLC
Chambersburg PA
CBHW062033090426
42740CB00016B/2888